A Centennial History of the Southern Association of Colleges and Schools

1895-1995

James D. Miller

Contents

Chapter One

Origins

At 10:30 in the morning of November 6, 1895, a group of Southern educators gathered in the chapel of the Georgia Institute of Technology in Atlanta, Georgia. By the end of their meeting and "after considerable discussion," they had organized the Association of Colleges and Preparatory Schools of the Southern States (ACPSSS).[1] The grand title reflected future expectations more than present realities. For one thing, it was a small gathering. The first meeting, and a second one later that day at the YMCA, attracted representatives from only twelve colleges and universities, albeit drawn from among the region's best institutions of higher learning. Of the twelve, only half became founding members of the Association.[2] Despite the new Association's name, none of the founding participants represented preparatory schools, while the six founding institutions were drawn from only four of the Southern states. Yet from these limited beginnings, the ACPSSS would grow tremendously over the following century. Through various name changes and 100 years of involvement in Southern education, by the time the Southern Association of Colleges and Schools held its 100th annual meeting in Atlanta in 1995 it had become one of the South's most important and influential educational organizations, more than meeting the claims implied in its original title.

Long before its centennial year, however, the Southern Association of Colleges and Schools would become an organization of wide-ranging significance and influence in Southern life. At times the Association has been involved in the great public debates and controversies of the region's modern history. Over time its expanding influence has been felt in everyday ways by every community in the South, often in ways that even those most affected have not fully realized. Whatever its varied impact on Southerners' lives, at the heart of the Association's activities has been the vast number of people who have given, for the most part voluntarily, their time, their effort, their spirit and their intellect to its service. Anything like a complete record of this organization and the thousands of people who have been part of it cannot be presented in a single book. One study can only focus on so much, and the aim of this one is to provide a general account of the place that the Southern Association of Colleges and Schools has occupied over the last century in the society and history of the southern United States. Even with this specific focus, not all people or events can receive their due. Rather than an exhaustive account of many events, therefore, this history will instead tell the story of particular events and people that represent the enduring themes and qualities of the Southern Association's life and work. It explores the historical and social forces that shaped the Association's creation and development. As important, however, it illuminates the role of the Southern Association and its thousands of members in shaping the direction of Southern education and society over the past century. This is a book, in other words, about the lives as well as the times of the Southern Association of Colleges and Schools. We begin, in this chapter, with an account of the Association's birth and infancy. This account focuses on the aims and expectations of the Association's founders and pays close attention, as the founders themselves did, to the unique educational and social circumstances of the time and the place.

In seeking to know something of the founders—their backgrounds and beliefs, their educational ambitions, and their social circumstances—a good place to begin is with what they decided to call themselves. First, they formed as an "Association." This hardly made them distinctive Americans. At least since French traveler Alexis de Tocqueville's consideration of *Democracy in America* in the 1820s, observers of the American scene had commented on Americans' propensity to form voluntary associations in pursuit of public goals beyond the reach of individuals acting alone.[3] Yet even for America, the last decades of the nineteenth century witnessed an unparalleled expansion of such activities in every walk of American life. It was an era of association.

There were contemporary as well as historical reasons behind this unprecedented commitment to cooperative activity. If it was an era of association, it was also a time of bigness. It was a time of big business, such as banks, steel and railroads, and of big men, like Andrew Carnegie and J.P. Morgan, who dominated them. It was an age of mass population movements to America and to and fro within America: from coast to coast and from the country to the city. It was an age when towns became big cities and the big cities of Chicago and New York needed a new word—metropolis—to capture the novelty of their mammoth stature. In giant cities a new kind of giant building—the skyscraper—symbolized those revolutionary times as their skeletons of new steel allowed them to rise to unprecedented heights. The power of steel, and iron before it, had also fueled the nation's horizontal expansion as railroads came to bind the nation together in unbreakable ties; economic, social and cultural. By the beginning of what publisher Henry Luce would later call "the American Century," the United States was truly a continental nation, truly a nation of global economic stature and political power. "An age," according to one of its leading historians, "never lent itself more readily to sweeping, uniform description: nationalization, industrialization, mechanization, urbanization."[4]

In the years between 1870 and 1900, the population of the United States almost doubled to just under 76 million. This growth was fueled by the natural increase of the existing population, but also by the arrival of almost twelve million immigrants in the same period. Many new immigrants arrived from familiar locations in northern and western Europe, but increasingly new Americans came from southern and eastern European countries like Italy and Russia, as well as the Asian nations of China and Japan. This mass, diverse, immigration helped to transform the religious and cultural face of America, adding especially to the numbers of Roman Catholics and Jews among its citizens, while multiplying the languages and customs heard and seen in the nation's homes and streets.

Mass immigration fueled, in turn, the rise of massive centers of population. The word "metropolis" became common as a description for the great cities of New York and Chicago, while dozens of other major cities grew or developed. Almost as large a contributor to the nation's rocketing urban population was the flow of internal migrants from countryside to city. Pushed by falling prices, rising debts or the increasing mechanization of agriculture, and pulled by bright lights, expanded employment and hopes of greater independence, millions of Americans adopted an urban way of life in this period. By 1900, with just under 40 percent of Americans living in towns and cities (up from about one quarter thirty years earlier), the United States was the most rapidly urbanizing country in the western world.

New demographic patterns were bound up with the industrialization of America. Whatever the diversity of their beliefs and customs, these new arrivals shared the desire to find work in the new factories and plants that increasingly dominated the urban landscape and employed over half the country's labor force by century's end. The industrialization of America went hand-in-hand with the increased exploitation of its natural resources through logging, mining and agriculture; and by the processing of livestock and crops, lumber and minerals, in the nation's mills, refineries and meat-packing plants. Technological innovation and increased mechanization brought vastly increased productivity and an always-expanding range of products for Americans to consume. From the spread of refrigeration and telecommunications to the new popularity of chain-pull toilets and mass-produced tin cans, everywhere Americans looked they seemed to see the benefits of new kinds of industry and commerce. By the turn of the century, Americans lived in the world's most productive industrialized nation, a land that also produced more food and raw materials than any other on earth.[5]

If one development stood as a symbol of this modernizing age, it was the expanding railroad system that had fueled much of the nation's expansion. As total track miles almost quadrupled (from 53,000 to 199,000) between 1870 and the turn of the century, railroads joined a growing West to the eastern portions of the nation.[6] The Union Pacific and Central Pacific lines were rapidly constructed at a terrific pace by thousands of laborers fresh from the battlefields of the Civil War or from the emigrant ships that arrived from Ireland and China. In May 1869 they met at Promontory, Utah, completing the first line to span the entire nation. The railroad system not only bound East to West like never before, it played a crucial role in multiplying the economic ties between city and country, linking the mines and fields of the one with the factories and plants of the other. New connections involved more than economic relations. Railroads carried culture as well as cargo. If the railroad carried products from field to factory, it also carried products back that brought aspects of urban culture to farms and villages. If it took rural people—black and white—to the city, it also took something of their values and practices. The railroads also had a profound psychological impact, changing Americans' perceptions of their country, their communities and themselves, seeming to "shrink" the vast distances between the nation's regions and places now joined together by the iron bands of the railroad. No nearer physically, places now seemed to exist in closer proximity, brought together by the flowing back and forth of people, products and values. As historian Robert Wiebe suggests, "great numbers of Americans came to believe that a new United States—stretched from ocean to ocean, filled out, and bound together—had miraculously appeared." By the 1880s, the word "nation" had acquired new meaning, according to Wiebe, indicating a "sense of a continent conquered and tamed. It was a term that above all connoted growth and development and enterprise."[7]

Few Americans remained unaffected by the great population shifts, economic changes and cultural transformations of those years. Whether Americans responded to change with optimism or anxiety, or, as was often the case, with both, many believed that the era required new forms of collective and consolidated action if its myriad challenges were to be met effectively. The expanding American economy seemed to offer models for more efficient, orderly and productive ways of conducting society. In this period, massive corporations, and later "trusts," came to dominate industries such as steel and oil. By the 1890s, corporations like General Electric and Westinghouse Electric had expanded the technological breakthroughs of individual inventors like Thomas Edison into vast corporations that came close to monopolizing various essential products and services. The railroads also offered a lesson in the benefits of large-scale, often centralized, organization at the heart of the developing idea of "big business," their influence symbolized in the introduction of national time zones to replace the increasingly unworkable method of local time-keeping.

American workers and farmers were often less convinced of the benefits of bigness and change, and they sought to counter the growing power of business through their own associations and organizations. Faced with long hours and low wages, industrial workers joined unions capable of challenging the power of capital. Often, these conflicts took the form of strikes or lockouts, some of them violent. Bitter disputes between railroad owners and workers had broken out in the 1870s, and serious conflicts such as the famous Pullman Palace Car company strike surfaced again in the wake of the economic crash of 1893. In the face of falling prices, rising debt and crippling transportation rates, farmers became increasingly resentful of the power of the railroad companies, in particular, and of new economic circumstances, in general. Rural Americans' desire for fairer economic and social relations also found expression in large-scale protest organizations, most notably, the Populist Movement. With their roots in earlier rural associations, such as the Grange movement of the South and Midwest and the Farmers' Alliances of Texas, the Populists had become a force in national life and politics by the late 1870s and 1880s. Although its power declined toward the end of the century, the Populist Movement represented millions of Americans' fears for the survival of traditional communities in a world that simultaneously seemed larger yet more confining, more welcoming yet more frightening.[8]

The urge to associate was confined neither to those leading the industrial charge nor to those concerned about being overrun by it. A growing "middle class" also sought to put its collective mark on the age. Then, as now, a somewhat amorphous entity, this "middle class" consisted of men and women drawn from two broad and expanding areas of American working life: business and the professions. The business "wing" of the middle class included the self-employed but also the expanding numbers of Americans who filled the clerical and management ranks of the country's expanding corporations. The professional "wing" also presented a varied collection of the old, the new and the transformed. It is the growth of the professional portion of the middle class that is of greatest significance in charting the development of the ACPSSS.[9]

Whatever the many differences among these proliferating professionals, they shared a general preoccupation with what historian of the era, Robert Wiebe, identifies as a "search for order." The rising middle class pursued order within their businesses and professions, but also in society as a whole. Within particular fields of endeavor and expertise, members worked to improve both standards and organization. The 1890s saw the reorganization and modernization of local associations of doctors, for example, activity that prompted, in turn, the reorganization of the older American Medical Association in 1901. American lawyers' efforts to organize (the American Bar Association was founded in 1878) "became a flood" in the same decade. Efforts to improve the standards of the professional schools in the nation's universities also reflected this impetus toward the "professionalization" of the professions and the drive to increase and maintain standards within them.[10]

The middle-class' "search for order" also extended to the wider society to such an extent that this period of new and varied social reform efforts has led historians to give the name of the Progressive Era to the period between 1895 and World War I. Middle-class, mostly urban, Progressives shared some of the general concerns of the rural Populists. They worried, for example, about the tremendous power wielded by railroads and corporations. But, whereas the Populists challenged the very nature of a system they believed had to be radically transformed, middle-class reformers often focused on the need to reform negative side-effects of social and economic change, which for the most part, they enthusiastically welcomed. Themselves among the beneficiaries of change, members of the middle class wanted to eradicate the darker, more disruptive aspects of industrial and urban growth. An expanding industrial economy was a national achievement, spreading slums a national embarrassment. Rising output and opportunity were good, rising unrest and poverty were bad. The progressives of the middle class thus sought reform, not revolution.

Progressives had faith that successful crusades could be waged against social evils through both government legislation and voluntary organization. Thus many members of the middle class joined a myriad of associations aimed at reforming society. The nation's drinking, eating and voting habits, among others, became the subject of crusading organizations, such as the Anti-Saloon League, founded in 1893. Many of these groups had a profound impact on such issues as food safety and child labor, often prompting changes in public attitudes and precipitating government legislation. Reform associations provided many middle-class women with a chance to pursue the kind of public contribution otherwise denied them by their general exclusion from business and the professions. The proliferating professional and voluntary associations of the era speak to the desire for greater regularity and standardization within professions and for greater order and efficiency in the organization of society, generally. Their development also suggests how, for reformers, both professional and social progress were inextricably linked. For example, a broad field, such as medicine, could see the development of specific fields and interests within it. With urban growth and its attendant problems, for example, public health grew in importance, becoming by the 1890s a "profession within a profession," with, after 1912, its own professional school located at the Massachusetts Institute of Technology.[11]

These dramatic changes had a profound effect on the nation's education, both in terms of how it was conducted and of how people thought about its pedagogical practices and social purposes. The last third of the nineteenth century would prove to be one of unusual ferment in the world of American education, as educators sought to reform from within at the same time as they worked out the place of education in the changing American nation. Historian of American education, Lawrence Cremin, describes the period between 1893 and the end of World War I as "an extraordinarily creative one in American educational history." According to Cremin, it is in this period that we find "rooted many ideas and outlooks which have since become basic in pedagogical theory and practice." Cremin chooses 1893 as the start date for this period of unusual significance because that was the year that what became known as the National Education Association published its enormously influential report on curriculum reform: an issue at the heart of educational debate. Under the chairmanship of Harvard University President Charles W. Eliot, the group that would become famous as the "Committee of Ten" was initially formed to explore the issue of uniform entrance requirements. Their eventual report, however, proved to be the catalyst for extensive and wide-ranging debate. The 1890s, then, in the phrase of education historian Herbert Kliebard, proved to be the "seed-bed" for this major debate of curriculum reform with the Committee of Ten's report its "single most significant event." At the heart of the curriculum debate lay the persisting questions of what education could and should be, and what place or role it should have in modern America. These questions would run like a central theme through the history of the Association that also came to life in that decade.[12]

Debates over the curriculum, or indeed other aspects of life within schools and colleges, were inextricably bound up with wider questions that addressed the appropriate role of education in a modern, mass society. This debate was characterized, as Kliebard

describes, by a "growing tendency to see education not simply in
terms of individual development of intellectual powers but in
broad social terms." Educational philosophers like John Dewey,
author of *Democracy and Education*, helped shape discussions of
how existing educational practices and philosophies might be
reformed to increase the role and significance of education in
shaping social developments. Taking center stage in much of this
debate was the vast expansion in the public school system that
took place over this period. In 1870, 7 million Americans were
enrolled in public schools. By 1910, a combination of a growing
population and the compulsory-attendance laws passed by many
states, had raised the number to 18 million. Over the same period,
the number of public high schools increased from 500 to more
than 10,000. The rise of the public school system was seen by
many as central to this task of turning education toward social as
well as personal ends.

Many saw it as the "democratization" of American education, a goal valued by reformers not only for reasons of fairness
but also of social order in a chaotic, changing, heterogeneous
world. "More often than not," as Kliebard explains, the tendency
to see educational reform in terms of social goals "emerged from a
concern for social stability in the face of a rapidly changing society." Thus the insistent "search for order" evident in the wider
professional world was reflected in the world of educational
reform: arguably the area of professional life in which changes in
practice and philosophy had the most widespread public impact in
a democratizing society increasingly intent on providing education for all.[13]

This was the wider social and educational context for the
Association's formation. As educators, its early members were
attuned to developments within their profession, and shared the
desire for greater professional and social order. As citizens, they
were also acutely aware of the changes transforming American
society in the last third of the nineteenth century. Like other professionals around the nation, they sought both to encourage
reform within their profession and to act, as a profession, to
reform and improve their society. Convinced that such aims could
best be achieved through collective effort, they formed an
Association in whose early activities we see reflected both the

desire to reform Southern education and the assumption that such reform would inevitably foster the advance and improvement of the South as a whole.[14]

Taking the question of professionalization first, several aspects of the founders' educational background and experience encouraged a sense of collective interest. The men who attended that first meeting, and those who filled the Association's upper ranks in its early years, frequently represented the best and most prestigious institutions that the South of the time had to offer. Those visiting were welcomed by the host institution's president, I.S. Hopkins. The public universities of North Carolina, Tennessee, Alabama and Mississippi were represented by President George T. Winston, Professor J.B. Henneman, Chancellor R.B. Fulton, and Professor R.W. Jones and Professor T.W. Palmer, respectively. Seven of the region's private colleges and universities were also represented: the University of the South by Professor William Peterfield Trent, Washington and Lee University by Professor S.T. Moreland, Trinity College by Professor Edwin Mims, Mercer College by Professors J.T. Sellers and P.D. Pollock, and Wofford College by Professors H.N. Snyder and A.G. Rembert. Also in attendance were James Hampton Kirkland, chancellor of Vanderbilt University, and Professor W.M. Baskervill of its English department, representing what many considered to be the South's best university at that time.

As their titles suggest, these men occupied places of prominence within these prominent institutions. Many were well-respected scholars in their respective fields. Edwin Mims, an influential member of the Association in its early decades, noted how the Vanderbilt triumvirate of Baskervill, Kirkland, and their colleague Charles Foster Smith (who was not at the meeting) were all "well-trained scholars—none more so," prepared "to do work that would place them among the best scholars of the country." Smith had done "excellent work" in editing Thucydides, while Baskervill had "made important contributions" to Anglo-Saxon and Southern literary studies. James Kirkland had edited, "with rare success," the *Satires and Epistles of Horace*.[15] Other early members were noted for their scholarship. William Peterfield Trent of the University of the South, for example, had produced pioneering work on the slave South's most famous novelist, William Gilmore

Simms. Many of these men had also become administrative forces within their institutions, none more so than James Kirkland, who at a young age already occupied the chancellorship that would allow him to dominate Vanderbilt's development over the coming decades. George Winston, the Association's first president, would soon leave North Carolina to take up the presidency of the University of Texas. Prominence and power within their own institutions and in their local communities would continue to be characteristic of many of the Association's leaders and volunteers over the coming years, both at the postsecondary and secondary level. This would be a significant factor in explaining the Association's ability, over the coming years, to gain support and expand its influence beyond its own organizational boundaries.

Individual members of the Association in those early days were also likely to have taken similar educational paths toward their current positions. The three Vanderbilt men had all attended Wofford College as undergraduates, while Trent had studied at the University of Virginia. If receiving an education of the quality offered by institutions like Wofford and Virginia was a relative privilege in the Southern United States at that time, then a graduate education of any kind was rarer still. Again, the Vanderbilt trio all enjoyed one. Furthermore, their specialized graduate training was undertaken in Germany, at that time the recognized center of modern scholarly methods. Kirkland received his Ph.D. from the University of Leipzig in 1885, while Baskervill and Forster also studied in that city. The educational background of what Vanderbilt's historian has called this "Wofford-Leipzig junta" had much in common with many of their fellow reformers. They, too, had usually been the beneficiaries of the best college education their home region had to offer before going on to further study at the great German graduate schools or at the growing number of American graduate schools established on the German model. Henry Nelson Snyder of Wofford had done graduate work in Europe, for example, while William Peterfield Trent was greatly influenced by his time at Johns Hopkins University in Baltimore. Francis Preston Venable, another early member of the Association who assumed the presidency of the University of North Carolina in 1900, was a chemist with a Ph.D. from the University of Gottingen in Germany. As historian of Southern education, James Leloudis, points out, a doctoral degree, whether from Europe or America, remained "a rare credential in late nineteenth-century America." It was rarer still in the South. Thus at a relatively early age some of the leading figures in the Association had received an education that set them apart even from most other college-educated Southerners. [16]

Their education and training also set them apart from their predecessors in the South's institutions of higher learning. Their rise to positions of influence in the region's universities coincided with determined efforts to set aside the considerations of politics, popularity, family connection and sectarian interest that in the past had often been the guiding priorities in the selection of faculty. James Leloudis describes the transitional nature of a period in which "clergymen and tutors disappeared from the faculty roster" to be replaced by a younger generation who represented a new approach to education as a profession and brought with them the graduate qualifications that signaled their commitment to a more professional and orderly way of doing things. This shared background clearly encouraged a professional solidarity of the kind evident within other professional groups at this time. [17]

It was from this small group that the early leaders of the Association were drawn. A shared sense of professional endeavor need not, however, have led to a shared commitment to educational reform. From one perspective, "the natural thing" for these men to do, as Edwin Mims suggested, would have been "to devote themselves" to their academic specialties and "do critical work after the order of their masters in Germany" or in the graduate schools of America. Yet their interests in education extended beyond their own scholarly interests to encompass the entire system within which they lived and studied. Like-educated and like-minded men, their sense of themselves as successful professionals also encouraged their desire to band together to bring higher standards and greater order to their profession. [18]

The early members of the ACPSSS were acutely aware of the status and condition of the system within which they worked. In turn, they took an intense interest in the relation of education to the wider society and held strong opinions regarding education's potential as a progressive influence on that society. Many would have agreed with Walter Hines Page, a Southern writer and reformer living in the North, that these new educators were no

"mere teachers of children as the widow and the old scholar and
the old preacher" had been. Rather, insisted Page, they were "the
builders of a new social order." The historian of Southern
Progressivism endorses this view to an extent when he identifies
"the voices of criticism" coming from the South's colleges and
universities as "especially significant" for being "the product of
the region's first modern intellectual community." Like most "progressive" people of the time, they believed strongly in the power of
organization to achieve goals that would otherwise remain beyond
even the brightest and the best individuals acting alone. Thus, they
chose the path of reform activity in part because their sense of
their own growing role in education blended with an expanding
sense of education's role in society.[19]

This combination of personal interest, professional solidarity
and social awareness is evident in the specific aims of the
Association. James Kirkland was adamant "that the new organization . . . must commit the members to a definite program of
work and to definite standards."[20] What was this "definite program" to consist of? Again, the Association's title provides a par-
tial clue. It was to be an association of preparatory schools and
colleges. But that left the question of how these institutions should
be associated and to what purpose. The stated aims of the
Association, enunciated at the first meeting by James Kirkland,
suggest the answer. The Association's purpose was:

1. To organize Southern schools and colleges for cooperation and mutual assistance.
2. To elevate the standard of scholarship and to effect
   uniformity of entrance requirements.
3. To develop preparatory schools and cut off this work
   from the colleges.

On its face, "cooperation and mutual assistance" between two
interrelated levels of education seems an obvious goal. To understand why the Association's members considered the reform of
these relations an urgent priority, we must look to the wider educational circumstances of the time.[21]

Few areas of the South's life needed organization and cooperation more than an educational "system" that hardly seemed to
warrant the name. Impoverished and lacking in resources in so

many areas of its life, the South's educational deficiencies seemed especially striking to those who believed that educational improvement was the key to all other economic, social and cultural progress. While problems were myriad, the issue that focused the attention of the Association's founders was how to bring order to the relations between the region's colleges and secondary schools. With the help of an early Association member, President F.C. Woodward of South Carolina College, we can relate the Association's specific aims to this wider educational situation. Speaking in 1899, Woodward described the situation in his own state, but could just as easily have been describing almost any part of the region. Woodward described how the region's traditional preparatory school system was in steep decline. Historically, very few Southerners had attended college, and the private academies that had traditionally been charged with preparing them to do so had been more than able to cope with the small number of students involved. As higher education expanded across the nation in the post-Civil War era, pressure was exerted downward on the institutions expected to fill new college classrooms with more, and better-trained, students. This role increasingly fell to the growing number of public high schools as well as, or instead of, the private preparatory schools. This shift was welcomed and encouraged by many American educators. In the 1870s, for example, the University of Michigan began to certify the best public schools in the state in order to facilitate their graduates' entrance into college.[22] The public high schools' assumption of a preparatory role fueled the decline of private schools already doing an adequate job of meeting the growing demand for qualified, college-ready students. Yet the expanding public system was not sufficiently developed to assume this role. Indeed it remained an open and hotly debated question whether preparing an elite for higher education should be a priority for a public system intended to meet the needs of the broad population. The overall "result," according to Woodward, was "a grievous falling off of in the preparation of students seeking to enter our colleges, and that despite of an accompanying increase in the number of such applicants."[23]

Compounding the problem was the commonplace practice of colleges and universities offering their own preparatory classes designed to raise incoming students to the educational level which, ideally, they should already have reached before entering. College preparatory departments further undermined preparatory and secondary schools by prematurely attracting their "advanced pupils." Students, according to Woodward, combining "a natural desire to avoid their stricter discipline" and "a false ambition to be ranked as collegians" were eager to "desert the secondary schools at the first opportunity." With students "drawn away to the colleges by the enticements of few and easy entrance examinations . . . and unexacting discipline, it is no wonder that the high schools languish and even perish," concluded Woodward. The subtraction of their best students both weakened the secondary schools while diminishing the quality of education for those who remained, including those intending to enter employment rather than academe upon leaving secondary school.[24]

The premature addition of insufficiently prepared students hardly proved an unmitigated blessing for the colleges. In Woodward's unsparing indictment, a college's preparatory departments functioned as "a sort of collegiate hospital for intellectual weaklings and scholastic delinquents." Furthermore, actual college-level classes were "burdened and hindered by the necessity of carrying ignorant and unprepared students," Woodward complained. Overall, the effect of preparatory departments was to breed a "sort of hybrid collegianism" and "to lower . . . standards of discipline and scholarship" in the colleges that operated them. A system of preparatory departments that blurred the lines between the school and the college damaged both institutions alike, not to mention the students entrusted to their care. Woodward accepted that "pressing need" rather than blameworthy intentions had often "compelled" colleges "to enter the proper field of the schools." He accepted that in his own state, at least until recently, colleges "would have been almost empty if they had depended on the schools to send them students." Their choice had been stark: "Open preparatory departments or close their doors." Nevertheless, an arrangement once "desirable and excusable only as an expedient to meet the exigency of a necessary transition from an old to a new order" now "persisted, with the effect of increasing the disorder it was intended to correct." Now was the time to bring order to a "system" that encouraged mediocrity rather than excellence, decline rather than progress.[25]

Given the pressing need for reforms that seemed so self-evidently for the eventual good of all, why had so little been done? As Woodward's earlier comments suggest, present competition rather than future cooperation tended to dominate the thinking of academics and administrators facing their institution's demise. A further reason frequently cited was what Woodward called the "disconnection and indifference" prevailing between schools and colleges that seemed "to discern no mutual relations, to acknowledge no reciprocal obligations." Woodward described a situation in which "The public high schools affect independence of the colleges, and the colleges seek, through their own preparatory departments, to do without the help of the high schools." Woodward was far from alone in worrying that this mutual isolation was "threatening to crystallize into custom." He argued instead for more "understanding and interdependence" between institutions that should be "natural allies" rather than competitors or enemies.26

The Association's founders recognized both the need for future cooperation and the vicious cycle of disorder and disconnection that prevented its being achieved in the present. The priority they gave to overcoming the one in the interests of the other is evident in the Association's first stated aim of "organiz[ing] Southern schools and colleges for cooperation and mutual assistance." One of the Association's tasks would be to promote mutual cooperation by facilitating an atmosphere in which the interested parties might come together to debate their often divergent understandings of what and how mutual progress might be achieved. This role as forum for debate would prove to be a major element of the Association's work over the coming century.

Yet even if cooperation could be encouraged, there remained the question of the more specific steps that schools and colleges could take to improve the system. The Association's response to this question is revealed in the third of its stated aims: "To give the preparatory schools the right to exist by insisting that colleges refrain from doing preparatory work." As Woodward put it five years later, "Nothing short of the disestablishment of this provisional and now hurtful system of college preparatory departments will restore health and vigor to both colleges and schools, and make possible educational solidarity and efficiency." Achieving this end, Association members believed, would have several beneficial consequences. By refusing them admission, higher institutions would "force" unqualified students "to remain in the secondary schools where they belong." This, in turn, would help to "foster and build up" secondary institutions. The beneficial consequences would also be felt by colleges and universities now free to concentrate on their legitimate role of providing higher, not remedial, education. It almost went without saying that a system reformed in this way would benefit all secondary students, college-bound or not, and all college students.[27]

Many educators would, no doubt, have sheepishly admitted their participation in a system that harmed many individual students and undermined the cause of education generally. Yet many would just as surely have offered the age-old rationale that if they did not do it, someone else would. A further barrier to change was the widespread fear that short-term drawbacks would overshadow the long-term benefits. Some institutions, as Woodward suggested, might be unable to survive if limited to admitting only the genuinely qualified. The Association challenged these arguments head-on. In doing so, the new organization gained its confidence from the success that Vanderbilt had already enjoyed in breaking the cycle of disorder and moving toward greater articulation and organization to its relations to the schools that provided its students. In 1888, Vanderbilt changed "from the school system to the college system" by abolishing its own preparatory department. Initially, enrollment suffered quite severely. The academic department for example, lost forty of its 188 students in the first year of the new system, and by 1890, enrollment had dropped to 112. According to Henry Snyder, Wofford professor, Vanderbilt alumnus and Association founder, this "disheartening loss" brought Vanderbilt "all sorts of criticisms, even from its friends." But the university "bravely kept its faith fixed in its high policy" and the tide began to turn, and "year by year these scant numbers" had grown to 238 students by the academic year of 1897-98.[28] The Vanderbilt experience also provided support for the belief that reform would ultimately benefit secondary schools. Existing institutions, "encouraged and sustained by the action of the university," according to Snyder, "at once confidently took up the work thus relegated to them." Furthermore, fifteen new preparatory schools could, "making all due allowance for other influences," be seen "as the direct concrete expression" of Vanderbilt's new policy. In effect, Vanderbilt had created its own miniature association, gradually building up a cadre of associated schools whose standards they could depend upon to prepare students for full university courses without resort to remedial or preparatory classes once on campus.[29]

Encouraged by their own success, the Vanderbilt men, especially James Kirkland and William Baskervill, became the driving force behind the creation of ACPSSS. In March 1895, Baskervill presented a paper to the Vanderbilt faculty "inviting Southern scholars and colleges to cooperate in a movement for the formation of a Southern Association of Schools and Colleges." A motion appointing a committee "to promote this movement" was passed, and a Vanderbilt faculty meeting on October 22, 1895, appointed Kirkland, Baskervill and H.C. Tolman as delegates to the meeting in Atlanta. Their efforts did not receive the official support of the university, but it seems that most of the faculty was sympathetic.[30]

Their own reforming successes imbued the Vanderbilt contingent with a single-minded sense of how best to organize the Association as a vehicle for widespread reform. According to Kirkland, "the purposes of that meeting were already distinctly formulated in the minds of the Vanderbilt delegates." A strong sense of what he wanted, and a determination to get it, would characterize much of Kirkland's subsequent activity as the dominant figure in the Association's first decades of existence. William Peterfield Trent, a fellow participant in that first meeting, remembered how he had "envied" Kirkland's "sound political sens" and believed that he "had the tact needed to persuade recalcitrant members of backwoods Southern colleges to throw their influence in favor of the association." As we shall see, these "backwoods" college men would not always share this positive view of the chancellor's diplomatic skills. But Trent's view that Kirkland's central role in the Association's creation made him "one of the most important pioneers in Southern education" would come to be widely shared. Clearly working with their own and Vanderbilt's interests in mind, Kirkland and his colleagues were optimistic that similar reforms could also do for other institutions what they had done for Vanderbilt and its associated schools.[31]

What, more precisely, did they believe would bring about these desirable ends? Their answers to this question were shaped by various factors. For Kirkland and his colleagues, central to the goal of properly ordering *relations between* secondary and postsecondary institutions was the necessity of establishing order and excellence when it can to *standards within* institutions. This is evident in their second stated aim "to elevate the standard of scholarship and to effect uniformity of entrance requirements," for students going on to college. In other words, any benefit accruing to Southern education from a clearer demarcation of secondary and postsecondary spheres of activity would be largely dissipated if it were not accompanied by significant improvement in the standards of teaching and learning within those spheres. The question of educational standards at the secondary and postsecondary, and later at the elementary school level, would prove to be another central theme of the Association's work and history. As we shall see, it would prove to be arguably the most contentious issue throughout the Association's history, as a growing and diversifying organization became the site of long-running debates and disputes over questions of educational practice and philosophy. Specific debates over school or college standards would seldom take place uninfluenced by broader questions of the role education should play in a complex, modern society. Again, these were questions of great interest everywhere in America, but they took on acute and often distinctive aspects in the Southern states. The founders and their successors understood the many mutual influences shaping Southern schooling and society. If these were privileged men of their educational time, they were all the sons of a particular geographical place. Like Kirkland, born in Spartanburg, South Carolina, on September 9, 1859, most were native sons of the small-town South. Many had lived and taught, or continued to do so, in communities like Spartanburg or Macon, Georgia, and Sewanee, Tennessee. Thus while they saw themselves as part of a wider community of intellectuals and educators, they also saw themselves as the product of specific places. They were Southerners as well as scholars.[32]

Thus it was of great importance to the founders that they formed an "Association of Colleges and Preparatory Schools" that was also *"of the Southern States."* Addressing the Association's fourth annual meeting, W.E. Boggs of the University of Georgia emphasized regional identity when he welcomed the organization "as an Association of *Southern* Colleges and Universities." Boggs was quick to insist that "the name smacks of nothing narrow or sectional," and that it should not obscure an "abiding and friendly interest in educational work everywhere." Rather, Boggs claimed that there were "conditions peculiar to the colleges and universities of the South" that made a regional association desirable. Most of the founders shared the view that the South was a distinctive society, that Southern education was distinctive, and, therefore, that Southern educational reform would follow a distinctive path.[33]

How was the South distinctive and what were the implications of this difference to efforts to give the region an educational system worthy of the name? Like many advocates of change, Association members tended to define their region's distinctiveness in terms of what they believed to be wrong with it. This did not necessarily mean that the South's problems were unique, just more severe. This was true of the Association's major focus of concern. To a greater or lesser extent, poor articulation between the secondary and college levels and inadequate standards within institutions were problems in all parts of the country. But as Professor George Mellen of the University of Tennessee explained, there was a "special need in the South for cooperation and mutual help on the part of schools and colleges" since "the line of demarcation has been but dimly drawn, the spirit of helpfulness has had but a faint existence, and the principle of cooperation has been but feebly put in action." Thus, there was a "greater need," in Mellen's view, "for the work of just such an association" as the one he had joined.[34]

Thus, the South's problems were often more acute versions of those evident in other parts of the country. At times, however, the South's extreme poverty seemed to transform quantitative differences into qualitative distinctions. Most reformers in the South, including Association members, located the acuteness of the region's education deficiencies in a wider set of economic, social and cultural problems. Sometimes the obviousness of this was simply assumed. President Woodward, for example, did not bother to elaborate on the "obvious reasons" why the "makeshift policy of college preparatory departments" had prevailed only in the South. To many reformers, the most "obvious" reason for the severity of the South's educational problems was its pervasive poverty.

Whether they believed it to be the legacy of slavery or the result of contemporary social and economic circumstances, many observers of the Southern scene agreed that, in the words of one of its historians, poverty was a "hallmark of the South's historical experience." To some it was clear that economic poverty went hand-in-hand with cultural backwardness. George Winston, for example, first president of ACPSSS, lamented that the South had "hitherto failed to make adequate contribution to the literary and scientific culture of the world." Poverty's specific educational legacy was to be found in the limited ability of communities to support local schools, in the region's sparse collection of colleges (many not deserving of the name), and in the inescapable conclusion that the South was the weakest region in the nation when it came to education. It could often seem, indeed, that there was nothing distinctive about the South at all, except its material and cultural problems.[35]

Alongside this often bleak picture of Southern conditions, reformers were nevertheless quick to recognize the ways in which the region seemed to be making economic and cultural progress. Southerners of all kinds seemed to be active participants in the same kinds of changes sweeping the rest of the country. Perhaps the most startling aspect of the South's changing face was the growing number, size and importance of its cities, towns, and even its villages. When Greenough White of the University of the South addressed his fellow ACPSSS members in 1898, he talked of how the South was being transformed by "rising cities" growing "with remarkable rapidity." The region's urban population soared in the 1880s, and, by 1910, more than 7 million Southerners, almost one-fifth of the region's population, lived in towns and cities.[36] Older cities like the Tennessee trio of Knoxville, Nashville and Memphis shared in this growth. But the most striking increases were to be found in places like Jacksonville, Florida, Little Rock, Arkansas, and the Texas cities of Dallas, Houston and San Antonio that had been small or even nonexistent a short time before. The Southeast also saw the expansion of cities like Atlanta, Birmingham and Chattanooga, "the A, B, C of the new South" as Greenough White called the cities which, like their Northern counterparts, owed their growth to the region's industrial and commercial expansion.[37]

As White recognized, this "centralization of population" was

inextricably bound up with the "industrial revolution" also sweeping the region. As in the rest of the country, many Southerners left
the countryside for the workshops and factories. Long a land of
cotton fields, the postwar South became a place of cotton mills
and factories, too.[38] Birmingham's mills spun steel, not cotton,
while the electric-powered streetcars transforming the nation's
urban patterns of living had been designed in Montgomery,
Alabama, and Richmond, Virginia. In the final twenty years of
the century, sawmills and lumber mills, turpentine camps and coal
mines, cotton processing plants and metal foundries became
increasingly visible elements of the Southern landscape. "Every
measure of industrial growth raced ahead in the New South," concludes historian of the New South Edward Ayers, "consistently
outstripping national averages." Large factories, plants and mills
were increasingly likely to be the workplace of Southerners
involved in industry rather than the small workshops that had been
the norm as recently as 1880.[39]

Yet Southern urbanization and industrialization remained distinctive. Unlike Northern cities, the mass of new Southern urban-
ites were joined by relatively few immigrants from abroad. "The
rise of the urban South in this period is all the more impressive," as
historian of the urban South Don Doyle points out, "because it
was generated almost entirely by internal regional migration." With
only ten percent of its urban population in this period foreign-born,
the South's white population remained relatively homogeneous
compared to the rest of the country. Southern cities and towns also
remained for the most part small relative to their counterparts in
the North. Furthermore, although by the 1880s the South was
urbanizing as rapidly as the rest of the country, it remained much
less urban than most of the country. By the 1880s, although about
ten percent of the Southern population lived in towns and cities,
this was the level of urbanization already apparent in the
Northeastern states by the 1820s. As the twentieth century began,
agriculture remained central to both Southern economy and culture. Thus the South in this period experienced the same high rates
of urban growth as the rest of the country, but did so from a qualitatively more rural starting point. These circumstances encouraged
a double vision of the South undergoing startling urban and industrial growth and yet remaining profoundly rooted in rural life.[40]

Given the pace and extent of change, some observers felt justified in talking, boasting even, of a "New South." Many had no doubt that 'new' meant 'better.' Rapid economic and social change encouraged the view that, for once, the South was fully participating in wider patterns of national development. In the 1880s the most optimistic outpourings regarding the South's future came from public figures like Atlanta newspaperman Henry Grady who sought to convince Northern investor and Southern skeptic alike that the South really was "New." This New South ideology—some would say mythology—was an effort not only to describe but also to prescribe social and economic change in the region. Thus, in one aspect, it was an exercise in exhortation, an effort to encourage Southerners that new ways of living were both desirable and achievable. Especially from the perspective of the expanding white business and professional classes, it seemed that this was a blessed generation of Southerners, privileged to be present at the birth of a "New South."[41]

Some seemed so intent on the future that the past could seem little more than a drag on their efforts to speed forward. Many Southerners remained to be convinced that new was necessarily better, or that the blessings of change outweighed its problems. Again, as the Populists' strength in the South indicates, doubt and opposition there shared much with popular anxieties in the rest of the country.[42] Yet popular resistance to change also had uniquely Southern roots. Many white Southerners disliked the prospect of a Southern future modeled on a Northern society they still viewed with suspicion, if not outright enmity. This suspicion of "Yankee" values *and* of their Southern promoters revealed a powerful and continuing attachment to Southern tradition. Thus if the New South was in part the creation of new events, it remained in significant part the product of distinctive cultural and social traditions. What people believed about Southern "progress" could not be separated from their attitudes toward Southern "tradition." The optimistic and the cautious, the anxious and the antagonistic, all played into the wider cultural atmosphere of the New South. If it was new, it was still linked to the old. It was an American story certainly, but one told with a distinctively Southern accent.

Atlanta was the New South's spiritual and ideological hub, the city that had risen from the ashes of the past's defeat to become the self-declared capital of a re-born region.[43] Thus it was perhaps appropriate that the ACPSSS held its founding meeting in the city that for many was the leading source and symbol of the region's new ways. The Association's founders were very much part of this new cultural setting. Most of the beliefs and attitudes, hopes and fears, that blended and clashed in the culture of the New South, were evident in the varying words and thoughts of ACPSSS members. This was true of eager voices such as that of Greenough White, who believed that the social and economic change he described was laying the foundations for a "new civilization." It was true also of the more critical champions of Southern change, those who saw change as self-evident good and resistance to change as the product of impoverished and reactionary thinking. White, for example, described how "the forces of conservatism are giving away all along the line" in the face of modernity's relentless attacks.[44]

Greenough White did concede that the "conservative" Southerner could find these "new and untried" circumstances "depressing." But he also insisted that there was "nothing but to make the best of it; the South is being drawn into the current of the world's life."[45] If conservatives found these circumstances "depressing," they often found remarks like White's condescending and dismissive. The idea that the uniqueness of their region lay in nothing more that its supposed economic and cultural backwardness did not sit well with many white Southerners. They heard a lack of sympathy, and they heard, they believed, a failure to distinguish between what had to go and what should remain as part of the South's continued life. For many white Southerners, their society was the sum not just of its flaws but also of a unique set of cultural traits and beliefs that required preservation and propagation. They viewed their society, not with the eyes of the pathologist, but rather with those of the patriot.

This group also included many reformers, including many in the Association. Most reformers were aware that they could not be entirely dismissive of the South's past. Many did not want to be. Again, the reformers' own social background and experience was important. Most were too young to have participated in the Civil War, but many came from families with members who had. James Kirkland, for example, saw three brothers enlist in the Confederate

forces, one of whom, Allen, had been badly wounded.[46] And perhaps many tough-talking reformers felt freer to criticize precisely
because of their strong sense of commitment to the region. As
well, the struggle to overcome the very real barriers of reaction
and nostalgia that did exist must sometimes have seemed to
demand nothing less than an all-out assault on old attitudes.
Ultimately, most Southern reformers sought to cheer progress
while paying their respects to the past by arguing that their shared
society was renewing itself in ways that fulfilled rather than forgot
the best characteristics of the Southern past. It was a "New" ideology, but it remained an ideology, of, by, and for "the South." In
various ways, differences and tensions between change and conservatism within the Association, as well as the Association's
efforts to mediate those tensions and differences in the wider educational realm, would prove to be another recurring theme
throughout the next century.

Reformers' efforts to blend tradition and progress were
nowhere more apparent than in the complex and contentious
world of Southern race relations. The Association began life on
the cusp of a nationwide "Progressive Movement" devoted to
change and improvement in the cause of order and progress. It
was also born in a decade in which white Southerners' efforts to
restore a stable social order founded on white supremacy took
increasingly violent and discriminatory forms, sometimes enforced
by the lynch mob, increasingly held in place by a pervasive net-
work of new segregation laws being introduced across the region.
This restoration of white power was justified in the name of tradition and of order. Many white Southerners, and many
Northerners too, subscribed to a growing myth of the earlier
Reconstruction era as a period of great tribulation in which the
twin social pillars of white rule and home rule had been pulled
down. If Reconstruction was, in this view, an objective lesson in
the chaotic dangers of black rule and Northern interference, the
subsequent "Redemption" of the white South had begun the journey back to a stable social order in which white and black once
again knew their places and were all the happier (and safer) for it.

The racist morality play of Reconstruction chaos and
Redemptive order was a staple of white supremacists' justification for the progressive destruction of black freedoms and the

permanent retention of social and political power by white Southerners over the following years. This broad mythology of Reconstruction was, as Dan T. Carter writes, "ultimately shared by most Southerners, rich and poor, educated and illiterate, even black as well as white." This included most white reformers and most members of the Association.[47] White supremacy was a given of almost all of the reforming class to which ACPSSS's members belonged. More moderate white Southerners may not have expressed their views so virulently or violently as the less-educated; they may have preferred "Negro" to "nigger," but without question it was the rare white reformer in the South who did not share the basic assumptions of white supremacist thought.

From a later perspective, such views hardly seem "moderate," far less forward looking. But there was no easy correlation between racism and reaction or between a commitment to reform and "progress" and a desire for racial justice. In fact, if racial inequality seemed right to most white "moderates" *as* white Southerners, the legal and orderly forms through which it would be preserved in the modern segregated South seemed right to them *as* reformers and progressives. In fact, racist and progressive attitudes were in significant respects complementary. White supremacist thought and action possessed many of the characteristics of progressive thinking. For one thing, they both placed a tremendous value on social order. The re-imposition of a racial order acceptable to the white majority represented a form of continuity amid the flux and upheaval of so much else that was changing. Both held out the hope of social stability in which a leadership elite could effectively shape the future of the larger population, whether white or black. In this regard, many reformers argued that segregation would help to curtail the violence directed against black Southerners by the more extreme or unruly elements in white society.

Reformers also argued that, once sufficiently placated and pacified, the white majority would grow less hostile to other kinds of social change, including reforms that would help black Southerners. "So far as most whites were concerned," historian Jack Temple Kirby explains, "counting out Negroes politically and socially made possible nearly every other reform they might undertake—from building better schools to closing the saloons." Thus

the new patterns of race relations taking shape in the late nineteenth and early twentieth century proved attractive to many
reformers not least because segregation was itself a modern product of the New South. Segregation combined two powerful elements of progressive thought: the search for order and the desire
for elite control of social policy. Thus, as Kirby puts it, "the great
race settlement of 1890-1910 . . .was itself the seminal 'progressive' reform of the era."[48] For the white South, then, the political
disfranchisement and social segregation of black Southerners was
itself a reform.

To black Southerners, the new order smacked of aggression
and regression rather than the peace and progress of New South
propaganda. What white Southerners saw as "Redemption" and
reform, most "Negroes" saw as the severest manifestation of their
own "white problem." Facing the overwhelming force of white
power married to white prejudice, black Southerners were forced
to give up many of the limited gains made under Reconstruction.
Black Southerners' struggle to hold on to what they could and
their fight over the coming years for equality in education as in
other areas of Southern life would prove to be a major theme of
American history in "the American century." As a central part of
the ongoing blending of progress and tradition, freedom and
oppression, racism and equality, it would prove central to the
twentieth-century history of the South, of Southern education,
and, therefore, of the Southern Association.

Although it would undergo revolutionary change during the
course of the following century, the relationship between race relations and education would prove an enduring theme in the history
of this *Southern* organization. Other persistent issues, the
Association's varying and developing relations to different levels of
government, for example, would also be significantly shaped by the
wider values and attitudes of Southern society. Yet over the course
of the coming century, the Association's priorities would also come
to be increasingly shaped by major trends in American life generally, thus to a significant extent diminishing the significance of a
characteristic clearly viewed as centrally important by its founders.

Other themes relating to the Association's focus on the relations between the standards within schools and colleges would
also persist. Later name changes would reflect the ways in which

the categories encompassed by the Association's original aim
would change and expand to include a far wider range of schools
and colleges, and of Southerners, than the founders originally
envisioned. In turn, the Association would be transformed, gradually assuming new roles and responsibilities that would greatly
extend the Association's reach and influence in Southern education and society. These changes would also, at times, generate conflicts of such severity within the Association, as to call into
question the very idea that it really was an "association." The
determination of various groups to preserve their autonomy and to
advance the interests of the institutions they represented would
often make the organization a battleground for wider philosophical battles and power struggles. But it would also prove to be a
place where diverse interests and ideas could find common
ground. Thus a further persistent theme of the Association's life is
the way in which, through conflict and compromise, the interests
of reform and conservatism have been reconciled to produce great
educational change.

The major events and themes of the Association's history
also offer important signposts along the path taken by Southern
education and society over the course of the twentieth century.
Over time, education has increasingly become both battleground
and proving-ground for wider social attitudes and experiments
regarding such fundamental matters as race relations, the role of
government, economic development, and the values that should
shape personal behavior and community life. These inter-connec-
tions will be pursued as we go along, but the overarching trajectory
to bear in mind is the movement of education from the backwaters
of Southern society to the very center of the region's private and
public life. Indeed, much of the Association's travels toward educational influence illuminates the journey education has made
from the periphery to the center of Southern life. The evolution of
the Southern Association of Colleges and Schools thus mirrors the
changing nature of education in the South and of the South itself.

For the Association of Colleges and Preparatory Schools of
the Southern States, 1895 began a century of forward movement,
but also one of consistent turning and returning to the questions
and themes at the core of Southern education and society. One of
the most consistent, and insistent, of these themes can be suggested

in the form of a question: "What is the meaning and purpose of education?" It is to the Association's efforts to answer these questions in the early decades of its existence that we now turn.

Endnotes

[1] *Proceedings of the First Meeting of the Association of Colleges and Preparatory Schools of the Southern States* (hereafter cited as *Proceedings*) 1895: 1, 3-4. Guy E. Snavely, *A Short History of the Southern Association of Colleges and Secondary Schools* [Reprint from the *Southern Association Quarterly* (hereafter *SAQ* 9 Nov. 1945)], 5-6. At the Second Session, additional representatives reported from the University of Mississippi, Chancellor R.B. Fulton and Prof. R.W. Jones; from Tulane University, Prof. J.H. Dillard; and from the University of Alabama, Prof. T.W. Palmer.

[2] The six charter members were Vanderbilt University, University of North Carolina, University of the South, Washington and Lee University, Trinity College and the University of Mississippi. Representatives of Mercer University, Wofford College, University of Tennessee, Tulane University, University of Alabama, and the host, Georgia Institute of Technology also attended one or both of the meetings. Prof. J.B. Henneman of Tennessee, Prof. J.H. Dillard of Tulane, and Prof. T.W. Palmer of Alabama signed as charter members on behalf of their institutions but had their names withdrawn when they returned to their campuses.

[3] Alexis de Tocqueville, *Democracy in America* (Garden City, NY: Doubleday & Company, Inc., 1969), Ed. J.P. Mayer, 189-95.

[4] Robert H. Wiebe, *The Search For Order, 1877-1920* (New York: Hill and Wang, 1967), 11-12.

[5] See, for example, Mary Beth Norton et al, *A People and A Nation: A History of the United States* (Boston: Houghton Mifflin Company, 1994), 530.

[6] Between 1870 and 1890, the population of the region between the Mississippi River and the Pacific Ocean grew from ten million to seventeen million. The West's increasing growth, and its integration into the rest of the country, is indicated by the admission to statehood of Montana, the Dakotas, Idaho, Wyoming and Washington in 1889 and 1890.

[7] Wiebe, 11-12.

[8] Quoted in Norton et al, 613. The Grange began as social organizations that organized family and educational events in part as a means to overcome the isolation of rural life. In 1892, Northern and Southern alliance members met at a People's party convention in Omaha where they drafted a platform that described America as a country "brought to the verge of moral, political and material ruin," in which "the fruits of the toil of millions are boldly stolen to build up colossal fortunes for a few."

[9] Wiebe, Chap. 5.

[10] Ibid, 115, 117. See also George Jackson Allen, Jr., "A History of the Commission of Colleges of the Southern Association of Colleges and Schools, 1949-1975" (doctoral dissertation, Georgia State University, 1978), Chap. 1.

[11] Wiebe, 115.

[12] Lawrence A. Cremin, "The Revolution in American Secondary Education," *Teachers College Record* 56, (1955): 295, Teachers College, Columbia University, New York). Reprinted in Stan Dropkin, Harold Full, and Ernest Schwarcz, eds., *Contemporary American Education: An Anthology of Issues, Problems, Challenges*, 2nd ed. (New York: The McMillan Company, 1970), 133; Herbert M. Kliebard, *The Struggle for the American Curriculum, 1893-1958* (New York: Routledge, 1995), xiii.

[13] Norton et al, 635; Kliebard, 8-14, 53ff

[14] Dewey W. Grantham, *Southern Progressivism: The Reconciliation of Progress and Tradition* (Knoxville: The University of Tennessee Press, 1983). xv. "The origins of the progressive impulse in the South," according to Grantham, "can be found in a confluence of internal and external developments in the late nineteenth century," such as industrialization, urbanization, "and the growing importance of a new middle class made up of business and professional elements."

[15] Edwin Mims, "The Work and Influence of the College Professor Outside the Class Room," *Proceedings* 5 (1899): 76.

[16] Snavely, *A Short History*, 4, 7-8, for Snyder; William S. Knickerbocker to Franklin T. Waler, Sept. 25, 1940, William Peterfield Trent Papers, Southern Historical Collection, Chapel Hill, N.C. (hereafter cited as SHC). Knickerbocker was editor of the *Sewanee Review*, while Walker was considering a Ph.D. on Trent. James L. Leloudis, *Schooling the New South: Pedagogy, Self, and Society in North Carolina, 1880-1920* (Chapel Hill: UNC Press, 1996), 57, discusses Francis Venable and other reform-minded educators associated with the University of North Carolina.

[17] Leloudis, 57. Leloudis' description is of teaching changes at the University of North Carolina, but it has much wider applicability and is relevant to the experiences of many early members of the ACPSSS.

[18] Mims, "Work and Influence," 76.

[19] Page cited in Leloudis, 73; Grantham, *Southern Progressivism*, 27. Writing of the mill towns of South Carolina, for example, historian David Carlton notes how "Organization was to the townspeople the great lever of Progress, the tool with which men could shape their own lives rather than have them shaped by implacable external forces." David Carlton, *Mill and Town in South Carolina, 1880-1920* (Baton Rouge, Louisiana State University Press, 1982), 38.

[20] Alfred A. Meyer, "A History of the Southern Association of Colleges and Secondary Schools" (doctoral dissertation, George Peabody College for Teachers, Nashville, TN, 1933), 10.

[21] Snavely, 3. Or, as William Baskervill put it a year later, the new association aimed at creating what "might be called a cooperative endeavor to accelerate the movement and to lighten the task of correlating high schools with colleges, [and] of defining the metes and bounds of preparatory and collegiate instruction." W.M. Baskervill, "The Work of the Southern Association of Colleges and Preparatory Schools [sic]," *Proceedings* 2 (1896): 17.

[22] Wiebe, *Search for Order*, 118.

[23] F.C. Woodward, "The Correlation of Colleges and Preparatory Schools," *Proceedings* 5 (1899): 55.

[24] Ibid., 59. Meyer, 18, writes that at the time of the Association's organization "practically all of the colleges of the South were offering preparatory work."

[25] Woodward, 58-9, 57.

[26] Ibid., 56-7.

[27] Ibid., 57, 59.

[28] Quoted in ibid., 61-2.

[29] Ibid., 61-62. See also Paul K. Conkin, assisted by Henry Lee Swint and Patricia S. Miletich, *Gone With the Ivy: A Biography of Vanderbilt University* (Knoxville: The University of Tennessee Press, 1985), 87ff

[30] Minutes of Vanderbilt faculty meetings, March 26, 1895, and October 22, 1895. Cited in Snavely, 4-5. According to Snavely, these are the only two mentions of the forthcoming meeting made at Vanderbilt faculty meetings. Kirkland later recalled that "It would seem that Vanderbilt University did not officially issue the call, not even the faculty of the College of Arts and Science." Kirkland's recollection was that he and Baskervill signed the call, which was, according to Kirkland, "a request of an unofficial character addressed to various institutions and suggesting a meeting in Atlanta." James H. Kirkland, "Personal Letter and Memorandum" from Kirkland, dated April 6, 1933. Cited in Meyer, 9.

[31] Ibid.; William Peterfield Trent to Thomas O. Mabbott, 17 Nov. 1930, William Peterfield Trent Papers, SHC. Kirkland's life and role in the Association's affairs will be discussed in Chap. 2.

[32] Snavely, 4.

[33] W.G. Boggs, "Address of Welcome," *Proceedings* 4 (1898).

[34] George F. Mellen, "The Public High School as a Preparation for College," *Proceedings* 2 (1896).

[35] Woodward, "Correlation of Colleges and Preparatory Schools," 57; Winston, "Annual Address," *Proceedings* 2 (1896): 11-12; William A. Link, *A Hard Country and a Lonely Place: Schooling, Society, and Reform in Rural Virginia, 1870-1920* (Chapel Hill: University of North Carolina Press, 1986), x.

[36] Greenough White, "The South Past and Present," *Proceedings* 4 (1898): 9; Edward L. Ayers, *The Promise of the New South: Life After Reconstruction* (New York: Oxford University Press, 1992), 2; Don H. Doyle, *New Men, New Cities, New South: Atlanta, Nashville, Charleston, Mobile, 1860-1910* (Chapel Hill: University of North Carolina Press, 1990), 9-10.

[37] Grantham, *"Southern Progressivism,"* 5; White, 4, 12. Birmingham, founded in 1871 close to iron ore and coal deposits in Alabama, soon became a focus for railroads and investors. A cornfield half a century earlier, by 1920 Birmingham was home to 178,806 people. Birmingham's growth was unparalleled but other cities also grew rapidly. John B. Boles, *The South Through Time: A History of An American Region* (Englewood Cliffs, NJ.: Prentice Hall), 385.

[38] White, *Proceedings*, 4, 12. From the "beginning of the cotton manufacturing boom in the 1880s and the approximate end of the Progressive era in 1920," according to David Carlton, South Carolina, for example, "became the third largest textile producing state in the Union. The number of wage earners employed by the industry increased over twenty-two times, from 2,053 in 1880 to

48,079 in 1920; in the latter year an estimated one-sixth of the state's white population resided in its mill villages." The Bureau of the Census reported in 1900 that the increase in cotton manufacturing in the South was "the one great fact in its history during the past ten years." David Carlton, *Mill and Town*, 7; Twelfth Census of the United States. Taken in the Year 1900. William R. Merriman, Director. Census Reports, vol. 9. Manufactures, pt. 3; Special Reports on Selected Industries (Washington, DC, 1902), 28.) Quoted in Grantham, 3.

[39] Norton et al, 563, Ayers, 22.

[40] Doyle, 11-12, 3; White, 9. Despite its rapid urbanization, the level of Southern urbanization on the eve of World War II was the same (35 percent) as the Northeast's at the outbreak of the American Civil War. See Grantham, 3.

[41] Boles, 377-82.

[42] Norton et al, 612. In 1890, for example, Alliance members controlled four governorships, eight state legislatures, forty-four seats in the U.S. House of Representatives and three members of the U.S. Senate. In historian John Boles' judgment, the Southern Alliance "developed the most sustained mass critique of unrestrained free-market capitalism in American history, and it was by far the most far-reaching and radical protest political movement in the South from Reconstruction to the 1960s (390)."

[43] By the 1890s, Atlanta had survived the depression of the 1890s and, according to Don Doyle, "had triumphed as the new interior metropolis of the Southeast, both as a commercial and financial center and as the quintessential symbol of the New South." Doyle, Chap. 2, compares the development of Nashville and Atlanta.

[44] White, 10-12. See also, for example, Winston, "Presidential Address," *Proceedings* 2 (1896): 11-12.

[45] White, 11.

[46] Edwin Mims, *Chancellor Kirkland of Vanderbilt* (Nashville: Vanderbilt University Press, 1940), 15-17.

[47] Dan T. Carter, "Southern Political Style," in Robert Haws, ed., *The Age of Segregation: Race Relations in the South, 1890-1945* (Jackson: University Press of Mississippi, 1978), 52. Carter summarizes the power and extent of a myth in which "the lurid and inflammatory exaggerations of the Reconstruction became a historical object lesson that exemplified the dangers of granting political rights to black Southerners."

[48] Jack Temple Kirby, *Darkness at the Dawning: Race and Reform in the Progressive South* (Philadelphia: J.B. Lippincott Company, 1972), 4. See also, C. Vann Woodward, *The Strange Career of Jim Crow* (New York: Oxford University Press, 1966), 67ff.

Chapter Two

Shaping Society, Shaped by Society

In the fall of 1921, the football team from little Centre College in Danville, Kentucky, traveled to Cambridge, Massachusetts, to play Harvard University. In an era when that famous university's athletic firepower equaled its academic prowess, few gave the Praying Colonels, so named in honor of their college's Presbyterian and frontier origins, much of a chance. Prior to the game, the Centre president, W.A. Ganfield prayed, and Albert B. 'Happy' Chandler, future Kentucky senator and commissioner of Major League Baseball who was studying law at Harvard at the time, sang "Down the Trail to Home Sweet Home," "a song then dear to the hearts of Southerners." Moved to tears, the team set off for the stadium where 45,000 excited spectators saw them pull off one of the great upsets in the history of college football. Whether they credited the praying, the singing or the outstanding blocking that allowed star quarterback Bo McMillin to dash thirty-one yards for the game's only score, Centre's 6-0 victory amazed and delighted Americans everywhere. Centre players became the darlings of Kentucky, the South, and indeed the nation, as Americans from coast to coast hailed the plucky small-town Davids who had downed the establishment Goliaths.[1]

The Praying Colonels, and especially McMillin, already had a national reputation, in part as a consequence of a losing, but heroic, performance the previous year at Harvard. But the national attention focused on the team that year was intense. On the way to San Diego for an end-of-season bowl game, for example, the Praying Colonels stopped off in Hollywood, where the team "attracted so much interest . . . that several movie stars followed them to San Diego for the game and socialized with the players on the train and in the hotel." They arrived as "conquering heroes" in San Diego to find themselves on the front page of the local newspaper's special "Centre College edition."[2] Although many players contributed to the victory, Bo McMillin drew most of the attention. On the evening of the victory, he "was showered with kisses by the beauties of the Ziegfeld Follies," while he signed autographs and read congratulatory telegrams "from dozens of important and ordinary people." In Hollywood, he was "photographed as he playfully tackled the movie queen, Gloria Swanson, who had obligingly tucked a football under the arm of her stylish jazz-era dress." Frequent rumors that McMillin would turn professional also testified to the interest his on-field exploits generated. Taken together, the two Harvard games cemented McMillin's growing reputation as the most famous college football player of the time. One Cincinnati sportswriter insisted that McMillin was to football what Jack Dempsey and Babe Ruth were to boxing and baseball. Children all over America could revel in Bo's exploits by reading *First Down Kentucky,* a "biographical novel" based on the quarterback's early life, while the governor of Kentucky, Edwin P. Morrow, "appointed the Centre quarterback a colonel on his staff, Kentucky's highest honor." In achieving such fame, McMillin also helped to make his previously obscure college a focus of national attention. A popular speaker at various banquets given in honor of the Centre team, McMillin "took the podium even after the coaches and president," according to his biographers. President Ganfield even quipped that, whereas in the past he had been introduced as president of Centre College, now he was introduced as the president of Bo McMillin's football team.[3]

Not everyone found this remark funny, or the inversion of priorities it suggested acceptable. Unfortunately for Centre, the leaders of the Southern Association were among the unamused. The 26-year-old quarterback and his teammates had attracted somewhat less adulatory attention from the Association's leadership who placed the college under investigation for various alleged infractions. More broadly, the prominence of athletics at Centre came to stand for many within the Association as a symbol for the corrupting impact of modern culture on academic life. Thus, another of Centre's enduring rivalries in this era would be with the men from the Association as they fought to deny the charges made against them and to win the accreditation that also increasingly represented success and stature in the public eye. The attention Americans paid to the Centre-Harvard games and the star treatment they accorded McMillin provides a vivid glimpse of the kind of country that was emerging, relatively unscathed, from the global catastrophe of the Great War. Centre's smaller, less welcome, place in the history of the Association of Colleges and Preparatory Schools of the Southern States also tells us something of that organization's place in the related realms of education and society after a quarter century of growth and activity. This chapter looks at the wider, rapidly changing culture that provided the context for the Association's work, and examines how that work developed and changed in its aims and methods. In doing so it emphasizes how the interrelationship of Southern culture and the Association's development reflected and shaped significant changes in both education and society. It follows the Association's development through its early days, then through the significant social, educational and organizational changes of the 1920s and 1930s to the eve of America's entry into World War II.

In the early twentieth century, Americans continued their highly mobile ways, with the West, especially California, their favorite destination. Towns and cities, especially the growing industrial centers, continued to draw Americans from the countryside, while America as a whole continued to be a magnet for people of other lands. In 1910, the Census Bureau introduced the term "metropolitan area" to recognize the unique nature of vast sprawling cities like New York, which alone had almost five million residents. By 1920, Americans had become more urban than rural in terms of population, with 52 percent of them (out of a total of 106 million) living in towns and cities. Demographic fluidity remained inextricably bound up with the nation's continued industrialization. Despite the severe economic depression of the mid-1890s, that decade saw the United States surpass the United Kingdom in iron and steel output, and continue to undergo ceaseless change in its patterns of production and consumption.[4]

The country's growing stature in the world encouraged many Americans to believe that their society should overcome its frequent tendency to isolate itself from global affairs and instead take on a larger role on the world stage. The depression of the 1890s had focused attention on foreign markets as a means to maintain high production levels when domestic demand failed to meet supply. In turn, it was hoped, a more stable economy would reduce the social and political conflicts that often accompanied hard times. Some felt that America's assumption of a larger role in world affairs was simply inevitable. "Whether they will or not, Americans must now begin to look outward," insisted famed Naval strategist Alfred T. Mahan in 1890. "The growing production of the country requires it." The following years would see America heed Mahan's appeal. Through war, trade and diplomacy, America would take control of Cuba, Puerto Rico, Guam and the Philippines as a consequence of the Spanish-American War of 1898; push for a canal across Central America and an "Open-Door" policy in China as means to further the nation's global trading power; and develop an ideology of what might be called progressive imperialism to justify such expansion as not only good for America, but good for a world assumed to be in need of being more like America.[5]

The single greatest indication of America's growing might and stature was its inability or unwillingness to stay out of the Great War of 1914-18. Having joined the conflict in 1917, by the time war ended on November 11, 1918, about two million American troops were in Europe, two-thirds of whom had seen some action. More than 50,000 of them lost their lives, while a further 60,000 died from other causes, most of them in the great flu epidemic of 1918-19. While hardly small, these losses paled beside the 8 million Europeans killed in the conflict. And, of course, America had entirely escaped the devastation to land and property that Europeans had wreaked upon one another. Thus, while America's entry into the World War can be seen as its adoption of a larger world role, the state in which it emerged from the war left it well-positioned to pursue and to benefit from that role.[6]

In boom times and slumps, these years also saw economic disorder and social dislocation. The early years of the twentieth century saw the development of the "Progressive Movement" that had begun to take shape in the last years of the nineteenth century. The Progressives' impact was felt throughout society in efforts to eradicate or ameliorate urban slums, sweat shops, unfair trading monopolies, political corruption, crime and drunkenness, and other social ills. A significant feature of this widespread and varied wave of reform activity was that it provided many new public roles for American women. Still excluded from many areas of work and most professions, growing numbers of middle-class women turned to social reform as a means to make a greater impact on society. Related to these efforts was the resurgence of the woman suffrage movement, which sought to correct another major injustice of the age: the denial of the vote to women. The movement had been making inroads for some time, meeting its fiercest resistance in the Southern states, and eventually won passage of the Nineteenth Amendment in 1920. An important factor in the suffrage victory was the recognition of American women's massive contribution to the nation's victory in World War I. In the war's aftermath, however, hundreds of thousands of soldiers returned to economic depression, social dislocation and labor unrest. These troubled years saw urban riots aimed at black Americans, as well as political and legislative actions aimed at curbing immigration and eradicating the Communism supposedly undermining the American way of life.[7]

But economic depression lifted, and after 1922, the "Roaring Twenties" brought tremendous economic growth and accelerating demographic change. Of greatest significance to the South was the role that black Southerners played in fueling this change. In the "New South" of the late nineteenth century, many African-Americans had moved from country to town within the South. In the 1920s, hundreds of thousands turned northward, forming a "great migration" from "field to factory" and to new lives in expanding industrial centers like Detroit and Chicago. Overall, in the 1920s the nation saw the first net decline in the number of farmers in its history. The postwar era saw, then, the continuation and acceleration of trends begun long before the war.[8]

The 1920s also saw tremendous change in the way Americans lived and worked, and consequently in how they understood themselves and their country. Economic and cultural change went hand-in-hand, as the 1920s saw the birth of many of the features of the "consumer" society that we take for granted today. No single individual symbolized the era's revolution in manufacturing and marketing, work and life, better than Henry Ford. The Michigan automaker combined technological innovation in the production and assembly of cars with new marketing methods to make his Model T automobile an ubiquitous symbol of modern America. By 1925, Ford's continuously moving production lines were turning out 9,000 cars a day. Mass production required, as Ford also realized, mass consumption. Unlike earlier industrialists like Andrew Carnegie, Ford was determined to "get the prices down to the buying power" and so ensure sufficient customers to buy the staggering number of cars his workers were producing. In compensating his employees for their mind-numbing production-line toil with the highest wages paid to industrial workers anywhere in the world, Ford championed the "high-wage" economy that would give workers more money, money that they and their families could then spend in their developing role as "consumers." The postwar era saw the mass production and consumption of many other products and services such as radios and airplanes, motels and service stations, magazines and movies. Ways to make this disposable income easier to spend also came to the fore. By the end of the 1920s, the Atlantic and Pacific Tea Company (A & P) had 15,000 stores across America, and other "chain stores" like Woolworth and J.C. Penney had become readily recognized features of the urban landscape. Consumer society seemed to be working. Encouraged by the explosion in advertising and the greater availability and acceptability of credit during the 1920s, Americans purchased 15 million new cars, and Ford became a folk hero and a billionaire. By the middle of the decade, "a typical middle-class household owned an automobile, a radio, a phonograph, a washing machine, a vacuum cleaner, a sewing machine and a telephone." The 1920s saw the real beginnings of that variant on the American Dream that had at its heart the paradoxical concept of "affordable luxury." [9]

Advertising was, in many ways, what held the developing culture of modern America together. It was also central to the development of a mass culture that could also be "consumed," as radio shows, magazines, fashion, the movies, and, of course, sports. Advertising blended into the new world of mass entertainment being born in what many called the "Jazz Age." Advertising brought the glamour and desire of entertainment to the wishes and necessities of everyday living, linking them both to an economy increasingly oriented toward the individual consumer. In turn, the sovereignty of the individual in the marketplace was reinforced by the celebrity of the movie star or sports hero. Americans increasingly defined themselves in terms of what they consumed rather than, or as well as, what they did. They also developed new perspectives on their relations toward others, becoming more likely to define community in terms of "shared styles of consumption" rather than "shared values." For many Americans these rapid and qualitative changes in work and culture made the 1920s "an important watershed in the development of a mass national culture" that fundamentally reshaped American life forever, bringing permanent "changes in manners, morals and personal identities." [10]

Not everyone welcomed the change. For one thing, many

Americans could not afford the material blessings of the new consumerism, not even on "the installment plan." In the 1920s, the
income of 65 percent of American families was still less than
$2,000, while the income of the poorest 40 percent averaged only
$725. Nor was everyone leaving the American countryside. Many
of those who stayed saw the values of mass culture as distinctly
urban in content, and thus at odds with the priorities of their traditional way of life. As historian George Moss points out,
"beneath the surface unity of consumerism and mass participation
in new games, sports and recreations, cultural conflicts and tensions seethed." The 1920s also saw, then, a "profound divide
between those who embraced a modernist culture and those who
retained traditional values." Thus, an event like the Centre College
victory over Harvard could be greeted by some Americans as a
victory against the cultural power of urban America and its alien
values. As is usually the case in America, those centers of power
were themselves quick to pander to those who resented them. As
"the Sportsman" columnist of that great defender of the rural
sensibility, the *Boston Globe,* put it, "George Bernard Shaw may
never have heard of Bo McMillin, but his name is on the lips of all
the kids of this broad land, and he is an outstanding figure with all
red-blooded men and women." Many adult Americans who
resented what they saw as the power and elitism of the East, also
saw Harvard as the perfect symbol for what they did not like and
were happy to adopt Centre as a "surrogate alma mater."[11]

Despite sharing to a significant extent in the economic expansion of the time, the South still contained a disproportionate share
of poor Americans, both black and white. Despite its rapid urbanization, it remained qualitatively more rural than many other
regions of the nation. In the South the rural-urban divide blended
with a continuing sense of regional distinctiveness, especially
among white Southerners. Much of this sense of distinctiveness
had its roots in continuing resentment toward the North and deep
ambivalence or outright antagonism toward many aspects of modern life closely identified with the North. As with the New South of
the late nineteenth century, there were those who saw the spread of
mass culture as, in effect, the destructive imposition of "Yankee"
culture and power. The sectional angle to the Centre celebrations is
suggested by a story told of Coach Moran's pre-game pep-talk. "I

know you guys have been royally entertained by these Harvard
chaps," the coach reportedly told his huddled players, "but just
remember one thing . . . Every one of those bums votes the
straight Republican ticket." Whether true or apocryphal, the very
popularity of the story suggests how a sporting event could take on
wider cultural and political meaning in a region still uncertain of
its relation to the rest of the nation.[12]

Thus, diverging and ambivalent attitudes regarding the pace
and consequences of modern life blended with other familiar divisions in American society—between rural and urban, South and
North—in shaping responses to change. As in the latter part of the
nineteenth century, social and cultural change encouraged in many
Americans a sense of greater openness but also deeper introspec-
tion, enthusiasm for the power of a growing "national" culture
but also a concern for the preservation of local identity. From
Danville to San Diego, these related yet conflicting attitudes and
emotions can be observed in the celebration of Centre's famous
victory: the desire for national fame, an attraction to celebrity, a
sense of local pride, feelings of sectional suspicion or rural resentment, even, of course, the love of a good football game. The
power of events such as the Centre game, and of sports in general,
was a consequence of their ability to be all things to all people in a
shifting, complex, often confusing cultural atmosphere. The
Praying Colonels could be modern, entertaining, All-American,
Gloria Swanson and the Ziegfield Follies. The Praying Colonels
could be traditional, inspirational, local, the small boy and the
small-time booster in the Danville street.

There was at least one place in America (other than Harvard
Yard) where the Praying Colonels' victory brought discomfort
rather than pleasure. For the Association of Colleges and
Secondary Schools of the Southern States, Centre athletics symbolized everything that was unwelcome about modern culture's
impact on education. Thus Centre College became involved in
another series of conflicts, still related to athletics, but with the
Association's leadership providing the determined opposition. The
Association's Executive Committee had been concerned for some
time about athletics at Centre, claiming to have information about
players being paid to play or being allowed to play despite neglecting
their academic responsibilities. There were, apparently, several

candidates for the role of ineligible hero, including Bo McMillin. Despite entering his fifth year at Centre, the 26-year-old quarterback remained 35 credits short of the 120 required for graduation. By many accounts an upstanding young man, it seems that McMillin had nevertheless focused with something less than laserlike intensity on his studies. His biographers conclude that McMillin should probably have been benched for his academic inadequacies rather than lauded, in the words of the *Louisville Courier-Journal,* "as Danville's Alexander the Great" leading "an expedition to Cambridge." There were other players whose eligibility was also questionable, but it appears that the Association's leaders were more concerned about what they saw as pervasive corruption at Centre College.[13]

Beyond the accusations of specific infractions at one college, to some Association leaders Centre appears to have been emblematic of a problem that had been developing for some time. Indeed, the Association had been concerned about the role of athletics in college life almost from its inception. Its annual *Proceedings* of these years are peppered with papers on the benefits and abuses of sport for students, with the emphasis increasingly on the sad decline of the scholar-athlete ideal. For many educators, the influence of society on college athletics and, in turn, athletics' pervasive impact on college life symbolized everything about the modern culture that threatened the world of education. In 1921, the closest, and from their point of view, most deserving target of these concerns was Centre College. The extensive publicity surrounding the game only intensified the unwelcome attention that the college had sought to avoid, and the Association soon brought formal charges against Centre for "subsidizing football players and laxly administering entrance requirements in admitting them." The Executive Committee of the Association then recommended that Centre's membership in the organization be suspended.[14]

The Centre administration vehemently questioned the validity of the charges, and at different annual meetings of the Association stoutly defended their institution. Complaining that the Executive Committee would not provide details of their supposed violations, they also questioned their detractors' motives. Some detected a strong corollary between those who wished to banish Centre and those who belonged to institutions, like

Vanderbilt, whose own football supremacy had been challenged by the upstart Colonels. Replying to a detailed letter President Montgomery had sent to all the trustees, Charles D. Gates, president of Turner, Day & Woolworth Handle Company of Louisville, Kentucky, expressed the not uncommon opinion that Centre's new athletic standing "weigh[ed] heavily" upon "envious" Association leaders. Another Centre supporter criticized those Southern colleges that, "unwilling to risk getting beaten" by Centre and "unable to get a clear claim to the Southern title so long as they run out on us," had instead been "active in circulating slanderous rumors discrediting the amateur status of athletics at Centre." Especially suspect in this respect, according to this Centre supporter, was Vanderbilt University and its chancellor, James H. Kirkland. Jealousy rather than principle, then, was deemed to be the motivation behind efforts to "get Centre."[15]

The Centre representatives also deeply resented what they saw as the high-handed way in which they had been treated by the Executive Committee. Many of the trustees questioned the value of belonging to such a disrespectful Association. Trustee Gates for one "doubt[ed] if it is of sufficient importance for Centre College to make any further sacrifice of your time and dignity than you have already made." Although probably as angry as anyone connected to Centre, President Montgomery had a much clearer idea than most of his trustees just how important membership in the Association had become. As he bluntly stated the case, "We are *unapproved* by *the* standardizing organization of the South." This "stigma" hurt Centre's ability to attract new students. It also harmed existing students' ability to transfer to other schools. Furthermore, "no approved secondary school dares to take but a very limited number of our graduates" as teachers, Montgomery explained, since they were bound by Association standards regarding faculty qualifications. At least one trustee was convinced, despite his suspicion of the Association's motives, agreeing "that the thing of first consideration at Centre is to get right with the Association, and if at all possible, get accredited."[16] By the 1920s, educators and administrators like Montgomery understood that membership in the Association had become a valuable educational and social asset. Conversely, exclusion from membership was increasingly a serious hardship, even a threat to survival, as institutions had to compete for students with colleges quick to advertise their approved status. Thus, necessity as well as anger motivated Centre's vigorous and persistent efforts to rebut the charges against them.

Centre's claim that their "offenses" were no worse and often far less than other colleges is perhaps supported by the fact that the assembled membership took the rare step at that time of refusing to endorse the Executive Committee's recommendation that the college be dropped from the membership. The conflict with Centre would drag on for several years before being resolved with the college retaining its membership in the Association. While dramatic, the Centre conflict hardly represents a towering event in the Association's history. It does illuminate, however, some of the ways in which the Association was shaped by wider cultural changes. It also suggests the ways in which the Association developed as a venue for the era's widespread debates and disagreements regarding educational life and its relation to the wider society. The dispute with Centre also provides a sense of where the Association stood, both in the educational realm and in the wider society, after a quarter of a century or so of existence, as, by the 1920s, the Association had come to exercise a significant amount of power in both Southern education and society.

That the Association had come to possess this degree of influence no doubt pleased its leaders of a generation earlier as they watched their brainchild taking small, slow steps toward an uncertain future. The Association had a small membership to start with as only six of the colleges represented at the original meeting became charter members of the Association. Few others joined them in the ensuing years. After a decade of existence, the Association counted only fourteen member colleges across the entire South. After another ten years, 32 higher institutions belonged to the Association. The Association counted no secondary schools among its charter members, but thirteen private schools did join the following year. By 1902, the secondary school membership totaled only 45 institutions; but even that modest figure dropped back to 38 a decade later, having dropped as low as 30 in the intervening period. The Association's slow growth concerned its leaders. Addressing the eighth annual meeting, Edwin Mims of Trinity College acknowledged that there had been "much to discourage" even the more optimistic who saw in the Association's creation "a great forward movement in higher education." Mims conceded that the Association had "faltered" in the face of higher education's problems. "Many of our meetings," he lamented, had turned into "confessions of failure" and had even led some members to "wonder if it is worth while to come here from year to year only to realize more vividly the difficulty of the task we have undertaken."[17]

Given the severity of the challenges facing the Association, a slow start was perhaps inevitable. Yet other organizations formed in response to the same social and educational circumstances had already made a significant impression on the public consciousness. Notable among them was the Southern Educational Board (SEB), formed in 1901 through the combined efforts of Southern educators and reformers and Northern business people and philanthropists. Through propaganda and public meetings, the Board proved successful in rallying white Southerners to the cause of developing tax-supported schools throughout the region. Mims agreed on the "overwhelming importance" of "awakening the Southern people to their duty." He praised the successes of SEB rallies where big crowds were "raised to a high pitch of enthusiasm" on behalf of the "forgotten man" of the South and in support of his educational advance, and he acknowledged "the unprecedented generosity of Northern benefactors" who had helped to make the crusade a success.[18]

Mims acknowledged that the Association's own work had been "obscured somewhat" by the far greater public visibility of these other efforts. But he insisted that the success of the SEB did not in any way diminish the need for the Association. "For the working out of some of our problems," Mims argued, "enlightenment rather than agitation is needed, the deliberation of the few rather than the enthusiasm of the many." James Kirkland also distinguished the Association's work from these "general educational gathering[s]." The demands for such meetings "were already supplied," he later opined, "and we had no desire to add to the list." In the words and tone of Mims and Kirkland can be detected a hint of defensiveness and/or of the suspicion of "enthusiasm" that educated elites in America have often felt for camp-meeting style crusades.[19]

Their words suggest more, however, about how the founders

conceived the function of their Association in advancing the cause of educational reform. Whatever their disappointment at the Association's lack of public impact, educators like Kirkland and Mims had not in fact set out to create a mass organization dependent on public support but rather a professional association founded on professional cooperation. In pursuit of this goal, they were just as committed to "talk," to debate and persuasion as other groups. Recognizing that they began as a minority among Southern educators, they understood that an essential part of their early work would be to persuade fellow educators of the value of their aims and of the Association's potential for bringing them about. Achieving the necessary level of professional solidarity required that the Association develop as a venue for the discussion and debate of educational ideas and concerns. Even Chancellor Kirkland was not always so dismissive of "talk," noting that the founders had "in mind an annual gathering where the peculiar problems of schools and colleges might be discussed and illuminated."[20] William Baskervill, Kirkland's colleague and co-founder, perhaps grasped best the priorities of the situation when he recognized that "the first work of the Association is largely preliminary, consisting mainly in meetings, which should be well-attended," where educators could "make the personal acquaintance" of each other "as teachers and fellow workers in this great undertaking." As part of this endeavor, interested non-members were also encouraged to attend annual meetings. "The social ties and friendly exchange of experiences and opinions may not easily be overvalued at this time," Baskervill believed. Through such steps the Association could become "a large and influential body," focused on the South's educational problems and thus in a position to "strengthen the position and help to alleviate the difficulties of all institutions of learning within its bounds." If the Southern Educational Board had set out to "evangelize" the public, the Association would set out to persuade the profession. Baskervill also "recognized at the outset" what Mims and others noted later, that the construction of a cooperative foundation for educational leadership could be achieved "only after long and patient as well as united effort." Thus as Mims well knew, delegates to the annual meetings did more than congregate for the purpose of questioning why they had bothered to do so.[21]

Nevertheless, the Association's limited membership had other causes. One was the ethos and focus established by the founders. Almost all the early members of the Association were drawn from the ranks of the region's colleges and universities. Not surprisingly, this gave it a distinctly postsecondary perspective on educational matters generally. That perspective was more tightly focused still on higher institutions in what might loosely be termed the liberal arts tradition. This could include liberal arts colleges such as Trinity College or larger institutions like Vanderbilt University, in which the humanities nevertheless occupied a central role. A clear picture emerges from the early resolutions and by-laws of the founders' strong underlying beliefs as to what a college or university education should entail. As with much else about the founders, their ideal was a blend of the traditional and the modern. Many of them had trained in the modern German and American cathedrals of secular education and warmly embraced modern "scientific" methods of, for example, literary, theological and historical inquiry. Nevertheless, they retained a quite traditional idea of the subjects, such as mathematics, Latin and Greek, that should be studied. In the long term, the founders' shaping of the young Association in their own image would be a source of great conflict as other educators with other philosophies and interests came to challenge what they referred to as "the liberal arts crowd." In the short term, however, the founders' commitment to this particular educational ideal was itself a major cause of the Association's slow growth as, among other things, it limited the types of institution likely to be interested in joining.[22]

There was a further cause of slow growth: the stringency of the Association's standards. The Association adopted a set of standards as the basis for judging whether educational institutions should be admitted to membership. In doing so they acted similarly to many other professional organizations and associations, which shared their aim of bringing order and improvement to the conduct of their profession. The period between 1895 and 1920 was, as one historian describes it, "The Age of Standards."[23]

The Association's "fundamental principles" and standards were set out in five by-laws, drawn up at the first meeting. No college offering "preparatory instruction in any subject as part of its college organization" would be eligible for membership (by-law I), nor would any preparatory school conferring degrees (by-law V).

(The need for such a by-law speaks eloquently to the extent of the confusion and lack of demarcation that the Association sought to remedy.) No college that admitted students under the age of fifteen was to be granted membership (by-law IV), a stipulation that, had it been in force at the time, would either have kept Wofford College out of the Association or the precocious fourteen-year-old James Kirkland out of Wofford! No college was to be admitted, or retained once admitted, that did not hold written entrance examinations, publish those examinations annually and deposit copies of them with the Association's secretary (by-law II). The exams mandated in by-law II were to meet, at least, the standards established in by-law III, which set out "minimum requirements for admission to college, the same to be binding on each institution belonging to this Association."[24]

Thus the Association's membership was expected to consist not only of schools and colleges committed to various general reform goals, but also, as James Kirkland later recalled, "pledged to certain standards." There was "a pledge, either expressed or understood," that the Association's "fundamental principles . . . would be observed." The Association, Kirkland explained, "was a compact," participation in which "was not an honor but an obligation," which would not be "without its inconvenience and cost." Thus the pursuit of this elite vanguard's aims would require not only a great deal of cooperation *between* its member institutions, but also place significant demands *upon* them. Clearly, it was not enough that an institution or its faculty shared the founders' desire for better relations *between* institutions. They also had to meet, or promise soon to meet, certain standards *within* their institutions.[25]

Meeting the obligations and demands set out in the standards proved initially beyond the abilities or inclinations of most of the South's educational institutions. If the Association's adoption of standards fit within a national pattern, its efforts to apply them, nevertheless, took place in the poorest part of the country with the least-developed educational system. Although perhaps not so onerous when compared to the academic ideal that inspired them, these standards were demanding given the disorder of the educational system and the poverty of the wider society. Despite Chancellor Kirkland's view that "care was taken that these provisions should be few in number and of reasonable import," very few institutions appeared either willing or able to meet them. Indeed, the stringency of its own standards is perhaps the most significant cause of the Association's glacial growth in the first phase of its existence.[26]

The slow growth of the early years bears out the judgment of Guy Snavely, an early member, and later a historian of the Association, who believed that the "rigid" membership "policy" set out in the by-laws made it "impossible to secure any college members" other than the original six. James Kirkland admitted that even their participation had only been "secured through concessions," since the Association's general requirements for admission were not to take effect until September of 1897, and that for the study of Greek until 1898. "Thus, and thus only," Kirkland concluded, "was the Southern Association brought into being." When even Kirkland acknowledged understanding why "few institutions were ready to accept the regulations agreed on," he seemed to acknowledge that what might be a "reasonable" goal for the future might not be a practical possibility in the present. Nevertheless, the founders' sense of their elite role in education and society and the nature of the standards they considered appropriate for schools and colleges were two central causes of the limited membership of the early years.[27]

Limited membership and influence would not prove to be among the Association's enduring characteristics. By the 1920s, as the Centre controversy suggests, the Association had gained a place among the most important educational organizations in the South. Its influence would only increase over the following years. Its increased influence was in part the consequence of its increased membership. Increased growth also brought greater conflict within the Association as to its goals and practices. Some new members and many more prospective members did not share the founders' commitment to the centrality of liberal arts in education or of their advocates within the Association. Out of this growth and conflict would emerge, by the 1930s, a much larger, more powerful Association. By then, it would have become an organization very different in form and function than the one envisioned by its creators.

In the early days, however, the Association's debates and activities followed fairly closely from the founders' original intention to bring order to the relations between different levels of the educational system. As Chancellor Kirkland remembered in 1912, "attention was first directed to one particular task, the adjustment of the relationship between the high school and the college."[28] Inevitably, however, the issue of articulation between colleges raised questions about standards within institutions. Thus, in the early years, the Association also looked closely at issues and concerns within secondary schools and within colleges. Indeed, in some ways the founders' predominantly college-oriented perspective encouraged close attention in this period to concerns within the secondary system, especially those that presented problems for the colleges.

The task of bringing order to the curriculum and standards of secondary schools attracted particular attention within the Association in the early years. This was true of both private and public schools. The great majority of early secondary members came from private schools, and their work was the subject of much debate within the Association.[29] At its first meeting, however, the Association placed itself on the record as "strongly sympathiz[ing] with the development of the state public school systems." Early papers also addressed topics such as "The Preparation of the Teacher for High School Work," and wider concerns such as "The Outlook of the Public High School in the South." Thus the rapid growth of the public school system and its future relation to the region's colleges also proved to be a major topic of concern. The founders' early resolution in favor of public schools illuminates not only their concern for all secondary education, but also how their perspective shaped those concerns. Although the major differences between private and public schools were clearly recognized, the Association nevertheless tended to view both from the same perspective: as places that prepared students before college. Thus, the resolution also maintained "that the best interests of popular education demand the insertion in the curriculum of the public high schools of four years' instruction in Latin, and as soon as practicable two years in Greek." This resolution does more than capture the blend of the progressive and the traditional that characterized the founding generation's thought and action. Its insistence on the importance of classical languages to a high school education indicates how, from their perspective, the public school's most important role was the preparation of students (albeit greater numbers of them) for further education at the college or university level. In the early days, the secondary school members of the Association were mostly private schools, and therefore inclined to endorse this understanding of the secondary schools' principle educational role.[30]

The founders did recognize that a public high school might have other functions beyond the preparation of students for further education, functions shaped by other educational responsibilities and social expectations. Indeed, one speaker at the Association's second meeting did acknowledge that, so far, "the matter of preparation for college has been secondary with the public high schools." Nevertheless, given their own sense of priorities, college preparation was the matter that was of primary concern for most of the Association's early members. "We have declared this Association to be the friend and champion of preparatory schools, whether private or public," Chancellor Kirkland declared in 1907, "and our main purpose from the beginning has been to exclude students from college who could not show a respectable career in some respectable preparatory school." The postsecondary priorities suggested by Kirkland's words dominated the first generation of Association activity. These priorities are evident in the Association's dual focus on bringing about the standardization of the secondary school curriculum while developing an efficient system of college entrance requirements. In a time of such educational and social turmoil, however, progress toward either of these related goals was not easy. Nor was it predictable. The Association began life as an attempt to shape the developing educational system by championing college values and priorities. Very soon, however, the growing influence of different, often conflicting, educational beliefs and priorities would begin to shape the Association, and to alter its aims, its activities, even its ethos.[31]

Change was a constant feature, for example, of *what* the Association evaluated within secondary institutions. This was a period of ferment and experimentation in education, fueled by the increasing claims made on it by a wider public both paying for and participating in public education on an unprecedented scale. Demands that education should be more amenable to public priorities were often heard among educators, too. Among the early victims of changing attitudes were the classical languages so valued by the founders. James Kirkland regretfully accepted that the

Association's plans for the teaching of Greek in schools had "failed," a defeat codified in the 1902 adoption of by-laws that allowed the study of Greek, as well as French and German, to begin in college. "We were trying to stem a tide too strong for us," Kirkland conceded, "and wisely decided to yield to the inevitable with grace and promptness." The tide did not stop at the school gates. Addressing the Association in 1912, Dr. Kendric C. Babcock, a specialist in higher education from the United States Bureau of Education, described how, "save for a few scattered walled towns of the rare old culture," most colleges no longer insisted on Greek as a requirement for a bachelor's degree.[32] The founders' reluctant acceptance of classical languages' declining importance suggests how despite the "progressive" character of some of their educational views and practices, in other respects they remained attached to more traditional beliefs and priorities, attachments that increasingly made them a minority within the world of educational reform. Furthermore, it increasingly made them a minority within the Association that they had founded.

At other times, there was greater consensus on the value of adapting to seemingly inevitable change. This was evident in the Association's largely uncontroversial acceptance of newly prominent subjects of study. Many of the subjects considered integral components of college curricula at the end of the twentieth century were largely absent or peripheral 100 years earlier. Gradually, however, subjects like the sciences, modern languages and history came, in Babcock's words, to be "accorded equal if not preferential treatment with the classics and mathematics." This trend was apparent in the South, whose colleges also increasingly accepted the physical sciences as "equal partners" with the classics and mathematics and in so doing effectively elevated the Bachelor of Science to the status of the Bachelor of Arts degree. Indeed, some Association members, otherwise committed to the liberal arts position, welcomed an expansion of subjects, and therefore of student choice. Edwin Mims, for example, used his 1902 presidential address to appeal for "greater freedom in entrance requirements," a development which, as Alfred Meyer writes, "implied the enriching of the schools' curricula" and the development of "a system of electives" in which students would have greater choice of subjects. Mims, though, was insistent that such a system not be taken too far and that high standards be demanded in the new subjects.[33]

The response of Mims, Kirkland and their colleagues to these changes illustrate their ability to blend attachment to traditional ideals with acceptance of innovation when it was either desirable or inevitable, and when they believed the improvement of education or the preservation of their own influence required it. A significant example of this came in their efforts to encourage school standardization. In 1906, the Carnegie Foundation produced a report that suggested ways to standardize the measurement of high school achievement: the unit of credit. Defining one unit of credit as consisting of 120 hours of instruction, the Foundation recommended that the completion of fourteen such units be required of students seeking to enter college. Chancellor Kirkland and his Vanderbilt and Association colleague, Dean Frederick W. Moore, were "convinced" that the Carnegie Unit represented "the wave of the future." Both men delivered addresses on the subject at the 1907 annual meeting. In Kirkland's view, there was "room for argument" with some of the Carnegie valuations, but on balance he recommended acceptance as "the wiser course." Such a course would require "some adjustment" on the part of the Association's members, since, as the current diverse state of things stood, units of credit were awarded for anything from 90 to 200 hours of instruction. The Association's own requirement of ten units for college admission would also have to be increased, although, as proponents of change pointed out, all but three of the Association's current members already exceeded this requirement. The changes in the Association's by-laws required by acceptance of the Carnegie proposals did not go unopposed. The proposed change was tabled for a year after failed attempts to alter it. A two-year delay in its implementation also suggests something less than unanimity. "Generally," however, as James Stiltner, historian of the Secondary Commission concludes, "participants at the annual meeting were receptive to the proposal to adopt the recommendations of the Carnegie Foundation."[34]

James Kirkland expressed his surprise at the members' openness to such major changes. Recalling how the Association had "struggled for fifteen years for the promotion of better standards," as well as "how difficult, if not impossible, it has been to secure advancement," Kirkland could not "withhold an expression of

surprise at the readiness with which old standards have been aban-
doned and new ones adopted in the presence of the stimulating
influence of the Carnegie report." One incentive, as Kirkland recognized, was that an institution's acceptance of the new requirements meant that its faculty became eligible for the pension plan
also funded by the Carnegie Foundation. This plan did not apply
to all institutions (public and denomination schools were initially
excluded), so it could not "be said that the motive is purely a mer-
cenary one," Kirkland acknowledged. But whatever the reason,
Kirkland was pleased that "the timely hour for which some of us
have been looking for so long has at last arrived, and Southern
institutions are ready to demand standard requirements for admission to college." The recommendations were adopted in 1907, to
come into effect in 1910, after which member institutions were
bound to require fourteen units from any student seeking "admission to any degree course in its literary department" or at least ten
units from irregular students. By 1913, Kirkland noted that the
Association "now has practically no other requirements than
these." By adopting the Carnegie Unit, "the Association took a
giant step toward the standardization of schools."[35]

The establishment of the fourteen-unit requirement did not,
however, resolve the question of whether or not a student should
be admitted to college. Colleges still sought further evidence of
suitability, especially with regard to what subjects, and not just
how much of them, the student had studied in secondary school.
College entrance was also, therefore, a much debated issue within
the Association, with many speeches and papers devoted to the
question of how best to measure students' suitability for college.
An early step toward this end was the plan, approved at the second
annual meeting, to set up several three-member committees "to
consider the minimum requirements for admission to college
adopted by this Association in the various subjects of study."
These committees reported back at the following year's annual
meeting, at which time their reports themselves became further
food for thought and debate.[36] In practice, most students were
admitted in one of two ways. Sometimes students were accepted if
they held a certificate from an institution deemed by the college to
be of sufficiently high academic standards. Some institutions, like
Vanderbilt, had their own individual systems, each encompassing

a few preparatory schools considered acceptable. Nevertheless, as James Kirkland later remembered, given the "absence of reliable high schools, public or private" whose certificates could confidently be assumed to be "satisfactory" by the colleges, "it was assumed that a considerable number of students would be examined" by the college. At this time, an entrance examination administered by the college was the most common means of testing prospective students.[37]

As its original by-laws indicate, the entrance examination was the Association's preferred method of student testing. At first, member colleges were required to hold entrance examinations, copies of which were to be deposited with the Association's secretary.[38] The Association's "Entrance Examination Committee," formed in 1904, reported back the following year, concluding, "with the enthusiasm essential for success" that a system of uniform entrance examinations represented "the crystallization of the purpose of this Association and the easiest and the most practical way" of putting it into effect. It was hoped that such a program would bring greater uniformity to the exams themselves and through them to the central task of improving school-college relations.[39] Despite the enthusiasm, the assumption in favor of college-administered examinations quickly proved mistaken. As use of the Association's uniform examinations declined significantly over the following years, a study commissioned to explore this lack of enthusiasm found "an almost unanimous preference for the admitting of students by certificate over the program of uniform entrance examinations." The study's authors, Dean Moore and Professor J.L. Henderson, came to the unequivocal conclusion that most member institutions "have little use for the papers . . . and any subscription on their part must be counted as purely a contribution to the work of the committee without any feeling of value received." James Kirkland himself sarcastically noted "the universal rebellion on the part of pupils and teachers against the hardship and indignity of entrance examinations." By 1912, although he and his Vanderbilt colleagues were still "trying to hold on to our traditions," even the Chancellor had to acknowledge the "almost entire abandonment of examinations as a means of entering college." The Association's uniform entrance examination program was discontinued that same year.[40]

As the testing of individual students by individual colleges proved increasingly unpopular, attention necessarily shifted to the testing of secondary schools in ways that would guarantee that students emerging from them were ready for college. The gloomy prognosis for entrance exams encouraged those who supported a system of school certification. Impetus toward developing such a system came from various sources across the nation. One source was the Association's participation in discussions and conferences with like-interested associations and organizations from around the country. Despite important regional differences, these organizations inevitably shared many concerns and aims, among them a desire for greater standardization of both high school curricula and college entrance requirements. The Association's acceptance of the Carnegie Unit, for example, was in part encouraged by participation in national discussions with like-interested organizations that also endorsed its adoption. A pivotal event in the development of this kind of nationwide cooperation was a meeting held at Williamstown, Massachusetts, on August 3, 1906. Representatives of the four regional associations and the College Entrance Examination Board responded to the appeal of the National Association of State Universities to meet in order to plan for greater cooperation in establishing and maintaining college admission standards that would be understood and accepted across the nation. In pursuit of this goal, the conference passed several resolutions, all unanimously, one of which called for the setting up of "a permanent commission to consider admission requirements and other matters of mutual concern." Originally named the National Conference Committee of the Association of Colleges and Preparatory Schools, its name changed in 1908 to the National Conference Committee on Standards of Colleges and Secondary Schools.[41]

Another resolution (the fifth) was more specific, recommending that the Association and its counterpart in the Middle States and Maryland "each consider the desirability of organizing a College Entrance Certificate board, or a Commission for accrediting schools," similar to those already established by the New England and the North Central Associations. Acceptance of this resolution "marked," according to Stiltner, "the first time that such an ideal had been formally sanctioned." In explaining the value of an accredited list, Moore focused on its usefulness for Southern students wishing to pursue their education elsewhere in the country. He insisted that "it would miss the whole purpose of the recommendation," as well as being "foolish and humiliating," for the Association to adopt lower standards than those in force elsewhere. When Moore spoke of a set of conditions that "any school, a member of the Association, which desires to be placed on the list" would have to satisfy, he also gave the impression that member institutions could choose whether or not to seek inclusion in the accredited list. In other words, accreditation would not be synonymous with membership. In this somewhat cautious fashion, Moore recommended "the authorization of an 'Accredited List,'" to be administered by the Executive Board, "upon the high plane indicated."[42]

Support for a secondary accrediting commission also came from within the region and within the Association, and was led by Joseph S. Stewart, professor of Secondary Education at the University of Georgia. Stewart had held this post since 1903, his chair funded by the General Education Board as part of its effort to improve the secondary school system. The purpose of these chairs, as Stewart explained it to the Association, was "to bring about unity of action and improvement to the high schools, extending their influence to every county, and properly correlating their work with the elementary schools and the higher institutions." Through a variety of duties, including classroom instruction in the university, inspection of schools, and legislative activity, "these professors are expected to aid in enriching, systemizing [sic], and extending the high school system of the South." Stewart had also been instrumental in forming the Georgia Accrediting Commission, which published the first list of that state's accredited schools in 1904. Encouraged by Stewart's success, the board eventually funded similar chairs in all the other state universities of the South on the understanding that, after a certain period, each state Department of Education would assume financial responsibility for them. Encouraged by the success of accrediting programs in Georgia and elsewhere, Stewart was "convinced" that accreditation "could work on a regional basis." Stewart presented a resolution to the Association's sixteenth annual meeting asking "that a permanent commission be formed to be called the Southern Commission on Accredited Schools and Colleges, to consist of the High School inspectors and Professors of Secondary Education in the several Southern States." Many in the Association strongly opposed the creation of such a commission as well as the system of certification and accreditation that it implied. Some opponents wanted at the very least to tie certification to the standards demanded by the Association's uniform entrance examinations. J. Carter Walker of the Woodberry Forest School, a representative and defender of private schools, proposed a counter-resolution requiring that no school be accredited "by any college or university included in the membership of this association" unless its students be tested by examinations prepared by the Association ("or others of equal difficulty") with the papers "graded by the professors of the college or university administering the test." Such opposition prevented, for the time being, any effort to create an accrediting commission. As Joseph Stewart recognized, the continuing debate over the issue "emphasized the wide difference of opinion" that still existed between the advocates of accreditation and the supporters of examinations.[43]

A compromise resolution was eventually presented by Chancellor Kirkland. It called for a "special committee" to examine how the Association might "regulate and improve the administration of the certificating system" and to "consider the advisability of establishing a permanent commission or board" to that end. Kirkland recommended that Association members J.L. Henderson, Bruce R. Payne, J.J. Doster, E.C. Brooks, and St. George L. Sioussat be appointed to this Committee on Regulating and Improving the Administration of the Certificating System. Importantly, Dr. Stewart was added to the members suggested by Kirkland. Under his influence, the Committee recommended to the following year's meeting in Tuscaloosa, Alabama, that a Commission be established "composed of two members from each State, to be named and appointed by the Executive Committee . . . for a term of two or three years." One member would be the state inspector of secondary schools, a position usually connected to the state university. The other would represent "some other college or school belonging to this Association." The report further recommended that this committee would be responsible for preparing uniform "blanks," or questionnaires, for reports of high school principals relative to organization, teaching force, attendance, library, laboratory, and other equipment. The committee would also "describe and define unit course study in the various high school programs" based on the Carnegie recommendations and the rules of the Association. Each state committee would be responsible for preparing a list of accredited schools in their state, and provide it to the commission for its decision on which schools would make "the Southern List of Accredited Schools."[44]

The acceptance of the report saw the creation of the Commission on Secondary Schools. As Theodore Jack, a leading figure in the early years of the Association later put it, the Commission was charged "with responsibility for the oversight of the secondary school members of the Association and for the approval of satisfactory non-member schools." The Commission was organized as a working group at a meeting the following April in Nashville, Tennessee. Nine representatives from six states attended the first meeting and elected Stewart as chairman and Professor Bert Young of Vanderbilt University as secretary. Work began on developing the Commission's rules, and some changes were made as it progressed. Perhaps the most important change was to increase each state's representation by one person, since the original plan had not allowed for any representatives from the secondary schools the Commission would be dealing with. Stewart and his colleagues quickly corrected this "oversight" by making a place for a third person on each state committee. A more symbolic recognition of the greater emphasis on public secondary schools was the Association's first name change, with the substitution of *Secondary* for *Preparatory*. That also took place in 1912, the year which, with the beginning of the Secondary Commission's work, "can be said to mark the beginning of the Association's role as an accrediting agency."[45]

The Association's transformation into an accrediting agency was further cemented five years later with the establishment of the Commission on Institutions of Higher Education. Given their own situations as well as their general interests, the Association's members were, of course, interested in conditions and standards within the South's colleges. As well as a strong focus on admissions to college, there was a growing effort to define what students could reasonably expect to find once they arrived at an institution that could legitimately call itself a college. Thus papers and debates at annual meetings studied existing institutions and their current capacity to meet their remit, as well as their prospects for improvement in faculty and facilities, subjects offered and standards demanded. Professor E.H. Babbitt, for example, of the University of the South, addressed "The Problems of the Small College in the Southern States" by analyzing numerous college catalogs in order to get a sense of the current state (not very good, as it turned out) of such institutions. Other speakers also focused on conditions and standards within colleges. The status and quality of faculty proved important matters, and were addressed in papers that studied the "Salaries of Professors in Southern Colleges" or asked "Should Freshmen Receive the Bulk of Their Instruction from Others than the Heads of Departments?" Papers explored "The Place of Laboratories in a Liberal College Course" and sought to define the status of "Scientific and Technical Education" within the academy.[46]

Out of these and related concerns, and given the shift to standardization and accreditation in the Association's secondary affairs, it was probably only a matter of time before a commission for colleges and universities was also created. At the 1916 meeting in Durham, North Carolina, the Association supported the Executive Committee's recommendation that a five-person committee be formed to develop a suitable plan. The following year in Atlanta, the report was presented and the Commission created. Originally it consisted of thirty-nine representatives; twenty-four elected from colleges and fifteen from secondary schools, drawn from all states within the Association's region. Each state had at least one secondary representative and usually two from the colleges. Members were elected for three-year terms, with one-third of those expiring each year. The Commission was then called upon, Theodore Jack related, "to prepare, subject to the approval of the Association, a statement of the standards to be met by institutions of higher education, which are members of this Association, and to rate any other institutions within the territory of this Association, which may apply for inspection, classification, and rating by the Commission."[47]

American involvement in World War I, as well as the influenza epidemic sweeping the nation, prevented the Commission from meeting until 1919. In December of that year, in Louisville,

Kentucky, it produced its first set of standards for colleges. The following year it established a list of approved member colleges, as well as a list of approved non-member institutions that came close to meeting the Association's standards. The creation of this second list was prompted by the rapidly growing need for qualified secondary school teachers. With the number of approved member schools far too small to supply the expanding secondary system, it was necessary to establish a list of non-accredited institutions whose graduates would nevertheless be accepted as secondary teachers by the Association. Indeed, one motivation behind the College Commission's creation had been the need for the better evaluation of teachers required by the secondary school accreditation process. Evaluation of the teachers required, to some extent, an evaluation of the institutions from which they had graduated.[48]

By the early 1920s, then, the Association was fully embarked on a course far removed from the one originally charted by its founders. Theodore Jack later summarized this unintended shift in the organization's role. "The Association was not organized as an accrediting body nor, as a matter of fact, as a public agency in any sense," Jack explained. Nor did it "set itself up to pass on colleges and schools in general in this territory" or "demand that institutions should meet its standards or seek its membership." James Kirkland's 1921 presidential address reinforced this sense of an organization pushed to assume a role neither intended nor wanted. The Association had not been "organized in order to be a standardizing agency for the whole South," Kirkland declared, insisting that "so far as we play that role today it has been forced upon us." Yet Kirkland's "we" neglected those already within the Association who applied some of the "force" behind the push to accreditation. The debate over accreditation reflected differences of philosophy and priority *within* the Association, conflicts that would only intensify in the following years. And however "forced" the transition to accreditation seemed to some, the logic inherent in a system of standards and membership requirements led inexorably toward the establishment of a corresponding system for assessing prospective members. As Theodore Jack understood, "by force of necessity and in the absence of any other organization, the Association gradually evolved certain requirements" for membership as well as "standards by which applicants for membership might be tested."

By its establishing of two commissions, "the Association actually if not officially, set itself up as an accrediting agency."[49]

Whatever the reluctance of some members, the establishment of the commissions and the shift to accreditation soon, as Jack Allen, historian of the Commission on Colleges states, "established the Association as a force in Southern education and made membership more desirable as an indication of quality." This was reflected in the almost immediate increase in secondary membership following the Secondary Commission's establishment. The year after the commission's creation saw a great leap upward in secondary membership from 38 to 161 members, a figure that had almost doubled (to 308) by 1915. This increase offers implicit evidence that many Southern educators did indeed view the accreditation list as a "roll of honor," and were eager to see their institution's name appear on it. By 1925, the Association had 759 secondary school members. In his 1921 presidential address, James Kirkland insisted that the commission was "entitled to high praise" for its work in "the inspection and classification of schools," and noted how its role as an accrediting body had given the Association's work greater visibility in the educational realm. So much so, indeed, that Kirkland jokingly recalled a recent speaker from the North Central Association who had confused the Secondary Commission (only eight years old) with the Association in claiming that the South's regional Association was younger than his own. "We congratulate our school commission," Kirkland drolly proclaimed, on having "loomed so large in the public eye as to obscure the whole association behind it." The College Commission's immediate impact is harder to gauge as its creation coincided with America's entry into the World War. But Kirkland duly noted that it, too, had "been diligently at work and bids fair to secure for us a degree of publicity equally as striking and perhaps more violent than that attained by the school commission." The college membership, thirty-two in 1915, had climbed to eighty-one by 1925. These numbers suggest the larger story of the Association's first quarter century of existence in the midst of great social change and educational ferment. What had started as a small cooperative association had grown into the region's preeminent accrediting agency. Increased membership brought greater responsibilities and also a higher public profile.[50]

Yet if the direction was new, the chief navigators remained the same. The Association emerged from World War I still largely under the control of the conservative, if adaptable, "liberal arts group" responsible for charting its original course. As the next quarter-century brought a continuation of many of the debates that had characterized the early years, the gap between changes in the Association's aims and ethos and the continuing power of its original leaders would prove a source of increasingly bitter conflict over matters of philosophy, practice, and power. These conflicts would come to a head in the "revolutionary" era of the 1930s, which brought significant change to the Association's constitutional and organizational structure.

In the pivotal year of the high school commission's creation, however, Chancellor Kirkland had felt able to report to the eighteenth annual meeting on the relative lack of conflict regarding the Association's activities. "The Association has never sought to interfere with the freedom of each institution," and had "exercised a wise self-restraint." According to Kirkland, "no complaint has ever been made of unjust legislation," nor, Kirkland proudly added, had an institution "ever withdrawn from our Association through a sense of wrongdoing or lack of sympathy with our purposes." Such relative harmony was not to last. The years between the two World Wars would see the Association transformed into an ideological battlefield on which many social and educational conflicts would be waged. Indeed, when in 1921 Kirkland spoke of the potentially more "violent" nature of the publicity surrounding the Higher Commission, he had in mind certain recent events that had raised the very kinds of complaints he claimed had once been non-existent. The year before, the Commission had issued its first list of approved institutions. The list, as Guy Snavely recalls, proved to be "a veritable bombshell." To their surprise and anger, eleven of the Association's existing members searched the list in vain for their own names. Previously, membership had been assumed to indicate approval. Now as the new commission formulated a new set of standards, it turned out that some members did not meet them. The embarrassment of these institutions was evident in several motions, all unsuccessful, to prevent the list's publication.[51]

In part, this somewhat embarrassing set of circumstances arose from the inevitable confusion attendant on a new enterprise.

Some new members were unsure of procedure; several institutions were tardy in returning necessary information. Perhaps most troubling of all was the poor attendance of commission members. According to Guy Snavely, "considerably over one-half of the membership appointed to this highly responsible task failed to put in their appearance." Whatever the cause, the excluded institutions came to the 1921 meeting in Birmingham looking for answers. Their concerns were met by changes that were put in place before the commission voted on the next approved list. From then on, membership and approval were once again synonymous, the former not being offered until the latter had been verified.[52] Nevertheless, the shock generated by the first list had a salutary impact on member institutions, encouraging greater awareness of the list's importance as well as greater participation in the commission's business.

Other conflicts would prove more enduring. The sources of conflict were several, including personal resentments, institutional rivalries, and philosophical differences. It is difficult, if not impossible, to separate intermingled causes that so often reinforced one another. Seldom far from center stage, however, were strong differences regarding questions of educational philosophy. Most fundamental of all, perhaps, was the broad philosophical question of just what social purposes education should serve and, in turn, how much influence should social values and priorities have on shaping what went on inside the region's schools and colleges. What support, for example, could institutions legitimately expect from the public, especially a public increasingly expected to fund education through taxation? What demands, in turn, could the public make of them? And, crucially, who was to define the meaning of "serve."

These debates had been a part of the Association since the beginning, but they took on greater intensity in the wake of the Association's own changed and expanded character, and also in the much-changed context of postwar American society. To many Americans, it was self-evident that a new kind of society required new kinds of education and instruction capable of preparing the mass of people for productive roles in an expanding, democratizing society. To an unprecedented degree, Americans of all groups and classes were called upon to pay for their educational system (as well as other government-provided services). Many Americans believed that the very least a system built with their hard-earned money should do was prepare them, or their children, to make more of it. Increased popular demand intertwined with increased appeals on the part of educators that they and their colleagues satisfy, but also shape, that demand. W.H. Heck, of the General Education Board, a guest speaker at the Association's 1904 meeting, argued that "More than any other part of our nation, the South is looking to its schools for leadership in all phases of its growing life." Heck was increasingly "enthusiastic" in his "hope for what might be called the socialization of the schools, vitalizing all instruction and connecting it more closely with social activities." The severe and enduring Great Depression that followed the stock market crash of 1929, placed, if anything, an even higher premium on the kinds of education that were seen as providing regular people with the basis for economic survival in the present and eventual progress in the future.[53]

Events and debates within the Association could hardly have been immune from these wider currents of social and educational thought, and indeed it is more accurate to say that it provided a major focal point for their discussion and development in the South. Increasingly, complaints were expressed that the Association was not responding appropriately to the many challenges presented to it by the rapidity and complexity of social change. An increasing number of members, and many more would-be members, agreed that the founders' educational tastes were too narrow, their preferred method of measuring academic success too limited, their understanding of education's relation to society too confining. There was no easy unanimity among the critics, whose general complaints often had specific sources. But a set of broad, interrelated concerns can be identified. At its heart lay the general belief that the Association's membership and standards must come to reflect a more expansive and diverse understanding of what constituted legitimate and worthwhile kinds of educational studies, institutions, and aims. Criticisms that were in some respects quite specific and not always consistent, together made a strong appeal for a radical rethink of the Association's aims and methods.

Just as the founders' attitudes reflected a mix of the traditional and the modern, so too criticisms directed at their running of the Association came from both traditional and modern perspectives.

On the one hand, the Association's definition of educational worth was criticized for embodying the worst aspects of the soulless materialism corrupting so much else in American life at the time. Institutions supported by religious denominations found especially troubling the Association's promotion of standards that seemed to run counter to their chosen mission in the wider society. This case was put most forcefully and memorably at the 1921 annual meeting in Birmingham, Alabama, by Dr. John E. White, president of Anderson College (which was not a member of the Association) located in the South Carolina town of the same name. White had found fault with the Association on previous occasions, and he began his address by acknowledging the Association's willingness to hear him "because of" rather than "in spite of" his previous criticism. Pointing to the more than $5 million they had spent over the preceding two years on improving both facilities and faculty, White was at pains to insist that denominational colleges shared the Association's "stand for increased efficiency in standards of education." But he also hoped that he could explain why "men of enlightenment, sincerity, and generosity" in those institutions, while also "oppressed by the backwardness of Southern schools and deeply conscious of the necessity for constructive standardization," nevertheless questioned the value of participating in the Association.[54]

These educators, White explained, were deeply concerned by the Association's concentration on quantitative and material measurements of efficiency. To a great extent, the Association's early standards did emphasize criteria susceptible to quantitative measurement. Close attention was paid to the financial health of an institution, the quality of its library and other physical plant facilities, the qualifications and remuneration of its faculty, and the size and content of classes. This emphasis was desirable up to a point, White agreed, but employed as almost the "exclusive" measure of an institution's worth, it made for an "inadequate" understanding of the standard school. White went so far as to argue that it tended toward "moral mischief" to the extent that it discouraged attention to less tangible criteria for the evaluation of an institution's worth and purpose. "Now is no time for denominational educators to accept as their exclusive and absorbing concern of standardization the definition of excellence and superiority which leaves Christianity out of consideration," White told his audience. In a materialistic age, argued White, more, not less Christianity was required in the nation's educational institutions. From this point of view, the Association's present standards strengthened the unwanted influence of secularism and materialism.[55]

Elsewhere in his speech, White criticized the Association for, in effect, not being "materialistic" enough in its evaluation, especially when it came to the difficult social and economic circumstances in which Southern educational institutions had to make their way. White also argued that the standards that were in place were too demanding given the South's grave social and economic circumstances. Despite the economic expansion that had taken place, the South remained by far the poorest section of the nation. Yet the Association took pride in having the higher standards of any regional association. "Is it unreasonable to wonder," White asked, why the accrediting association "operating in the most backward section of this country" had more "inaccessible" standards than those "in the wealthier and better advanced educational areas?" White proposed instead "a statesmanlike, standardizing movement" in the South that "should be built in patience and sympathy" and with greater recognition of the "actual conditions" that the region's educators faced. Despite the fierce assurance of White's speech, the ensuing debate offered some support for Kirkland's claim that "for the most part" denominational agencies "look to us hopefully and work with us sympathetically." Most of those present, including some of his fellow Baptists, did not share White's hard-line position regarding the relation of Baptist colleges to the Association. Nevertheless, White did give clear voice to a rising hubbub of complaint and anxiety that the Association's values and priorities were inappropriate for the educational and social tasks facing the region that it served.[56]

The most important group of critics, especially in terms of the Association's future development, was, in the words of one of them, what "might be called loosely the teachers' college crowd." According to Henry Hill, a later member, it was "composed of superintendents and principals of public schools, professors of secondary education at universities and colleges, and an almost solid membership of the Catholics, both Sisters and Fathers." Schools of education within large universities, such as Louisiana, Kentucky,

Tennessee, Clemson, and Georgia Tech played a large role. But the most powerful institutional role, especially in the second quarter-century of the Association's life, was assumed by George Peabody Teachers College in Nashville. Peabody joined the Association in 1915 under the presidency of Bruce R. Payne, who had already been a member of the Association's Executive Committee while at the University of Virginia. Peabody's growing influence stemmed in great part from the widespread participation of its alumni—as school superintendents, teachers, college professors and administrators—throughout Southern education. In an important sense, Peabody came to stand as the institutional embodiment of this group just as Vanderbilt University, its Nashville neighbor, did for those who adhered to the liberal arts tradition. According to M.C. Huntley, there were "many years of wrangling and sharpness" between Vanderbilt and Peabody that played itself out in the workings of the Association, but "they had great respect for each other," Huntley believed. Both "were giants," he remembered, "highly respected" leaders whose "judgments were highly regarded."[57]

Many in the "teacher college crowd" shared White's belief that the Association's standards were "practically prohibitive and discouraging," even for many of the region's "well-established, forward-looking" colleges. This group's perspective was, nevertheless, very different from that of White and the denominational colleges. From the standpoint of these educators, far from being too *materialistic,* the Association's standards were overly *idealistic.* If White found the standards too quantitative in their application, these critics found the goals that inspired them too qualitative in their conception, too committed to judging educational worth by the standards of the liberal arts ideal rather by the practical needs of a troubled, transforming society. Where White defended the traditional social role of the denominational school, these educators, as their institutional background would suggest, defended new kinds of education, and new ways of delivering that education to more people.[58]

Demands that the Association adopt a more open and expansive understanding of education's role in the twentieth-century South inevitably involved criticism of some of its existing values and priorities. Few were as unrestrained as Centre trustee Charles Gates, who felt he could "say without prejudice" that most of the leaders in educational associations were "mossbacks," "narrow and provincial" men with "faces turned toward the past instead of looking toward the future." Many advocates of change proved more measured, but there was much in what some of them argued to suggest that the educational ideals and standards of the liberal arts group would play a limited role in any new educational order of their design. Especially in what all admitted was a region of scarce resources and undereducated people, there were many who, even when they valued subjects like Greek and Latin, questioned the social utility of teaching them at the college level, never mind in the schools. H.M. Ivy, for example, who voluntarily taught classes in Latin and Greek in Mississippi, remembered how in his role as school inspector he stressed the importance of building up the sciences. In encouraging the development of study in biology and health, he received immediate support from the school boards, most of which contained a doctor. Ivy believed that this "practical" kind of program "gave something for the people themselves." In Ivy's view, "Greek and Latin did not mean much to the people of Mississippi."[59]

Not only the specialized academic nature of the classics but the perceived narrowness of the liberal arts curriculum generally came in for criticism. Sometimes it was in humorous vein. Henry Hill, for example, liked to say of his own undergraduate years at a liberal arts college, "that as a freshman at Davidson College, I had the privilege of taking five subjects [Greek, Latin, mathematics, English and Bible], all of them optional. That is, I took them all or I went home—that was the option." Hill, speaking in the 1970s, compared his "choice" with the vast range of options open to the modern-day student. Of course, as we have seen, by the period under discussion even the staunchest defender of the liberal arts tradition had accepted a wider range of subjects and a greater degree of student choice than had been available to Hill. Yet, for the most part, these new subjects also fell within many people's definition of "academic" studies. At the same time, many new fields and subjects whose social utility was scarcely in doubt continued to be excluded from most colleges and from many secondary schools. The pervasive impact of the liberal arts tradition in shaping both college and high school curricula had to end, the critics argued, before a transformed educational system could save the South. Whatever the positive and negative motivations for

demanding change, a consensus developed among those involved
with public education, land grant colleges, and related institutions.
They "knew," as E.B. Robert remembered, "that the philosophy of
classical Greek and Latin and the liberal arts philosophy was not
going to get the job done for education of the masses of the people
of the South."[60]

What *was* going to get the job done? At the heart of demands
for radical change were the related claims that educational institutions—through their curricula and their pedagogy—should better
serve the majority of students who looked to them for preparation
for employment rather than for further education. These broad
concerns fed a commitment to experimentation and reform in
many areas of educational philosophy and action.[61] Two of the
most significant concerns from the Association's point of view
were efforts to improve the training and quality of teachers and to
increase the diversity of instruction and education available to students. Henry Hill, in a later interview, drew the broad distinction
between the two groups' philosophies of teaching. The liberal arts
professors, according to Hill, "did not think professional courses in
education were necessary, that teachers were born more than
made." Others thought it less than "natural" for teaching, especially at the college level, to remain the only profession in America
that did not require a set form of training. Such laxity, it was
argued, too often attracted people unable or unwilling to enter
professions that did have set standards. Furthermore, even those
college professors who turned out to be good teachers, received
their own training as a teacher to some extent at the expense of the
students who encountered them as novices.

Increasingly, educational reformers thought it unreasonable to
assume that a specialized knowledge of one's field and a largely
self-taught approach to imparting that knowledge represented a sufficient guarantee of effective pedagogy. Some at the time put it more
grandly than the understated Hill. H.B. Heidelberg, superintendent
for schools in Clarksdale, Mississippi, and Association president in
1935, believed that the teacher would be a central figure in bringing
about a "New Age." Borrowing a phrase from a like-minded
Association member, H.L. Donovan, Heidelberg insisted that the
teacher would be "the architect of mankind," and in fulfilling that
role "wield more powerful influence in molding the structure of

civilization than ever before." It was clear to Heidelberg that society would not accept for much longer the filling of such an important role by "the untrained individual, posing as a teacher, with smug complacency in possession of a college diploma as sufficient evidence of ability to teach what he may happen to know." Heidelberg, "at the risk of being condemned for heresy" went on to "timorously suggest" to his Association audience that "a modicum of professional training or apprenticeship teaching" would bring about a "vast improvement" in most classrooms. Many educators agreed with Heidelberg, even when they did not express themselves quite so grandly. The need to train teachers at all levels of the system, and to do so in departments and institutions devoted to that task, was an item of faith for the teachers' college group. "With the coming of the teachers' colleges into our membership," as H.M. Ivy put it, "we shall probably see a great improvement of the teaching force in our secondary schools." For Ivy and his colleagues, teachers' colleges were essential additions to the Southern educational system.[62]

The expanding position of teachers' training colleges, two-year junior colleges, and vocational schools in society inevitably raised questions as to how they should be treated within the Association. Increasingly seen as essential and respectable by the wider society and by a growing number of educators, their goals and standards did not prove easily reconcilable with the kind of institutional and educational development the Association's founders wished to encourage. They did apply for membership, but their applications were judged on the basis of standards more applicable to liberal arts colleges or universities where the humanities occupied a significant role. C.C. Colvert, an important figure in the early junior college movement, remembered one Association visit to Northeast Junior College in Monroe, Louisiana, in the 1920s. "The committee did not look at any occupational programs we had," Colvert recalled, "they just closed their eyes and went on by. They accredited only the academic programs. That is all the committee was interested in." Colvert's words indicate the difficulties these institutions encountered when seeking the Association's seal of approval. They also suggest some of the resentment that such treatment increasingly generated among the practitioners and proponents of non-liberal arts education.[63]

These institutions often faced an unpleasant choice in trying to become accredited. If they gave priority to their principal mission, even excellent teachers' colleges or vocational schools could find it difficult to meet the Association's standards. In 1905, Brown Ayres, president of the University of Tennessee and of the Association that year, made the case for a more open stance toward such institutions. Ayres lamented that "present policy rejects institutions in most of the Southern States, which appeal strongly to the present sympathies and needs of the people of those states," institutions "whose duty it is to train by far the larger number of the future citizens of the South." In pursuing their mission, however, these institutions risked rejection by the Association as well as the loss of positive public recognition that came with membership. Yet if an institution pursued membership on the Association's terms, it risked neglecting the very purposes for which it had been created by diverting scarce resources toward those areas that the Association's standards emphasized. On a wider scale, an entire state might give priority to those public institutions that were of greatest concern to the Association. Thus a typical complaint, as Jack Allen describes, was "that state funds were being drained off by the liberal arts colleges to help them meet standards, or that non-liberal arts institutions were having to 'change their center of gravity' from their 'needed purposes' to meet the demands of the Association." Critics continued to insist that the Association's standards, combined with its growing power, were diverting scarce resources and good students toward liberal arts colleges and away from those institutions and fields of study that had greatest public and practical value (whether spiritual or material) in the struggle for Southern social advance. From this perspective, the Association's efforts, however well-intentioned, were doing more harm than good to the students, the institutions, and to the South.[64]

Calls for the Association to make room for new social goals and the educational institutions designed to meet them predated any significant membership of those institutions within the Association. They did have their supporters, however, often representatives of the large state universities with extensive and direct ties to the public and to the secondary system. Thus educators such as Brown Ayres of Tennessee praised the "wonderful change and improvement" evident in the Association's first ten years of exis-tence. Yet Ayres also noted its emphasis, "largely, if not exclusive-ly," on "the needs and problems" of liberal arts institutions, and wondered if "it would not be a useful thing" for the Association now to "enlarge its scope" by bringing in the growing number of public schools as well as the region's "large number of exceedingly valuable technical and industrial colleges." Ayres asked "if the time [was] not ripe for a greater democracy and a wider field of useful-ness for this very valuable association." Ayres' own particular appeal was for greater acceptance and encouragement of state agri-cultural and mechanical institutions, but his plea would be heard, at the time and down through the decades, from various groups at different times. In essence these appeals reflected the belief that the growing diversity and democracy of society at large should find its reflection in the aims and organization of the Association.[65]

The responses of Kirkland and his supporters to these appeals ranged from outright hostility to cautious acceptance. Like those who challenged them, the liberal arts group's responses reflected their beliefs regarding the ideal relation of education to society. Commitment to the classical liberal arts tradition not only shaped their definition of "education," it also informed their understanding of the role of the educational system (especially the college) in the wider society. Central to this understanding was the paradoxical assumption at the heart of liberal arts education generally—that the best way to prepare a student to serve society is to insulate that student from many of the influences and demands of that society while in college. Such an approach allows for the development of both personality and intellect. These shared beliefs nevertheless generated a variety of responses to demands that education should be more responsive to the changes taking place in modern society.

Speaking of Southern institutions, Edwin Mims offered an idealized and quietly optimistic view of the role that his kind of college could play in the modern world. Mims believed that, even in an age as modern as theirs, there remained a strong desire that "something of the old spirit that made men of culture and men of power" should be retained. Southern colleges, Mims believed, should respond to this desire by "send[ing] forth men who will be leaders in the intellectual and spiritual emancipation of this peo-ple—men not provincial because they are citizens of the world; . . .

men not bigoted because they have breathed an atmosphere of freedom and toleration; men not dominated by material ideals, but rather sentinels of the spirit in an age of intense industrial activity—heralds of a new day, prophets of God." It was a vision of education that demanded a commitment to learning as well as locality, to the life of the mind more than to the art of accumulation. It was an education that would not obscure from its students the needs and challenges of modern society, but which would emphasize their guardianship of that which was of timeless, universal value in human culture. Mims, for his part, also favored a judicious widening of curricular choice as part of a necessary and continuing effort to balance the priorities of the educational realm with the demands of the wider world.[66]

Other members were almost entirely hostile. In the torrid circumstances of the early twentieth century, the reasonable skepticism and quiet hope of a Mims regarding the nature and pace of modern change could easily slide into intemperate fear and loathing. For many educators, the early twentieth century was a dangerous and discouraging place, a world turned upside down, in which instead of education improving society, the worst that society had to offer was corrupting education. James Powers encapsulated this view in his 1901 presidential address to the Association. Powers lamented "the multiplication of colleges and universities, which had no equipment, no endowment, no reason for existence except the gratification of the greed for gain, or a sense of local pride, or to satisfy the ambition of rival church organizations." Powers identified the two kinds of institution that troubled educators like him most. One was the small, often church-affiliated, colleges which, despite or because of their considerable numbers, weakened rather than enhanced the region's educational system. This perennial problem of a South with far too many "colleges" but not nearly enough "education" was compounded in the current era of rampant "commercialism," Powers argued, by the proliferation of "diploma mills" that existed only to confer marketplace legitimacy on "graduates" who sought the economic benefit and social prestige of academic recognition without being willing to pay the price in intellectual labor that legitimate scholarly achievement demanded. The "coin of the educational realm" was increasingly circulating in "counterfeit" form, complained Powers, employing an apt metaphor. And as with currency, the "counter-feit" undermined confidence in the authentic. "If we know that there have been issued spurious A.B.'s," explained Powers, "it places a ban on every A.B., unless one knows whence it came." These institutions not only sold their own worthless "education," they threatened to undermine the credibility and mission of those who offered the real thing. Furthermore, Powers might have added, they made the Association's now-stated goals of greater education-al order and articulation even harder to achieve.[67]

The threat the new social order posed to college education went deeper, however. Other college men fretted that genuine col-leges and universities risked destruction by themselves becoming infected by the surrounding values of consumption, advertising and instant gratification. Another president of the Association, George H. Denny, also president of Washington and Lee University, asked his audience whether the commercial values of "a pushing, progressive, practical age," would "also dominate our life in its immaterial and higher interests" and "invade our acade-mic ideals." Speaking in 1904, Denny feared that this question had already been answered in the affirmative and went on to pro-vide a scathing critique of the pestilential impact of "academic commercialism" on educational life. He contemptuously listed the features of modern educational life that to him represented a sur-render to the crass commercialism that prevailed in so many other walks of life.[68]

The root of academic "commercialism" was the love of pres-tige, "almost universal in its reign," of "power and influence," and of "publicity." This desire generated many unwholesome prac-tices: a willingness to accommodate the interference of big donors; the shameless self-promotion characterized by "profusely illustrat-ed bulletins and other light literature lacking little save a tone of dignity and, in many cases, of candor;" the abuse of scholarships as inducements to attend particular institutions; the increasing number of public ceremonies and "pompous gatherings"—largely seasoned with commercial flavor and largely prompted by com-mercial motive—that made academic life "more and more . . . a rapid succession of processions, receptions, dinners, and speeches, with brass bands, caps and gowns, continually in evidence;" the new type of college president who "must be chiefly a business

man, a man of affairs, a man of executive skill," with particular
talents in matters of "revenue-gathering and attracting a large stu-
dent-body through advertising in its various forms;" and the creation of competition and the destruction of the "harmony,
sympathy, and cooperation" that should "exist among natural
allies engaged in a common cause." And so on. All in all, educators like Denny and Powers believed such alien intrusion
"degrades the tone of academic life and cheapens the value and
meaning of academic tradition" in existing colleges, and encouraged the "bogus school and the sham college, with their 'paper'
courses, calling little things by very large names, and professing to
open royal roads of 'rapid transit' to business, to scholarship, and
to culture. . . . It enthrones the seen and the material. It dethrones
the unseen, the immaterial, the ideal."[69]

The fear and disdain of men like Powers and Denny represented (in strident, and perhaps exaggerated form) a viewpoint
widely shared by many of the Association's founders, who gave
the overall impression of being very uncomfortable with any kind
of social influence on educational institutions that they themselves
did not approve or control. Their concerns are symbolized, in
many ways, by an increasingly critical attitude toward the place of
athletics on campus. In the early decades of the century, it was
common for educators to contrast the shining classical ideal of
college athletics—*mens sana in corpore sano* (a healthy mind in a
healthy body)—with the sordid present-day reality of business and
boosterism. In 1904, Denny extolled the "value and merit" of college athletics when "physical culture was the aim and ideal," but
bemoaned its decline into a "business" where "athletic prestige"
had become "one of the most effective forms of academic advertising," more important in attracting students to some institutions,
so Denny argued, than "sound scholarship."[70]

Such concerns only deepened as the social significance of
college sports grew in the early decades of the century. More and
more, the mania for athletics seemed to reflect the undue influence
of non-educators, whether local or national, the misuse of schools
and colleges for non-educational ends, and the use of illegitimate
means to achieve the legitimate ends of attracting students or
building institutional prestige. Viewed ideally as a way to prepare
the student to influence society for the good, athletics had increas-

ingly come to embody the ways in which society was influencing college life very much for the worse. Supposedly a source of physical strength, collegiate athletics had become the ultimate symbol of education's moral frailty; "a festering sore," in Denny's choice phrase, "upon our academic body." Intercollegiate sport, especially football, was the most visible manifestation of the forces of cancerous commercialism and reactionary localism threatening the academic world. This was why, for many, Centre College (whose enrollment, incidentally, had rocketed in the wake of the Praying Colonels' success) represented far more than an individual case of administrative wrongdoing. It represented rather the dual, largely negative, impact of both local and commercial influences on educational institutions.[71]

The "liberal arts group's" tendency to disdain the narrowly provincial or the merely materialistic infused their responses to many of the major questions that faced the Association in this period, often hardening their resistance to changing the aims and ethos of the Association. If White thought Christian values were needed more than ever in such times, men like Kirkland saw the maintenance of standards as a bulwark against both parochial and commercial assault. Thus Kirkland was clearly furious at White's suggestion, "perhaps the most serious" charge ever made against a regional accrediting body, that the Association's efforts tended toward "moral mischief." "Knowing the ideals of this body from the beginning," Kirkland fumed, "I resent with all the emphasis possible the charge that our earnest efforts toward the establishment of honest standards and faithful work has ever tended to work moral mischief." Given his own central role in the prolonged and bitter "religious war" with the Methodist Church over the administration of Vanderbilt, Kirkland was perhaps especially sensitive to religious efforts to shape the curriculum and character of colleges.[72]

But Kirkland not only attacked the standards' critics, he defended the standards themselves. He and others recognized that the standards were not always easy to reach. But surely that was in some ways the point, they argued. If, for example, one attended too "realistically" to education's social "context," might not a full recognition of the South's economic woes generate such profound pessimism regarding the value of setting any meaningful standards at all? Instead, the standards' defenders insisted, the aim was to

arrive at standards that would be demanding without being demor-
alizing, and that would be of lasting benefit once achieved. From
this perspective, quantitative standards were to be seen as the
materialistic means to high-minded ends. As Edwin Mims
expressed it, "Standards of scholarship, large endowments, well-
equipped laboratories, and well-stocked libraries are good only as
they are a means to an end—the development of men for the service of society." Furthermore, they insisted that the standards were
both limited in their scope and fundamentally reasonable in their
application. "In making standards for an association like ours,"
Kirkland claimed in his direct response to White, "we necessarily
confine ourselves to a few fundamental matters." "The effort," as
he argued on another occasion, "is merely to agree on a definition
that will fix a point of beginning, to draw a line below which no
institution will contentedly rest." There was no intent to hamper
any institution from developing in accord with its own particular
missions or character. Rather, "by sympathy and encouragement"
the "desire [was] to lift all colleges across this line and put them
beyond the point of criticism and condemnation." Once above
that line, every school and college had "the right of going far
beyond our requirements, and making all the additional requirements desired for the support of its own peculiar program,"
Kirkland insisted.[73]

Kirkland's insistence on the reasonable and fundamental
nature of the Association's standards still left unanswered the question of who defined "reasonable" and "fundamental." Defenders of
the Association's existing standards also resisted the implication
that they were an alien imposition, handed down from a distant
organization, one that often failed to recognize the diverse needs
and situations of the region's institutions. Rather, they pointed out,
the standards were the creation of the members themselves. But
Kirkland's attachment to "universal" standards, in fact, grew from a
very particular conception of academic value and excellence. As
John White insisted, to adopt particular measurements of institutional development was to encourage a particular *kind* of institutional development. Standards derived from a particular
educational ideal inevitably encouraged development toward that
ideal. Furthermore, educational ideals were inevitably shaped by
wider views about culture and society. As White argued, "The

standardization of schools involves vastly more than schools in the ultimate fact: It involves the standard of civilization." In other words, one could not speak of an ideal education without in effect saying something about one's ideal society. This view was shared by many educators who otherwise may not have had a great deal of sympathy for White's specific defense of denominational education.[74]

Everyone, of course, denounced the fraudulent diploma mills lambasted by Powers and Denny. Yet many of the more traditional members were also skeptical, and often condescending, in their evaluation of more directly practical, or "vocational" subjects and institutions. A guest speaker at the 1912 annual meeting captured something of the condescension and skepticism of many of those in the audience who subscribed to more traditional definitions of education. Dr. Kendric C. Babcock, a specialist in higher education from the United States Bureau of Education, noted how "Manual training, domestic science, agriculture, carpentry, typewriting, bookkeeping, and parliamentary practice," all parts of "a rich alluvial deposit from the great current of materialism," were "successful claimants for recognition in some quarters." As did many others, Babcock had an anecdote to suggest the supposedly absurd extremes to which this open defining of college subjects could be taken. He told of how "Not long ago the dean of a Southern university told me that his committee on admissions had offended a teacher in a neighboring high school by refusing to permit him to count a course in wireless telegraphy in place of the required physics." This disdain for manual or vocational training was also part of the broader concern regarding social influences on education, influences that resulted in the proliferation of fields of study that they believed had no place in college life. Some educators of the old school worried that consumer society's elevation of "choice" to an ultimate value had come to be too strongly reflected in curriculum changes designed to increase student choice in colleges and schools. "I have slowly come to the conclusion," Professor C.E. Coates from Louisiana told the Association, "that we are all in serious danger of being injured by educational fads." In Coates's "judgment," the high school student, whether college-bound or not, should be offered "a much more restricted course" than was generally the case in an educational world where "the elective idea has been overworked."[75]

The antagonism and suspicion of Kirkland and others toward institutions not founded on the liberal arts ideal implicitly illustrates what White and others made explicit: that, on a philosophical level, different sets of standards might well be incompatible. For while they were convinced that no institution could suffer through seeking to meet the Association's standards, they certainly felt that the Association would suffer from the admission of institutions that did not share the liberal arts ethos. This fear was scarcely alleviated by suggestions that potential problems could be resolved by the creation of separate standards for different kinds of institution. Yet this was the preferred solution of many of those who favored a widening of the Association's responsibilities and membership. For educators like Brown Ayres, the best way to expand physically and philosophically without threatening the existing liberal arts membership or the standards they valued, was to devise a system of separate standards of judgment and measurement for institutions with very different aims and methods.[76]

The argument against separate standards was, in part, that separate would inevitably mean unequal or easier. Taking the example of engineering departments in universities, Kirkland observed that they drew their students from the same sources as a college's or university's literary departments. He argued, therefore, that to build up "genuine high schools in the South" it was "all-important that we maintain the same requirements for admission" to both kinds of courses. "Any other line of conduct is suicidal," Kirkland argued, because "we shall find the tendency almost irresistible for students to enter the engineering courses if they are to be admitted in these on less stringent demands than are made by the literary institutions." Such a view speaks to the depth of Kirkland's belief that *different* standards must necessarily be *lower* standards. When H.M. Ivy became the first superintendent of schools to be elected president of the Association in 1927-28, he remembered how "It took some time . . . to convince the entire [Executive] Committee that not all people in public education disbelieved in high standards." The assumption that the public education group was not committed to high educational standards was also rooted in the perception that its members were less qualified than their liberal arts counterparts. A further concern, therefore, was that a larger role for these "underqualified" people within the Association would inevitably damage the Association's reputation. M.C. Huntley, a leading figure in the College Commission before and after World War II, remembered believing at the time that "the liberal arts people in control felt that these upstarts in higher education, that is the professional education people, would tarnish, to a certain extent, the prestige of the organization." Thus "they steadily refused to consider them for inclusion in their membership." The founders' fears regarding the negative impact new standards and leaders would have on the Association's power and prestige was summed up by one speaker at the 1934 annual meeting who warned that, if it changed its ways, the Association would be reduced to a "regional debating society" with no authority in formulating or enforcing educational standards for the South.[77]

In response to appeals for further innovation, the founders also pointed to how much they had already changed. The Association's leaders could rightly insist that compromise and adjustment had been part of the Association's evolution from the beginning. As Kirkland acknowledged, the Association could hardly have been founded without compromises that allowed for exceptions to be made and for some standards to be phased in over a period of years. They could point to their acceptance of Greek's much-diminished role in both high school and college. They could also make the case that, by allowing students to begin study of modern and classical language in college, they were in effect compromising their goal of completely abolishing preparatory departments. They could also insist that such accommodations did reflect their understanding of the role that the circumstances and expectations of the wider society must play in shaping the Association's aims and policies. As Professor C.E. Coates of Louisiana pointed out in 1904, even those who, like himself, considered the Association's college standards to be "wise and conservative" recognized that it was often "more a goal than a standard, and must remain so in certain sections," unless educators were "to ignore facts" and run their institutions "on theory alone." Most striking of all, of course, by the 1910s, they could point to how they had accepted the fundamental transformation of the Association from a cooperative body to an accrediting agency.[78]

The Kirkland group was also quick to point out that membership was voluntary. When Chancellor Kirkland told John

White that "If membership in our Association weakens the general denominational movement of the Baptist church . . . then the Baptists have a right to insist that their own institutions remain outside," he made explicit what was at least implicit in other responses to calls for greater inclusiveness. The 1935 Report of the CIHE, for example, argued that a willingness to be a member of the Association signified a willingness to accept and to meet the standards of that Association. Consequently, if a college or school "does not, cannot or is not permitted by circumstances" to meet the standards, it "should not remain a member in good standing since the requirements that give meaning and worth to [a] whole organization are not being observed."[79]

In one sense Kirkland and others were right to insist that membership in the Association was wholly voluntary, and that Baptists, or anyone else for that matter, could simply leave if they considered membership contrary to their interests. But this "take it or leave it" posture hardly took sufficient account of the Association's growing prominence and influence and, therefore, of the increasing value of membership. As that CIHE report also acknowledged, "membership in a reputable association brings its members a certain degree of prestige and recognition." Yet for quite some time before 1935, the Association had been not *a* but *the* reputable general accrediting body in the South. In such circumstances the "prestige" of membership came to mean much more than simply the respect of fellow professionals. It represented a seal of approval in a wider society not especially knowledgeable about the details of accrediting. As Theodore Jack explained, "more and more institutions sought and obtained" an affiliation that was of increasing social value to them.[80] Questionable enough when the Association was a small, "cooperative" organization, the ideal that it remained entirely "voluntary" in the period of its growing prestige seemed, at best, unrealistic.

Or sought and *did not* obtain membership, Jack might have added. For standards of *inclusion* were also, inevitably, standards of *exclusion.* However much one claimed that membership was entirely voluntary, it was impossible to avoid the assumption that by "passing" some institutions the Association was "failing" others. Indeed a further complaint against its practices was that it explicitly drew such a distinction in order to boost the public reputation of its member institutions. "The way of power in the Association is propagandic *[sic]*," argued John White. He complained that the Association's coercive approach could be summed up as follows: "If you come into the Association and do not watch your step, you will be put out, with or without notice, and it will be published on you;. . . it will be impressed on the public that you are non-standard and inferior." One responder, a Father Walsh, agreed with White on this point, while another, Dr. Blackwell, thought it a "universal" and not unreasonable practice for accredited institutions to receive some public recognition of the fact. James Kirkland did not reply to this point directly, but it is safe to assume he would have been less than pleased to hear his Association's activities described in terms more appropriate to a protection racket than to a movement committed to educational improvement. Yet a growing number of Southern educators, even if they did not share White's particular perspective, shared his general concern that in a culture that increasingly valued both accreditation and educational variety, it was no longer enough for the region's accreditors to hold to a narrow ideal of educational excellence and an unrealistic estimation of membership's social as well as academic value. Such responses hardly answered the appeals of men like Ayres on behalf of institutions which, however excellent in their own right, had a hard time meeting standards that had not been formulated with them in mind.[81]

Whatever position people adopted on the question of who and what should constitute the focus of the Association's attention, the debate suggests a growing dissonance between, on the one hand, the Association's origins and initial aims and, on the other hand, its increasing power within educational circles and its growing profile in Southern society. This dissonance was in significant part an ironic consequence of the Association's transformation into an accrediting agency. For as a result of its growing power to bestow academic credibility on institutions, the Association had become an increasingly important public "player" in the very commercialism of academic life that so many of its members deplored. Indeed this may have been another reason for their reluctance to recognize the implications of their new role and power, and the resulting complaints of their critics. Yet the irony went deeper. For the founders sought to resist the encroachment of institutions that were increasingly valued by society as a whole at a time when the liberal arts tradition they defended had become a frequent target of public criticism, even mockery. In other words, when its founding ideals had never been less popular, the Association had never been more influential.

Despite the difficulties presented by the Association's standards, many secondary schools and higher institutions devoted primarily to the practical rather than the scholarly continued to seek membership. Their efforts to do so continued to find support among their allies in the departments of education in the state universities. Increasingly, they were successful. As membership in the Association grew, and grew increasingly desirable, it became clear that the differences at the heart of its continuing development would be resolved, not by the participants and their beliefs taking different organizational paths, but by their struggling within the Association in an effort to direct its path. This set the stage for a period of intense conflict within the Association, often acrimonious, culminating in major changes of organization and practice in the 1930s.

It was inevitable that a debate that many believed would decide the future role and character of the Association would often be fiery. Yet despite the explosive mixture of personality, principle, and power, these years of difference nevertheless also revealed that mutual respect could also be felt and common ground worked toward. Personal familiarity with ideological opponents could reduce the tendency to caricature their aims and ideas. H.M. Ivy noted his differences with the Executive Committee, but also his "high regard" for it. He also recalled how, during his presidency, "relations between the chairman and the Executive Committee [and himself] were wholeheartedly in accord." Ivy's own enthusiasm for the classics may have helped ease tensions in that particular case, but Ivy also described how other opponents of Kirkland's policies nevertheless expressed their respect for him as "a magnificent leader" in ways that went beyond the politely formulaic. The respect could be mutual. College Commission member M.C. Huntley did not downplay the way in which policy disagreements could take on a personal edge, acknowledging that some of his opponents "did not like me." Nevertheless, he recognized, and disagreed with, the tendency of some of his colleagues to dismiss their opponents' academic qualifications as inferior. Huntley believed that those who had degrees in professional education "were as well-qualified as those on the liberal arts side," and, for his part, remembered also finding them "very fine gentlemen." The mutual respect of at least some of the leading figures in the conflict meant that the period was not without efforts to soften attitudes or work toward agreement between the rival forces. M.C. Huntley, for example, periodically "protested to the Executive Committee" that it had to expand access to the presidency and the leadership to the "new area" of professional education "that had developed." Theodore Jack, also a member of the liberal arts group, also sought out a moderating position between the two camps, perhaps influenced by his service at the public University of Alabama and private Emory University in Atlanta. Inevitably, as Henry Hill remembered, "the question of personalities [was] all mixed up in it and there [was] a lot of froth on both sides," yet the ideological and organizational divisions of this period could sometimes be bridged rather than widened by the personal relations that developed among Association members.[82]

It was also the case that, despite their often outspoken views regarding the damage that an emphasis on liberal arts had caused, many critics did recognize the benefits that the Association's standards had brought to Southern education. As their power grew, they made a point of reassuring their opponents that they recognized these achievements. Many insisted that they wanted not the replacement of liberal arts colleges but a place beside them as different institutions serving different, yet nevertheless valid, educational and social interests. There was also a willingness on the part of some college men, especially as time passed, to augment their stout defenses of standards with acknowledgment of the problems that had sometimes attended their enforcement. W.D. Hooper, for example, president of the Association in 1925, reiterated the voluntary and service-oriented nature of the Association's work, also insisting that its standards were not "arbitrary" but "reasonable." He expressed the orthodox belief that "holding rigidly" to such standards was "a most potent force for the upbuilding of worthy institutions of every grade." But Hooper also recognized the radically altered circumstances in which these long-standing aims were to be pursued, especially the growing social significance of the

Association's educational decisions. The Association, Hooper acknowledged with some surprise, had "become so powerful as to awake some degree of concern in the minds of many of us—a compact body of 72 institutions of higher education and 592 secondary schools, having almost the power of the keys in the educational world of the South." Hooper also recognized the resentment caused by the Association's growing involvement in what amounted to consumer advocacy as well as the widespread perception that in this capacity it often exercised its power unreasonably. While he thought it should be a matter of "pride" that people looked to the Association for "advice, for sympathy, for assistance," he also insisted that it was "to be feared that some people think that the Association assume an attitude of exclusiveness—that it is cold-blooded and takes an actual pleasure in denying admission to worthy applicants, or is selfish and does not want to share its advantages with others." Hooper hoped that to the extent such resentment still existed, they could and would be "banished forever."[83]

Hooper's optimism on this last point may have been due to his speaking in a year in which the Association did see very significant changes designed to accommodate diverse institutions within its ranks. From all the contention and compromise had emerged a further significant change in the Association's way of doing things, one that sought to address the question that supporters of a more inclusive approach had been asking for years. Was it not possible, as President Ayres had put it back in 1905, "without in any way lowering our standards," to encourage the active participation of the agricultural and mechanical colleges and the technical schools, "and, by cooperation with them, help them to see more clearly their own place in the educational scheme, and make them co-workers with, rather than rivals" of the region's "academic colleges?" Ayres and like-minded colleagues had also offered a consistent answer to their question. They argued that a system of separate standards would allow the Association to bring in new kinds of institutions without undermining existing goals and expectations that had been advocated by the public school group. The "increasing demands" from both inside and outside the Association for such a step to be taken "led," as Jack Allen explains, "to the adoption of separate standards for arts and sciences colleges, teachers' colleges, and junior colleges." This 1925 change was reflected in the following year's *Proceedings,* which listed postsecondary members under those separate headings. Over the ensuing years, the seven teachers' colleges and nine junior colleges listed as members in 1926 would be joined by many others. These years saw, then, the gradual widening of membership and perspective that an increasing number of members, and prospective members, had called for.[84] The shift to separate standards did little to assuage the fears of those who felt the admission of new kinds of institutions, even under the previous standards, threatened the Association's legitimacy and credibility. In other respects, however, it seemed to offer the chance of accommodating the demands for greater inclusion as well as continued high standards, and of satisfying educators and administrators who wished to be judged by standards more appropriate to their institution's particular educational mission or social role.

But when President Hooper had hoped that conflict and resentment would be "banished forever," he hoped for too much. Change is as likely to increase as it is to diminish demands for more change. This proved to be true for the Association. Changes designed, at least in part, to make the Association more accommodating to a more diverse set of institutions and interests to a significant degree *heightened* rather than reduced the dissatisfaction of those members who represented those institutions and interests. The expansion and diversification of the Association's membership and the changes in its standards, although significant changes in their own right, for the most part had not been accompanied by a corresponding diffusion of power away from the founders. Once inside the Association, new members representing new interests faced an organizational structure they believed kept them largely outside the inner circles of Association power. Yet their increasing numbers held out the hope and the expectation of increasing influence and, gradually, the willingness to fight for it. Throughout the period, philosophical differences as to the social meaning and role of education would increasingly be bound up with questions of prestige and power within the Association. Change, then, proved to be a recipe for more change.

From its beginnings, much of the Association's institutional power rested with its Executive Committee. Originally the Executive Committee consisted of the president and the secretary-treasurer, as well as three other members. In 1906 the constitution was amended to increase the Executive Committee's *ex officio* membership to five, but this still represented a very high concentration of power in very few hands, especially as, in 1906, it was also decided that "there shall not be more than two changes in the Executive Committee in one year, except by death or by resignation, in which case the Executive Committee shall have authority to fill such vacancies." The Executive Committee membership was increased again, in 1933, this time to seven, in a further limited concession to demands that it be more representative.[85] The Executive Committee assumed responsibility for many aspects of the Association's work, from the planning of annual meetings to the nomination of institutions for membership. In effect, it had a leading say in most of the decisions made regarding admission or expulsion of member institutions. Executive Committee recommendations, prior to the late 1920s, were routinely endorsed by the Association as a whole. Indeed, the membership's refusal to go along with the recommendation to drop Centre College was remarkable because it was so rare. As the Association developed as an accrediting force, the power exercised by its Executive Committee loomed ever larger. Its tight control of increasing power, as well as its self-perpetuating character, continued after the creation of both the college and secondary commissions, drawing increasing complaints directed against what some critics called a "closed corporation." Despite their quite different ways of operating, the structure of both commissions' membership also tended to favor the liberal arts group. Furthermore, the election of commission members to the Association's Executive Committee was conducted in such a way as to perpetuate the power of a relatively limited number of people as well as the dominance of a viewpoint increasingly at odds with that of many members.[86]

How this power was exercised proved a further source of long-running contention and resentment. Many Association members may well have had little sympathy for the plight of Centre College, but when an outraged President Montgomery described the Executive Committee as the most autocratic kind of "star chamber" that he had ever had to deal with, many would have nodded in sympathetic agreement. Even when standards were deemed to be desirable, many were angered by the manner of their enforcement. Examples abounded among the Executive Committee's critics of the rigidity and pedantry with which it inspected applicants. The "loss" of Arkansas was, for some, an especially irksome example of the Executive Committee's arrogance and pedantry. Henry Hill remembered how, despite meeting the other standards, his school, in Walnut Ridge, Arkansas, had been denied membership in 1924 on the grounds that a teacher voluntarily offering a physics class "did not have a major in physics!" C.C. Colvert recollected the University of Arkansas' unsuccessful efforts to gain membership during the same period, describing a process in which the university's president would submit all the required reports, only for the Commission on Higher Education to "tell him to go back and do certain other things." When he did so, according to Colvert, "they would say that's good, go back and do this." In the end, "he got tired and walked out" and then successfully "petitioned every high school and college in the state" to join the North Central Association. "We lost Arkansas," an aggrieved Colvert concluded.[87]

College Commission people were more likely to favor the explanation that, as M.C. Huntley put it, "being in the west," Arkansas "was nearer to the North Central Association." Huntley, whose position as executive secretary involved him in many visits to hopeful applicants also remembered that although some places were turned down, several times perhaps, "there were few instances, I might say, where an objection was made to my [negative] recommendation." Nevertheless, angry disenchantment with Association procedures and not merely geographical convenience seems to have played a significant role in an episode that, for many, was indicative of a pervasive high-handedness. Hill, and others in Arkansas and in the Association, believed that what they saw as shabby treatment was due to the "complete domination of the accrediting procedure" by "what used to be referred to as the "Liberal Arts Crowd," and that Arkansas' joining of the North Central Association represented a "protest" against a group that, in Hill's view, "took a considerable amount of pleasure in their noble work of keeping schools out" of the Association. The differing understandings of the leaders' status became evident in many ways. At the annual meetings, for example, the Executive Committee was in the habit of appearing in "formal cutaway suits." Even after this tradition ended, they still appeared at the Thursday evening dinner, according to Guy Snavely, "in full dress or tuxedo," often accompanied by their wives, and presenting "an impressive appearance" to the assembled members. Indicative to themselves of "the dignity of their place," this sartorial symbolism "caused as much resentment among the 'dispossessed' members of the Association" as did the College Commission's 'much-talked-of secrecy' or the closed character of the Association's organizational structure."[88]

Just as a gulf had developed between the Association's original ethos and aims and its later status and circumstances, so too, at least to those excluded from power, there appeared to be an ever-growing gap between the growth of the Association's educational and social power and the continued concentration of control within the organization. This strong and growing sense of resentment fueled demands that a change in power had to come. Yet it would be some time before those demands were translated into major changes and before an increasing numerical superiority could be translated into organized action capable of winning control from the liberal arts group, which retained control of the Association for quite some time after it had come to represent only a minority viewpoint within it. Yet several events provided hints of what was to come. One of the most significant dated from the mid-1920s. In 1922, a Joint Committee of Ten on College Entrance Requirements had been appointed from the two commissions. Although the committee was prepared to report in 1925, a vote was taken to postpone consideration of it until the 1926 meeting in Jackson, Mississippi, when a minority report would also be available. Clearly there was disagreement over the report within the Committee reflecting divisions within the Association as a whole. At the heart of the disagreement were two conflicting understandings of college admission requirements and how they should be assessed and administered. The majority report, favored by the "teachers' school group," proposed, according to Guy Snavely, "that any student graduating from an approved high school with fifteen units be acceptable to member colleges—unless they wished to make specific additional requirements—provided he presented a minimum of three units in English and at least three sequences of two units from three of the following four groups: foreign language, history and the social studies, mathematics, and science." The minority report—signed by W.D. Hooper, Professor W.J. Battle of the University of Texas, and Superintendent Julius T.

Wright of the University Schools, Mobile, Alabama—pointed out that the nine minimum prescribed units were so broad as to amount to no actual requirement except high school graduation. The minority report also "deplored" the "further duplication of offerings between high school and college" that would arise from the greater need for introductory college courses in the subjects that would no longer be required for admission were the report to be approved. A further source of contention, according to H.M. Ivy, who was on the committee, was that state high school supervisors wanted more than an approved list of schools whose graduates could enter the Association's member colleges without examination. They also wanted to assume responsibility for deciding who should be on the list (a claim based on their having greater familiarity with local circumstances than the representatives of higher institutions). For the teachers' college group, such change represented a widening of opportunity for more students and greater recognition of the circumstances in which most lived and studied. The report "argued strongly" in favor of allowing students the chance to attend college even if they "did not plan their high school course with college entrance in mind" from the beginning, providing they could meet the new recommended minimum requirements. To its opponents this represented a retreat to the indeterminate standards and lack of school-college articulation that had brought the Association into being in the first place.[89]

The Jackson meeting proved to be a "bitter" one, with much maneuvering by both sides. In essence the teachers' college group, led by C.A. Ives of Louisiana State University (another member of the Committee of Ten), pursued a strategy that he hoped would eventually allow for a direct appeal to the entire Association. Chancellor Kirkland, for his part, made counter proposals designed to give as much final weight as possible to the pro-liberal arts commissions. Ives carried most of the attack himself, only one other member of the Committee speaking on the report's behalf in the end. In the end, Ives' motion was tabled, and the matter remained unresolved. This debate did, however, reveal the growing discontent of those who believed that their influence was not a fair reflection of their numbers. Many remained unwilling, however, to translate that discontent into decisive action. But this meeting did establish Ives as the leader of the forces that would eventually develop the will and the organization to successfully challenge the existing leadership.[90]

Continued pressure and debate eventually brought matters to a head in the mid-1930s. E.B. Robert remembered how "the tremendous increase in enrollment of State institutions, land grant colleges, teachers colleges and public high schools simply gave them an overwhelming control, and when they got organized . . . they practically took over the operation of the Southern Association." Rufus Harris, who would play a prominent role in the College Commission in the 1940s and 1950s, remembered "a real contest for power" in the 1930s between supporters of the liberal arts tradition "and the teachers colleges and the vocational colleges." This period saw heated meetings in Nashville in 1933 and Atlanta in 1934. In Nashville, H.M. Ivy presented a resolution invoking the "widespread sentiment" that the membership of the commissions was "largely self-perpetuating and not as representative as the best interests of the Association require." Seconded by Ives, the motion called for the president of the Association to set up a committee (consisting of the chairmen and secretaries of both commissions and three others who were not members of either commission) "to prepare the necessary amendments to the constitution and/or by-laws to remedy the condition." "After sharp discussion," the resolution was adopted. The greater strength of this challenge is further suggested by the three non-commission members of the committee—Dr. Ives, J.T. Davis of John Tarleton Agricultural College in Stephenville, Texas, and Dr. H.L. Donovan, president of Eastern Kentucky Teachers College in Richmond.[91]

The Committee on Revision of the Constitution reported the following year. Their report included a resolution calling for rotation in Commission offices to begin immediately. There was great acrimony and unsuccessful counter motions led by Chancellor Kirkland. According to Guy Snavely, the 1935 meeting at which the new constitution was accepted was less contentious. One reason was the calming influence of Theodore Jack, who commanded respect on both sides. Another reason for the calmer atmosphere was, as Snavely describes it, that Dean Ives and his supporters "increased in temperance of expression and willingness to conciliate as they approached their objective." As imminent victory bred greater magnanimity, they insisted "that they merely wished [a] broader basis of leadership" rather than a change in "the fundamental nature of the organization." The Louisville meeting, at which the new constitution was adopted, "was serious because it was realized that new leaders were replacing the old; but there was practically none of the bitterness that had flared at the two preceding meetings."[92]

It was probably one of those meetings E.B. Robert had in mind when he remembered how "as a result of this tremendous fight and tremendous reorganization that took place, I had, I would almost say, the pleasure of seeing Chancellor Kirkland walk out of the meeting" upon the failure of "his last effort at keeping the Southern Association in channels on which it had been run since it was established in 1895." Thus, however decorous the 1935 meeting, the pleasure at seeing victory symbolized by Kirkland's departure from the assembly he had for so long dominated clearly suggests that old wounds remained. M.C. Huntley, for example, accustomed to attending Executive Committee meetings, remembered how, once he had assumed the presidency, Dean Ives had "let me know in no uncertain language that I was not wanted in that room." It was inevitable that change would be interpreted in terms of victory and defeat rather than simply in terms of organizational restructuring and reform. It could hardly have been otherwise when matters of organizational structure and institutional power were so tightly interwoven with fierce clashes of personality and profound differences of educational philosophy.[93]

Given the level of conflict and the extent of the changes wrought in that year, it is quite understandable that, to many of the participants, the events of that time came to be known as "the Revolution of 1935." And certainly the 1930s saw great change. The new Constitution brought a "democratized power structure" with greater representation from the various junior, technical and teachers' colleges that now made up a majority of the College Commission's membership. The following years saw a succession of "firsts," with presidents elected from a junior college (John Tarleton Agricultural College), a Catholic institution (Loyola University of New Orleans), and a state college for women (Florida State College for Women). Only the second president to come from a teachers' college was elected, Dean Ives himself occupying the post. Yet in some respects the changes in this period

looked less like a revolution and more like a coup, albeit a constitutional one, in which a "transfer of power" to the "teachers' college
group" took place. Its members would, in turn, prove themselves as
adroit as their predecessors in the manipulation of procedures and
the monopoly of positions in pursuit of their ends. "So far as this
writer has been able to discern," Guy Snavely dryly expressed the
matter ten years later, "these gentlemen have carried on the tradition of office as well as their liberal arts predecessors." To the extent
that "revolution" implies a tremendous re-ordering of the very
structures of the Association, the events of the 1930s do not for the
most part qualify. Deeper structural and philosophical questions
regarding the meaning of "democratization" for both education
and the Association remained to be asked and argued in the coming
years. As in the wider society, tensions between democracy (with its
emphasis on majority rule) and a more republican or confederated
approach (with its emphasis on the recognition of group rights and
interests) remained unresolved within the Association.[94]

Nevertheless, a real "revolution" had taken place in the character and affairs of the Association since its small beginnings in
1895. Hundreds and thousands of people, with diverse personalities and representing diverse institutions and philosophies, had
come together, in conflict and compromise, acrimony and accommodation, to fuel the growth of what had become, by 1935, one of
the most influential educational forces in the Southern states. This
revolutionary evolution, as it were, of the Association's character
and role was closely entwined with the wider story of the
Southern states in these years. Few of the questions that taxed the
intelligence and fortitude of the Association's members could be
separated from a wider social context in which many individuals
and groups held strong opinions regarding the social purposes of
education. Arguably there had also been a revolution in the public
perception of education, and of what education could and should
do for the mass of people. Such questions had come to preoccupy
the Association's affairs far more, one suspects, than its founders
would have considered either possible or desirable.

The changing aims and ethos of the Association in this period developed out of both resignation and radicalism, conflict and
consensus. Its debates and activities in these years reflected a heartfelt focus on the improvement of Southern education. But because

felt focus on the improvement of Southern education. But because people look at the same things with similar intensity does not mean they see them in the same way. Indeed, the very intensity with which people pursued their visions of educational improvement served to increase the depth of the differences and disagreements that were part and parcel of reform efforts. Reform was ardently debated not only because the Association attracted committed educators, but also because diverse individuals and institutions inevitably represented different educational interests and priorities and espoused diverging philosophies both of education and of education's place in society. General agreement on broad goals left a wealth of potential disagreement over how to achieve them. If the debates of these years suggest the growing diversity and differences within the Association, they also suggest the increasing impact of the social and the political on the educational realm, especially the dramatically expanded popular expectations as to how education should serve society. That such concerns preoccupied the Association, and that it seldom succeeded in resolving them finally or definitively, speaks less to its failure than to its growing participation in a wider society that itself continued to confront familiar challenges and issues in ever-changing circumstances. In this respect, as in others, the Association's history from its creation to the "revolution of 1935" reflects the ways in which it was shaped by, and increasingly helped to shape, the character of the society from which it came.

Endnotes

[1] Charles W. Akers and John W. Carter, *Bo McMillin: Man and Legend* (Louisville, KY: The Sulgrave Press, 1989), 56ff. This account of the game and the events surrounding it follows that of Akers and Carter, whose book provides a highly informative and entertaining account of McMillin's life as well as his career as player and coach. The game took place on October 29. The Harvard team had not lost a game since going down 6-3 to Yale back in 1916.

[2] Ibid, 63-4.

[3] Ibid., 61, 63-4, 55, 52, 49. M.C. Huntley, later a leading figure in the Association, remembered Bo McMillin, having interviewed him as a reporter for the Jackson, Mississippi, Clarion-Ledger, when the sports star came to town.

[4] James Henretta et al., *America's History Vol. 2: Since 1865* (New York: Worth

Publishers, 1993), 609; George Donelson Moss, *America in the Twentieth Century* (Upper Saddle River, NJ: Prentice Hall, 1997), 118-19. By 1930, of a total population of 123 million, 69 million lived in urban areas.

5 Mahan cited in Henretta et al, 674.

6 Ibid., 669ff.

7 Moss, 42ff. See also Dorothy and Carl J. Schneider, *American Women in the Progressive Era, 1900-1920* (New York: Anchor Books, 1993). The relation of the Association to women's education and colleges will be discussed in Chap. 3.

8 Moss, 118-19.

9 Moss, 120.

10 Ibid 120-24, 117-18; Henretta et al., 728, 734.

11 Moss, 117; Henretta, 735, for income figures; Akers and Carter, 61, who also use the phrase "surrogate alma mater," for newspaper cites.

12 Quoted in Akers and Carter, 58.

13 Ibid., 56. Despite having failed one of the courses he took in the previous semester, which should have made him ineligible according to the standards of the Southern Intercollegiate Athletic Association to which Centre belonged, McMillin was allowed to play against Harvard. Others had feared he would never play in that game for another reason, his flirtation with the possibility of leaving college for a career in professional football.

14 Ibid.; 56; Guy E. Snavely, *A Short History of the Southern Association of Colleges and Secondary Schools* [Reprint from the Southern Association Quarterly (hereafter SAQ) 9 (Nov. 1945)], 30.

15 Charles D. Gates to R. Ames Montgomery, 10 Jan., 1924; R.J. Caldwell to Bruck Dudley (Sports Editor of the Louisville Courier Journal), 23 Jan., 1924, Centre College Archives, Danville, Kentucky.

16 Charles D. Gates to R. Ames Montgomery, Jan. 10, 1924; President's Report to the Members of the Board of Trustees, Jan. 7, 1924, 11; R.J. Caldwell to R. Ames Montgomery, Jan. 15, 1924, Centre College Archives, Danville, KY.

17 Snavely, 8-9, who also provides a list of the schools; Edwin Mims, "Presidential Address," *Proceedings 8* (1902); 5-7. The eighth meeting was held at the University of Mississippi in Oxford, Mississippi.

18 Ibid., 6. Some of the leading figures in the board's creation were Southerners J.L.M. Curry, Walter Hines Page, and Edwin Alderman and Northerners such as financier and manager of Wanamaker's department store, Robert C. Ogden, William H. Baldwin, a railroad magnate, and various members of the Rockefeller family. See Raymond B. Fosdick, *Adventure in Giving: The Story of the General Education Board, A Foundation established by John D. Rockefeller* (New York: Harper & Row, Publishers, 1962), 7. See also Jack Temple Kirby, *Darkness at the Dawning: Race and Reform in the Progressive South* (Philadelphia: J.B. Lippincott Company, 1972), 101-02. The influence of Northern philanthropists and the importance of their ties to Southern educators, especially in relation to the education of black Southerners, will be explored more fully in Chapter 3.

19 Mims, "Presidential Address," 6; James H. Kirkland, "The Past and Future Work of the Southern Association," *Proceedings* 18 (1912): 38.

[20] Quoted in Snavely, 5.

[21] W.M. Baskervill, "The Work of the Southern Association of Colleges and Preparatory Schools," *Proceedings* 2, 17-18. For the similar nature of another regional association, see Mark Newman, *Agency of Change: One Hundred Years of the North Central Association of Colleges and Schools* (Kirksville, MO: Thomas Jefferson University Press, 1996).

[22] Interview with Henry Hill, July 18, 1972, 4 (hereafter Hill interview), Southern Association of Colleges and Schools Archive, Decatur, GA (hereafter SACS Archive).

[23] Hugh Hawkins, *Banding Together: The Rise of National Associations in American Higher Education, 1877-1950* (Baltimore: The John Hopkins University Press, 1992), 78.

[24] Those standards were as follows: In English—Requirements of the Association of Schools and Colleges of the Middle States and Maryland. In History and Geography—United States history and general geography. In Latin—four books of Caesar and four orations of Cicero (or their equivalent), with accompanying work in grammar and prose composition. In Greek—three books of Xenophon's Anabasis (or equivalent), with accompanying work in grammar and prose composition. (Operative in 1898). In mathematics—arithmetic and algebra through quadratics, or algebra to quadratics and three books of plane geometry. Of the above subjects, examinations in history, geography, and English shall be required of all students admitted to college, provided that students pursuing technical subjects in not more than two subjects may be excused from these examinations. Examinations in Latin, Greek, and Mathematics, respectively, shall be required of all students expecting to continue these subjects. Certificates covering the above requirements may be accepted from duly accredited preparatory schools in lieu of entrance examinations.

[25] James H. Kirkland, "Past and Future Work," 38-9.

[26] Ibid.

[27] Ibid., 18, 38ff. Of the other institutions represented at those first meetings, Mercer did not join until 1911, while it was over two decades (22 years) before Wofford signed up, and almost three (28) before host Georgia Tech did so. The representatives of Alabama, Tennessee, and Tulane signed up at the meeting but had their decision reversed afterwards. For Alabama and Tennessee, membership was delayed only until 1897, but it was a further six years before the New Orleans institution joined the compact. For a more detailed discussion of membership requirements and procedures, see Snavely, 11ff.

[28] Kirkland, "Past and Future Work," 39.

[29] See, for example, "Report of Committee on Program of Studies for Preparatory Schools," *Proceedings* 5 (1899), submitted by J.H. Kirkland, chairman. The problems facing private preparatory schools were exacerbated during what was a period, as F.C. Woodward noted, of "transition from private fitting schools to public preparatory schools" that increasingly attracted some of the students that they would have attracted previously. See Chap. 1.

[30] Resolution in *Proceedings* 1 (1895): 8, cited in Snavely, 7, and Snavely, 35; P. Harrington (University of North Carolina), "The Preparation of the Teacher for High School Work." *Proceedings* 2 (1896): 19-21; P.H. Saunders

(University of Mississippi), "The Outlook of the Public High School in the South," *Proceedings* 2 (1896): 15-16: 25-6. See also Alfred A. Meyer, "A History of the Southern Association of Colleges and Secondary Schools," (Ph.D. Diss., George Peabody College for Teachers, 1933), 17-18, who also notes the slow initial growth, but also that it "soon drew into its membership many preparatory schools," and that "For many years the secondary membership was predominantly that of private schools." See for example, Professor Addison Hogue (Washington and Lee University), "Greek in the High School, Time and Method of Study, Text-Books Etc.," *Proceedings* 8 (1902): 71-91.

31 J.H. Kirkland, "Requirements for Admission to College," *Proceedings* 13 (1907): 68. See also James McGinnis, "The Public High School as a Preparation for College," *Proceedings* 2 (1896): 26. See also James H. Stiltner, "The Commission on Secondary Schools in Transition," (doctoral dissertation, Georgia State University, Atlanta, GA, 1982), 49. "The issue of entrance requirements accompanied by the search for a standardized high school curriculum dominated the efforts of the Association for the next fifteen years," according to Stiltner. For an example of the debate, see R.B. Fulton (University of Mississippi), "Uniform Requirements For Admission To College," *Proceedings* 2 (1896): 12-14.

32 Kirkland, "Past and Future Work," 42; Kendric C. Babcock, "College Standards as Affected by Diffusion of Entrance Credits," *Proceedings* 18 (1912); 51, 48, 50.

33 Ibid.; Mims, "Presidential Address;" Meyer, 28.

34 Stiltner, 57-9; Kirkland, "Requirements," 68-9. See also Frederick W. Moore, "College Preparatory Work in Southern Secondary Schools," *Proceedings* 13 (1907): 57-66.

35 Kirkland, "Requirements," 69-70; and "Past and Future Work," 43; Stiltner, 59.

36 See, for example, T.W. Jordan (University of Tennessee,), "Admission to College on Certificate," *Proceedings* 5 (1899); R.W. Jones, "Our Proposed New Requirements for Admission to College," *Proceedings* 6 (1900); Robert C. Tunstall, "Should the Association in its By-Laws Forbid Preparatory Departments and Require Specified Entrance Examinations for Admission to College," *Proceedings* 6 (1900): 21-26; and *Proceedings* 2 (1896) and 3 (1897) for material on various committees and their reports. See also Stiltner, 49-51, for a discussion of these committees and their members.

37 Kirkland, "Past and Future Work," 40-41. See also Meyer, 24ff, for debate between proponents of exams and certificates within the Association.

38 Kirkland, in "Past and Future Work," 40, recalled how this encouraged a certain degree of quality control as "Papers unreasonably easy were an object of ridicule. As these papers went into the hands of teachers, they offered a basis on which the work of the college might be appraised. Not only the entering freshmen were graded on these papers, but the professors and colleges as well."

39 P.H. Saunders, "Our Experiment in Uniform Examinations," *Proceedings* 11 (1905); 35; Stiltner, 60.

40 *Proceedings,* (1910); 25, cited in Stiltner, 61-2; Kirkland, "Past and Future Work," 40-43. Kirkland described how Vanderbilt was "falling back on a compromise measure, examining chiefly on the work of the last year and accepting certificates for the earlier years." "Financial statements of the Committee on Uniform Entrance Requirements indicated a lack of enthusiasm for the new procedure,"

according to Stiltner. The statements charted a declining number of exams being sold to member institutions and a declining number of members doing the purchasing, so much so that the sales and distribution numbers also "showed that Vanderbilt University had purchased half of all sets sold."

[41] Stiltner, 55-7; and F.W. Moore, "Report of the Williamstown Conference on Admission to College," *Proceedings* 12 (1906); 6-7. An important motivation for greater interregional cooperation and standardization was the increasing numbers of students seeking entrance to colleges and universities in regions other than those in which they received their secondary education. As well as the four regional associations, this new commission's members included the New England College Entrance Certificate Board, the College Entrance Examination Board, the National Association of State Universities, the office of the United States Commissioner of Education, and the Carnegie Foundation for Advancement of Teaching.

[42] Stiltner, 59; Moore, "Report of the Williamstown Conference," 9, 12-13. Moore's report contains the minutes of the meeting.

[43] James S. Stewart, "The High School Population of the South and a Plan for the Correlation of the High Schools and the Higher Institutions," *Proceedings* 12 (1906): 19; Stiltner, 63-5.

[44] Extracts from Walker's resolution quoted in Joseph H. Stewart, "The Work of the Southern Commission of the Accredited Schools," *Proceedings* 26 (1920): 89; *Proceedings* 16 (1910): 34-5, cited in Stiltner, 65-6; "Report of the Committee on the Accrediting of Schools." Reprinted in Stiltner, Appendix H, 228-9.

[45] Theodore H. Jack, "Presidential Address," *Proceedings* 32 (1927): 247; Stiltner, 69-70. For a full and detailed discussion of these events and of the early organization and membership of the Commission, see Stiltner, 63-75.

[46] E.H. Babbit, "The Problems of the Small College in the Southern States." *Proceedings* 7 (1901): 56-70; B.H. Locke, "Salaries of Professors in Southern Colleges," *Proceedings* 8 (1902): 48-55; W.D. Mooney, "Should Freshmen Receive the Bulk of Their Instruction from Others than the Heads of Departments?" *Proceedings* 2 (1896). See also, for example, Edwin Mims, "The Work and Influence of the College Professor Outside the Class Room," *Proceedings* 5 (1899): 72ff; John P. Campbell, "The Place of Laboratories in a Liberal College Course," *Proceedings* 7 (1901): 16ff; Charles W. Dabney, "Scientific and Technical Education," *Proceedings* 5 (1899): 7-17.

[47] Jack, "Presidential Address," 247-48; George Jackson, Allen, Jr.," A History of the Commission of Colleges of the Southern Association of Colleges and Schools, 1949-1975" (doctoral dissertation, Georgia State University, Atlanta, GA, 1978),19. Snavely, "A Short History," 97, lists the names and institutions of" all the original members.

[48] Allen, 6-8. The controversy generated by the first approved list will be discussed below.

[49] Jack, "Presidential Address," 247-48; James H. Kirkland, "Presidential Address," *Proceedings* 26 (1921): 74. See also Meyer, 23ff.

[50] Allen, 7; Kirkland, "Presidential Address," 76; Snavely, 8-9. There were 1,154 and 134 members respectively by 1935, 1,285 and 143 by 1945.

[51] *Proceedings* 18 (1912): 39; Snavely, 93; Allen, 7. Of 44 members, 33 were on the

list. See Snavely, 93ff, for a fuller account of these events, including the full report of the meeting that drew up the list.

[52] Snavely, 96. Only 13 of the 24 college members (with two others represented by proxies) and 2 of the 15 secondary school members were present when the original list was voted on and referred to the Executive Committee for ratification.

[53] W.H. Heck, "Citizenship in Southern Education," Proceedings 10 (1904): 63.

[54] John E. White, "The Denominational Colleges and the Southern Association," *Proceedings* 26 (1921): 110-12.

[55] White, "Denominational Colleges," 113.

[56] Ibid., 116; Kirkland, "Presidential Address," 77-8; Allen, 8.

[57] Hill interview, 9. Interview with M.C. Huntley, May 26, 1972, SACS Archive, 10-11. Hill was president emeritus of Peabody at the time of his interview. He served as vice president of the Association in 1940 while superintendent of the Lexington, Kentucky, public schools. Later he would be president of Peabody and of the Association in 1948-49. He was elected to honorary life membership in the Association in 1969. See also Snavely, 24, 38.

[58] White, "Denominational Colleges," 116.

[59] Charles D. Gates to R. Ames Montgomery, Jan. 10, 1824, Centre College Archives, Danville, Kentucky; interview with H.M. Ivy, May 19, 1972, 14, SACS Archive, Decatur, GA. Ivy was superintendent emeritus of the Meridian Public Schools at the time of the interview. He had been inspector of high schools in the state Department of Education in Mississippi, president of the Association in 1927-28 and member of the Executive Committee from 1928 to 1932.

[60] Hill interview, 23-4; Interview with E.B. Robert, May 24, 1973, 22, SACS Archive. Robert retired in 1964 after 24 years of service as dean of the College of Education at LSU, 1944-51 and "a central figure" in the Association on both the Executive Committee (1949-50) and as president.

[61] Hill interview, 5-6, for example, notes how the teachers' college group was more enthusiastic than the liberal arts group about such things as experimental schools and the Progressive Education Movement.

[62] H.B. Heidelberg, "Presidential Address: Education in the South for Changing Conditions in the National Recovery," Proceedings 40 (1935): 26-27; H.M. Ivy, "Presidential Address: Some College Problems from Another Viewpoint," *Proceedings* 33 (1928): 252.

[63] Interview with C.C. Colvert, May 21, 1973, 12, SACS Archives, Decatur, GA.

[64] Brown Ayres, "Presidential Address: The Place of the Agricultural and Mechanical College in the Educational Scheme of the South," *Proceedings* 11 (1905): 9. Allen, 10, citing a letter from A.A. Murphree to Frank McVey, president of the University of Kentucky, Nov. 25, 1925, Murphree Papers, University of Florida Archives, Gainesville, Florida. Allen adds that "Graduates of these schools [not meeting the standards of the Association] were finding it difficult to gain admission to graduate schools."

[65] Ayres, "Presidential Address," 8-9. See also Ivy, "Presidential Address," 252.

[66] Mims, "Presidential Address," 22.

67 James K. Powers, "Presidential Address," *Proceedings* 7 (1901): 11, 9-10. Powers believed that one benefit of the Association's "upholding proper standards" would be that it would eventually "educate public opinion and in time force careful legislation. . . . After a while spurious degrees, like counterfeit coin, will be detected."

68 George H. Denny, "Presidential Address," *Proceedings* 10 (1904): 5-6. It is, interestingly, a list that will seem strikingly familiar to anyone with more than a passing acquaintance with a modern-day American college or university.

69 Ibid., 8-17.

70 Ibid., 12. See, for example, Henry D. Phillips, "Inter-Collegiate Athletics and the College Faculty," *Proceedings* 26 (1921): 125. And also H.N. Snyder (Wofford College), "The College Literary Society," *Proceedings* 9 (1905): 90ff. Snyder lamented the growing influence of athletics on both the public's and the students' view at was important about college life, and the attendant decline in activities, such as participation in the literary society, once valued. The Association also heard expressions of concern regarding the abuse of athletics at the high school and other levels of education. See, for example, Superintendent Omer Carmichael (Selma, AL), "Report on Athletics in High Schools and Normal Schools," *Proceedings* 30 (1925). But with regard to such abuse as being indicative of wider problems in society and in the colleges' relation to society, the greatest emphasis was on college football. See also Edwin Mims, "What Should Be Done by Colleges and Universities for the Religious Training of Students," *Proceedings* 11 (1905): 15-16.

71 Denny, "Presidential Address," 12. The concern about the deleterious impact of athletics on education was not confined, however, to the liberal arts group. See, for example, H.M. Ivy, "Presidential Address: Some College Problems from Another Viewpoint," *Proceedings* 33 (1928): 249-50.

72 James H. Kirkland's Response to John White's "Denominational Colleges," *Proceedings* 26 (1921): 121. On Kirkland's long-running struggle against denominational influence at Vanderbilt. See Paul L. Conkin, *Gone With the Ivy: A Biography of Vanderbilt University* (Knoxville: University of Tennessee Press), Chap. 8, titled "The Bishop's War."

73 Mims, "Presidential Address," 21; Kirkland, "Presidential Address," *Proceedings* 26 (1921):77; and his response to White, "Denominational Colleges," *Proceedings* 26 (1921), 121. See also Snavely, 29. Kirkland frequently made the argument that "The colleges and universities constituting" the Association's membership "represent varying types and differ in a score of particulars. The points on which uniformity has been demanded have been a few essential principles accepted and approved by all (*Proceedings* 18: 39)." Yet what could look to one observer like fascinating and obvious diversity within a certain category, to others could appear a more general uniformity that excluded other categories of institution.

74 White, "Denominational Colleges," 113.

75 Babcock, "College Standards as Affected by Diffusion of Entrance Credits," 51; C.E. Coates, "The Interdependence of Schools and Colleges," *Proceedings* 10 (1904): 56.

76 Ayres, "Presidential Address," 10ff.

77 Kirkland, "Requirements for Admission to College," 80; Ivy interview, 22;

M.C. Huntley interview, May 26, 1972, 11-12. "Debating society" comment quoted in Snavely, 42.

[78] Coates, "Interdependence of Schools and Colleges," 56.

[79] Kirkland's response to White, 119; "Report of the Commission on Institutions of Higher Education," *Proceedings* 40 (1935): 49.

[80] Jack, "Presidential Address," 247.

[81] White, "Denominational Colleges," and responses to White, 115ff. Whatever the position participants took on the issue, the dispute, as Guy Snavely, 30, points out, "was noteworthy in pointing out the growing influence of the Association."

[82] Huntley interview, 11-12, 8-9; Hill interview, 11.

[83] W.D. Hooper, "President's Address," *Proceedings* 30 (1925): 307-08. Hawkins, *Banding Together*, 95, notes that as well as having benefits, standards in this period also "had many flaws," including "naively numerical criteria," which gave "leverage to rigid officials and not just enlightened ones." Against this, however, it might be argued, as indeed it was by James Kirkland, such standards actually made it easier to win membership than would more "subjective" standards, which might allow even greater scope for arbitrary or unsympathetic inspectors.

[84] Ayres, 8-9; Allen, 10; *Proceedings* 31 (1926).

[85] *Proceedings* 12 (1906); 4. Cited in Meyer, 35; Snavely, 40. See also Allen 18ff.

[86] For detailed accounts of the inner workings of the Commissions and the Executive Committee, see Snavely, 35-6; and Allen and Stiltner, passim. The distinctive evolutions of the Commissions' organization and practices, and their relation to one another and to the Association as a whole, will be discussed in Chap. 3. One important difference was that the Secondary Commission's meetings were open and any member of an Association school could have a voice in debate if not a vote in final decisions. The Commission on Higher Institutions, on the other hand, held most if its meetings in executive session. In part this was to protect the privacy of those institutions being expected. But privacy that was welcome enough if one's own affairs were being discussed, could look a lot like secrecy at other times, and this was a further source of discontent among those seeking change (Snavely, 36).

[87] Hill interview, 3-4; Colvert interview, 8-9.

[88] Huntley interview, 33, 7; Hill interview, 3-4; Snavely, 38. Hill did not consider the geographical explanation entirely groundless, but considered it much less significant than the factors he emphasized. For Hill, the view that Arkansas felt more oriented toward the North was "partly a good logical reason that has been thought up after the cool treatment received for several years." But he pointed out that Arkansas had lower salaries than most Southern states, and much lower than in NCA states. "I think the reason given is part of the picture, but the feeling engendered by what they considered harsh treatment by those of the 'liberal arts crowd' was the motivating factor (4-5)."

[89] Snavely, 31; H.M. Ivy interview, 17-18. As well as Ivy, the majority on the committee consisted of J.L. Patterson, E.D. Pusey, J.H. Highsmith, W.R. Smithey, G.P. Butler, and C.A. Ives.

[90] Ibid., 32.

[91] Robert interview, 18; Rufus C. Harris interview, Dec. 10, 1972, 6-7, SACS Archive, Decatur, GA. *Proceedings* 38 (1933): 46, cited in Snavely, 40-1. Harris was president of Mercer at the time of the interview and had held several important posts in the Association during the 1940s and 1950s, including chairman of the CIHE (1940-46) and elected member of that commission's Executive Council (1954-56).

[92] Snavely, 42.

[93] Robert interview, 16; Huntley interview, 8-9.

[94] Allen, 11; Snavely, 43. This period did see, however, the beginnings of the organizational developments that would eventually place these continuing conflicts and debates on a somewhat less acrimonious plane. Democratization of the Association as a whole encouraged the development of more autonomous commissions as members looked for ways in which to achieve a workable compromise between the need for the Association to change in socially responsive ways, and the concerns of different groups within it that such change might threaten their ability to pursue more specific goals. These developments will be discussed in later chapters.

Chapter Three

Black Education: Knocking for Admission

As the 1930s drew to a close, the Association had already developed into a very different kind of organization than the one envisioned by its founders. In important ways, however, it remained in the midst of unresolved debates as to the Association's future role in Southern education. In one respect, it was very definitely the end of an era. On August 5, 1939, at his home in Magnetawan, Canada, where each summer he pursued his passion for fishing, Chancellor James H. Kirkland died. Kirkland had been among the last surviving members of the founding generation. With his death, only two of the participants at the inaugural meeting, Henry Snyder and Edwin Mims, remained alive.

James H. Kirkland had been a dominant figure in Southern education for half a century. He had, in effect, two careers, both of which represented a remarkable record of achievement in its own right. By the end of his career, Kirkland had received extensive official recognition of his stature, including more than ten honorary doctorates. He had retired from the chancellorship of Vanderbilt University only just over two years before his death, finally withdrawing from the central role he had played in that institution's affairs for almost half a century.[1] He had retired from active Southern Association duty sometime earlier. Unwell and unable to attend the 1927 annual meeting in Fort Worth, Kirkland had asked his friend and colleague, Spencer McCallie, to offer his resignation from the positions he held with the Association. Instead of accepting the resignation, the Association made Kirkland its president emeritus as well as an *ex-officio* member of all the Association's committees and commissions. Kirkland, who according to McCallie "loved appreciation" just as much as the next person, "deeply appreciated" this gesture. The "Father of the Southern Association" continued to take a major role in the Association's business, especially the events and conflicts of the 1930s. However reduced in the decade's final years, the Chancellor's personality and influence infused the Association's affairs until the end.[2]

Kirkland had dominated an organization that, as one member put it, had not made an important decision in forty years of existence that the Chancellor had not endorsed. An acerbic opponent in debate, Kirkland could be a gracious and humorous companion and host in private. Few people who knew or worked with him failed to develop strong opinions about the man, his character, and his role in the Association and in Southern education generally. His possession of such great power and influence meant, inevitably, that assessments were sometimes far from positive. McCallie remembered how Kirkland was "opposed and vilified in the reorganization of Vanderbilt University" and how he had also "met bitterness and resistance" within the Southern Association. Yet he always remained, McCallie insisted, "supremely true to his convictions." This opinion was shared by many of those who did not share Kirkland's ideals, but nevertheless respected the determination and skill with which he pursued their fulfillment. E.B. Robert, for example, who could be less than complimentary about Kirkland's "medieval" philosophy of education, described the man himself as "a magnificent leader." For his friends and allies, on the other hand, no praise was high enough. Spencer McCallie, for example, while not blind to the Chancellor's flaws and foibles, believed that "It is not too much to say that as the Father of this Association he had more to do in advancing Southern Education than any other person." McCallie said that "Truly the chancellor was a great man. I pray God that this Southland may produce more like him. We need them; we can use them."[3]

Soon the whole country would be in need of a few million good men and women. Kirkland died in the same year that saw Germany's invasion of Poland draw a declaration of war from France and the United Kingdom, thus precipitating a second world war twenty short years after the end of the global conflict Woodrow Wilson had believed would end all wars. Once again, and however reluctantly, Americans were being drawn toward another profoundly important moment of national and global reckoning. That defining moment in modern American history had a date—December 7, 1941. That day the Japanese attack on Pearl Harbor, in the American colony of Hawaii, triggered the United States' entry into World War II. American involvement in the second World War far exceeded the limited participation in the first. The combined branches of the military eventually numbered more than 15 million men and women. Before final victory over Germany and Japan was achieved, 292,000 Americans had died and 671,000 had been wounded, fighting on every conceivable terrain, from the shipping lanes of the North Atlantic to the high seas of the Pacific, from African deserts to Asian jungles, from the beaches of Normandy to the sands of Iwo Jima.[4]

Mobilization for world war also brought an unprecedented transformation of the "home front" as production for victory became the number one economic and social priority. From the children who collected scrap metal to be recycled as munitions to the millions of Americans who flooded into the nation's plants, factories, and shipyards, there was hardly an American who did not make some contribution to the Allied war effort. The departure of existing workers for the military and the creation of millions of new jobs meant that an unprecedented number of women filled jobs and positions long considered the preserve of men. Exhorted by official advertisements claiming "It's A Woman's War Too!" or advising women that "Longing won't bring him back sooner . . . GET A WAR JOB!" many American women left "traditional" roles behind to become bomb-makers and aircraft-builders. Most American women scarcely needed such patronizing propaganda to impress upon them that this was their war, too. Many women, especially nurses, turned their peacetime professions to wartime service. By war's end, 19 million women made up more than one-third of the labor force. Alongside the millions of white women who joined the labor force in new roles or for the first time, many other Americans, African-American women, for example, were pleased to swap existing positions as domestic servants, field hands or office clerks in order to make a more fulfilling and better-paying contribution to the nation's war effort. Fueled by these new workers, American industry produced a staggering flow of fighting machines, including 86,000 tanks, 296,000 airplanes, 64,000 landing craft, 6,500 ships, and 15 million rifles and machine guns. Furthermore, the decline in unemployment and the entry into the paid work force of so many women greatly increased Americans' overall purchasing power, fueling increased consumption of household goods. As other forms of industrial output also soared, along with agricultural production, the nation's economy doubled in size in the first half of the decade, effectively ending the Great Depression.[5]

The war also had a great impact on the Southern Association. The bombs fell on Pearl Harbor, just two days after the 1941 annual meeting. The following year's meeting would be the last to take place during the war years, in part because the Federal Office of Defense Transportation discouraged conventions and assemblies. During this period, the Executive Committee acted for the organization as a whole. The 1942 meeting was devoted to discussing, in the words of President M.E. Ligon's address, "The Southern Association and War." Total cooperation with the war effort was both urged and discussed. Kentucky Senator A.B. Chandler—the same "Happy" Chandler who had inspired the Praying Colonels of Centre with his singing—addressed the Association on "the need for education to be flexible, to adapt to the needs of the country at war, and to keep an eye to the future when the war would be over."[6] Like other Americans, the members of the Southern Association re-evaluated their priorities to take into account the greater national need. Both commissions decided that no school or college should lose its accreditation for any violation of standards that might be a consequence of wartime problems that were likely to include the loss of teachers, professors, and administrators to the war effort. The Association also turned its thoughts and energies to how education could best serve the war effort. In North Carolina, for example, J. Henry Highsmith, director of Instructional Service in the state's Department of Public Instruction, and a leading figure in the Southern Association, described how school administrators, recognizing the obligation "to gear their schools to the war effort," had "not thought in terms of 'school as usual.'" This was a common situation across the region, as war curtailed much of the Association's regular activities and turned the attention of its members, as individuals and institutions, to the task of achieving military victory.[7]

In the years after the war, the Association returned to extensive participation in the educational life of the South. Perhaps confirming its apparent permanence in Southern life as it entered its second half-century of existence, the Association established its first head office. Located at 20 Ivy Street in Atlanta, the office opened on July 1, 1949.[8] The Association also resumed its role as a focal point for debating and researching the state of Southern education. These activities would reflect a certain continuity of concern, especially regarding questions of institutional organization, practice and philosophy. As always, however, new circumstances would have a unique impact on long-standing debates. In particular, the postwar years saw a qualitative leap forward in the "democratization" that had been a central trend of American education since the era of the Association's founding. It was to be an era of raised expectations in almost every area of American life, an atmosphere encouraged by wholesale changes in how Americans lived and worked, how they participated in all aspects of public life from buying to voting. These new expectations were increasingly evident even before the end of the war that had done so much to encourage them. Many Americans, especially women and African-Americans, had worked in wartime jobs previously considered inappropriate to their "nature" or their social position. Many were reluctant to surrender these advances when peace returned. Even more immediate in its impact was the flood of returning veterans. As it had done after World War I, the government brought the troops home with great rapidity. Twelve-million strong in 1945, the military had shrunk to three million by mid-1946, and to almost half that a year later. Returning veterans generated tremendous demand for places to live and places to work, helping to fuel an unprecedented explosion in Americans' economic and social expectations.[9]

The impact of these broad changes in attitude had an immeasurable impact on education. Increasingly, education was seen as both a citizen's right and, in a complex, technological world, a prerequisite of personal success in the world of work. Thus GIs were also among the millions of Americans who sought places to be educated. The government responded to this demand with the Servicemen's Readjustment Act of 1944. The GI Bill, as it was popularly known, gave legislative force to the feeling that those fighting to preserve the American way of life should themselves be rewarded with greater access to a free society's rewards. As well as medical and work-related benefits (including unemployment compensation and loans to start new businesses), the GI Bill provided subsidies for veterans to pursue further education or training. In the short term, this dramatically increased the size of the country's postsecondary student body, as more than six million students, nearly half of all veterans, enrolled in the country's universities, colleges and training programs. By 1947, half of those enrolling in college were veterans. The GI Bill also had an enduring impact on the educational system required to meet this demand. The providers of education grew in number, while many existing institutions increased their capacity to serve new students. Specific categories of institution—most notably the junior college—greatly increased in number.[10]

The GI Bill also helped to perpetuate Americans' changing perception of education, up to and including higher education, as a legitimate goal for most, if not all, Americans. As Hugh Hawkins points out, the GI Bill not only "promoted acceptance of older and married students," it also "created new awareness of academic possibilities among members of social classes that did not usually send their offspring to college." It is more accurate to say that postwar legislation encouraged an awareness and a sense of entitlement that had been steadily growing throughout the century. But it certainly speeded up the democratization of the academy by presenting vast numbers of people with educational opportunities they would not otherwise have enjoyed. The GI Bill, then, was both indicator and agent of the continuing democratization and openness of American life in general, and education in particular.[11]

The profound and complex impact of this continuing democratization on Southern education, and on the Association's life and work, will be the subject of future chapters. This chapter focuses on the Association's relation to black Southerners: a group who had contributed to American victory abroad and progress at home, but who were still denied, by law and majority custom, access to many of the fruits of that victory and progress. This chapter traces the challenges faced by African-Americans in the South in their pursuit of a better, fairer education, focusing in particular on black educators developing relations with the Southern Association. In turn, the growing ties between the Association and black education reflect many of the broader social and educational challenges posed by race prejudice and institutionalized inequality in the decades prior to the civil rights revolution of the 1960s.

If the GI Bill offered the most striking example of the way in which social and educational doors were opening for unprecedented numbers of Americans, other events of the immediate postwar era illustrated how many doors remained closed to black Americans. Many people, happy to see vast amounts of tax-payers' money expended on returning veterans in general, took a less generous view of the approximately 700,000 black Americans who joined the armed forces or for the hundreds of thousands more who had labored in war-related industries at home. Many African-American soldiers returned from fighting tyranny in Europe and Asia, only to face indignity and injury at home ranging from exclusion from restaurants and hotels to murder, sometimes in uniform, at the hands of lynch mobs. Although willing and able to embrace change in numerous aspects of daily and national life, many Americans showed a strong attachment to preserving, or restoring, the racial status quo.

Many black Americans, however, were unwilling to go from first-class soldiers and war workers to second-class citizens. Through acts of individual courage and collective organization, African-Americans in the postwar era intensified their struggle to win a full share of the rights and respect promised by American citizenship. This struggle for civil rights represents a major episode in the history of modern America. With the South and education two of its major battlegrounds, it is not surprising that the Southern Association played a part in these society-transforming events. The Association's involvement with black educators and institutions in the postwar years would bring the Association ever closer to the heart of Southern education and, therefore, of Southern life. By that time, however, the Association's history of relations with black education in the South was already an extensive, if ambiguous one, dating from the 1920s. This chapter will examine the Association's role in the development of a Southern educational system increasingly shaped by political and racial controversy, conflict, and change, from the period of the 1920s through to the civil rights revolution of the 1950s and 1960s.

As African-Americans stood on the brink of an era some historians have called the Second Reconstruction, it is important to look back briefly at their earlier struggles and, in particular, at the Association's expanding role in the life of the South's black schools and colleges. The year of the Association's creation had also been a crucial year for black education in the South. With all due respect to the creators of the ACPSSS, their meeting was scarcely the most important educational event to take place in Atlanta in 1895. In its immediate impact on Southern society, nothing matched the speech given at the Atlanta Exposition by the black educator,

Booker T. Washington. Born into slavery in Virginia in 1856, by the time he spoke in Atlanta Washington was a professor at the Tuskegee Institute in Alabama and an influential educator, well-known in the South and the nation. Washington argued that, in a rigorously racist South, black Southerners would have to pursue educational and economic advance in ways that minimized or neutralized white opposition to black advance and racial equality. Washington believed that black Southerners should focus on areas of education and training (especially agriculture, mechanical trades, and domestic service) and habits of conduct (thrift, good morals, and manners) most likely to convince white Southerners that black progress was good for the entire society. These skills and habits, Washington reasoned, would enable black Southerners to lay the foundation of future economic and social progress, diminish white hostility, and, of crucial importance, win the support of sympathetic white Southerners. Washington assured his white audience that "The wisest among my race understand that agitation for social equality is the extremist folly." Employing his famous metaphor of race relations, Washington insisted that "In all things that are purely social," black and white "can be as separate as the fingers, yet one as the hand in all things essential to mutual progress." Washington's blueprint for a mutual yet unequal Southern future brought forth heartfelt cheering from an audience largely consisting of middle-class white men and women.[12]

Many black Americans rejected Washington's approach. The most notable critic of what he called Washington's "Atlanta Compromise" was Harvard-trained historian W.E.B. Du Bois, a professor at Atlanta University and one of the leading American intellectuals of his time. He was also involved in the creation of the National Association for the Advancement of Colored People (NAACP), which followed from a 1905 meeting at Niagara Falls where Du Bois and others endorsed demands for "equality before the law, voting rights, integration, and equal education and economic opportunities for African Americans." "The way for a people to gain their reasonable rights is not by voluntarily throwing them away," Du Bois maintained, insisting that black people should work for full equality rather than a more livable form of inequality. For Du Bois, equality would include access to the same kinds of education enjoyed by white people, and he opposed

Washington's emphasis on practical training and vocational education as likely to reinforce African-American's second-class status.[13]

The different emphases of Washington and Du Bois were to
some extent grounded in differences in educational philosophies
largely unrelated to race. When historian John Hope Franklin
describes Washington as an educator who "did not deprecate the
study of such subjects as science, mathematics, and history," but
did consider them "impractical," he could have been describing
many within the Southern Association. Whatever white educators'
other reasons for supporting Washington, surely one was that many
of them considered his approach the correct one for most *white*
Southerners. And when Du Bois criticized Washington for preach-
ing a "gospel of work and money to such an extent as apparently
almost completely to overshadow the higher aims of life," he
sounds indistinguishable from many in the "liberal arts" wing of
the Association. In one sense, then, the Du Bois-Washington split
over educational priorities was similar to those apparent within the
Southern Association.[14]

Yet the challenges facing African-Americans were incalcula-
bly compounded by the racial prejudice and hatred directed at
them by millions of their fellow Americans. Black Southerners
pursued educational advance in the shadows cast by white
Southerners' determination to maintain their own economic, political, and social supremacy. Even as Washington spoke, many of
the social and political gains made by black Southerners during
Reconstruction had been eroded or eradicated. Indeed, the 1890s
saw what one historian has called the "nadir" of Southern race
relations. The period since 1877, which white Southerners named
"Redemption," had seen the gradual restoration of white Southern
power. Declining Northern interest in protecting the South's black
minority fueled this restoration, as did the desire among white
Americans of all regions for sectional reconciliation and greater
political and economic cooperation. White supremacy was
reasserted through both legal and extralegal means, from new laws
mandating the segregation of all aspects of public life to the widespread violence and vigilantism of terrorist groups such as the Ku
Klux Klan. The economic uncertainties and fears of the depression years of the mid-1890s fueled the racism of a region that
remained the nation's poorest. Economic hard times (and for

many white Southerners there was no other kind of times) brought forth a steady supply of racist demagogues ready to stir up an evil brew of fear and hate, and to encourage the belief that black gain must equal white loss. Money and race proved an explosive combination for people with little of one and a great deal of virulent prejudice regarding the other.

The most striking evidence for this rising tide of racism and discrimination was the introduction of a pervasive, legally-grounded system of racial segregation. Although racism was old, legal segregation was new, not appearing to any significant extent until this period. The first statewide segregation laws focused on the railroads. When their constitutionality was upheld by the Supreme Court's *Plessy v. Ferguson* decision in 1896, the principle of "separate but equal" public accommodations and facilities soon became the norm in all walks of Southern life.[15] The novelty of legal segregation is suggested by the opposition it aroused among white conservatives who, from their paternalistic perspective, viewed it as an unnecessary, even absurd, innovation. In 1898, for example, Charleston's conservative *News and Courier* published a scathing attack on the "Jim Crow" laws about to be applied to railroad carriages in South Carolina. Asking why, since the South had managed quite well without them for the past thirty years, such laws were necessary, the editorial poured satirical scorn on what it saw as the legislation's logical consequences. "If there must be Jim Crow cars on the railroads," the editorial insisted, "there should be Jim Crow cars on the street railways" and "on all passenger boats." Nor should it stop there. Jim Crow waiting rooms and restaurants, Jim Crow sections in government offices and jury boxes, even Jim Crow Bibles for witnesses to swear on. Yet, as C. Vann Woodward points out, what the conservative editor of the *News and Courier* "obviously regarded as an absurdity became in a very short time a reality . . . down to and including the Jim Crow Bible."[16]

Segregation's supporters were not confined to the ranks of the demagogic and the ignorant. If some elite Southerners viewed segregation as the absurd outcome of rabid racism, others saw it as a rational and orderly means to contain and control such prejudices. As Edward Ayers suggests of railroad segregation, far from seeing it as "a throwback to old-fashioned racism," many white Southerners accepted it as "a badge of sophisticated, modern,

managed race relations."[17] Many white "moderates" and progressives hoped that legal segregation, disenfranchisement, and the
confinement of black Southerners to particular economic roles
would reduce the extra-legal lynching and violence that those
same white Southerners abhorred. Segregation, it was hoped,
would also provide the breathing space the reformers required if
their efforts to build a progressive and stable South were to take
hold. Segregation was the product of an intensification of white
Southerners' long-standing racism, but it was also the child of
white Southern reformers' new ideas of how to bring social order
and cultural progress to their region. These reformers' support for
segregation tellingly illustrates how their thought and action was
shaped by both their adherence to the traditional attitudes of their
race and region and by their commitment to the progressive
assumptions of their class and time.

Separate and *equal* in theory, segregation seldom proved anything other than separate and hugely *unequal* in practice. This was
certainly true of education, where conditions, never ideal, seriously deteriorated. The difficulties faced by black education, and
the prominent role of whites-only government in creating and per-
petuating them, is evident in the comparative amounts spent on
black and white students. In 1900, for example, Adams County,
Mississippi, spent $22.25 on every white child and only $2 on
every black one. In Florida in 1898, the disparity was much smaller but the state still spent more than twice on white as on black
education ($5.92 to $2.27). Bearing in mind the serious inadequacy of the education most *white* Southerners received, these figures
offer some sense of the difficulties encountered by black students
and educators. In the face of such opposition, black Southerners
fought hard to preserve the educational opportunities that had
always been central to their conception of freedom. Educational
opportunities so painstakingly won would not be surrendered
without a fight. Notwithstanding many setbacks, education, as
John Hope Franklin notes, was the area of black life in which
Reconstruction-era gains were most successfully defended.[18]

What black Southerners defended was a system of schools
and colleges built up in the Reconstruction era through the combined efforts of the federal government's Freedmen's Bureau, various religious denominations, Northern teachers and philanthropic

foundations, the aid of some sympathetic white Southerners, and the efforts of black people themselves. When the bureau's educational work ended in 1870, it had spent more than $5 million on black education, including the establishment of 4,329 schools educating 247,333 students. In 1869, there were 9,503 teachers in the Freedmen's schools, a majority of the white ones having come from the North. Many colleges were founded, such as Fisk in Nashville, Howard University in Washington, D.C., and Biddle Memorial Institute (which later became Johnson C. Smith University), again with the help of many Northern educators. As with many white institutions at the time, many were closer to secondary, even elementary schools, than to colleges. Others, however, did serious college-level work.[19]

In the period between 1895 and 1925, these institutions continued to provide many young black men and women with the opportunity to study and to earn degrees. Assisting the efforts of African-Americans, philanthropic organizations such as the Peabody Education Fund (1867), the John F. Slater Fund (1882), the Anna T. Jeanes Fund (1905), and the General Education Board (1902), continued to send money south in the post-Reconstruction era. Founded on the wealth of rich Northerners and focused partly, or entirely, on the promotion of black education, these foundations had various motivations, from the wealthy family's sense of *noblesse oblige* to the industrial investor's desire to expand the available pool of cheap labor through the vocational and industrial education of black as well as white Southerners. And even in the darkest days of race hatred some influential white Southerners, such as those who applauded Booker T. Washington's Atlanta speech, remained ready to support certain kinds of black educational development. And given the scarcity of resources in their own region, white "moderates" and reformers welcomed, too, the financial impetus the Northern foundations gave to that development.[20]

White reformers' support for black education, and for Northern financing of black education, was hardly unconditional. Northern philanthropic assistance was welcomed provided two main requirements were met. The first condition was that the form and direction of *Northern* philanthropy be substantially determined by *Southern* reformers and educators. This condition was usually met. As the century progressed, Northern philanthropists increasingly deferred to their Southern colleagues' claim that, as educated white Southerners, they were best placed to understand the nature of what they liked to call their "Negro problem." As Northern philanthropists became more "understanding," their Southern collaborators became more comfortable with their participation and assistance. "As the North has grown more tolerant and sympathetic," James Kirkland explained in 1914 to a University of Pennsylvania audience, "the South has grown less sensitive and less isolated."[21]

The second condition related to the content of the assistance offered to black Southerners. As John Hope Franklin explains, a fundamental premise of any support for black education was that it should not lead toward social or economic equality. In most cases, this condition was easily met, since, however sympathetic they might be toward black Americans, Northern "benefactors showed little or no interest in establishing racial equality or of upsetting white supremacy." They also accepted the related assumption that even minimal black advance in education would be impossible unless the white majority was first convinced that it would not be harmful to their interests. As Henry St. George Tucker, president of Washington and Lee University, told a group of Northern philanthropists who would help to form the Southern Education Board, "If it is your idea to educate the Negro, you must have the white South with you." Tucker raised the image of "the poor white" in whom the sight of "the son of a Negro neighbor enjoying through your munificence benefits denied to his boy," would arouse "a feeling that will render futile all your work." "You must lift up the 'poor white' and the Negro together if you would approach success," Tucker advised. Tucker's words, according to the *New York World*, were met with such applause that it "drowned even the noise of the train" the reformers were traveling on.[22]

An important consequence of reform efforts being dominated by these conditions was that, even when black uplift was the declared aim, white Southerners often remained the focus of educators' attention. For many reformers, white education was the priority upon which all other progress depended. "The problem is not so much what to do to elevate the inferior race," as William Preston Few of Trinity College claimed, "as it is to save the whites from the blighting influences of narrow-mindedness, intolerance and injustice." Educators like Few did not believe that curbing white Southerners' bigotry would or should lead them to accept black Southerners as equals. They believed it would lead them toward the benevolence and friendship that the superior owed to the inferior. Once white Southerners had been rescued from their own ignorance and raised to a sufficiently elevated level of enlightenment, they would see that black education, provided it was suited to the needs of an "inferior" and subordinate people, would serve the South as a whole. [23]

The benefits that black schools and colleges derived from the efforts of Northern philanthropists and Southern reformers should not be minimized. They were, nevertheless, limited by the reformers' related goal of maintaining the inferior social and economic status of the people they were supposedly trying to help. In practice black and white were not lifted up "together," as Tucker had put it, but consecutively, if at all. In hard, practical terms, the reformers' policies meant preserving, indeed, hardening racial divisions in the present and curtailing the freedom of black Southerners in line with the supremacist beliefs and desires of the vast majority of the white population. A policy supposedly in the long-term interests of black education brought about, in the immediate term, a drastic reduction in the public money spent on black Southerners' education. These choices required not only the neglect of a group whose need was at least as great as any other, it required an absolute retreat from the levels and standards of education that had been achieved by black Southerners during Reconstruction. Black Southerners living in this "redeemed" South could be forgiven for wondering just who was leading who when it came to the satisfaction of white desires; for asking just which group of white Southerners—the reactionaries or the reformers, the elite or the ignorant—most threatened their advance.

As James Kirkland's favorable response to softening Northern attitudes illustrates, most of the Southern Association's early members would have shared some or all of their attitudes. Charles Dabney, for example, who according to Dewey Grantham "was as preoccupied with maintaining controlling direction over black destinies as he was in wiping out white illiteracy," was an early participant in the Association, and William Few would become one of its early presidents. From its inception until the mid-1920s, the Association stayed firmly on the white side of the color line that its members' class and generation had led the way in starkly drawing through the heart of Southern society.[24] For all the combined racial and educational prejudices that enveloped its creation and early years, the educators of the Association would eventually become involved with their black counterparts to an extent that was hardly commonplace in the South of the 1920s and 1930s. It would be three decades before the official ties established then would bring black institutions full admission to the Association. In those intervening years, however, contacts between black and white educators played an increasingly important part in the life of the Association. Inevitably the developing relationship was frequently characterized by ambivalence and ambiguity, by both acceptance and denial of responsibility, new closeness and continued separateness. Association members were to be found among the growing, if still small, number of white Southerners beginning to look more closely at the problems faced by their black neighbors and to accept their share of responsibility for alleviating them. A significant episode in the Association's own history, these developing connections also provide a window on the wider connections between race and education in Southern society during this period.

Perhaps the first encouragement the Association received to take a role in black education came in 1920 from Northern colleges and universities in need of help in evaluating student applicants from the South's schools and colleges. It was recommended, "after much debate," that "a separate list" of acceptable schools should be published, but, according to the historian of the Secondary Commission, "there is no evidence that such a list was ever published."[25] The strongest demands that the Southern Association take some responsibility for the evaluation of black institutions came from educators, black and white, working in the region's black schools and colleges. These educators pointed to the problems created for institutions which, in effect, lived in an accrediting vacuum. While black colleges and universities in the North, such as Howard in Washington, D.C., and Lincoln in Jefferson City, Missouri, were "eligible for accrediting" if they met the standards of the relevant regional association, comparable institutions from Virginia to Texas, "however worthy," could not even be considered "by reason of being in the territory of the Southern Association." Given that the vast majority of black institutions fell within this region, it was understandable that black educators should turn to the Association as the body best placed to rectify, or at least ameliorate, this unhappy situation. These educators' determination to reach out to their white counterparts, to make them aware of the problems they faced, and to challenge them to cooperate in overcoming them, proved to be the decisive catalyst for the Association's involvement in black education.[26]

Black educators' prompting of the Association began in the 1920s. In 1928, for example, Thomas E. Jones, president of Fisk University in Nashville and a leading figure in black education, approached Guy Snavely, then secretary-treasurer of the Association, with a view to eliciting the Association's help in establishing standards for black schools and colleges. That same year Dr. M.W. Adams of Atlanta University attended the Association's annual meeting in Fort Worth, Texas, seeking help in rectifying the unsatisfactory situation in which black institutions in the South were effectively denied any kind of accreditation. Based on previous efforts to seek the Association's help made by the Association of Colleges for Negro Youth [ACNY] and the U.S. Bureau of Education, including a meeting he had with James Kirkland and Theodore Jack that had not been "encouraging," Adams was not optimistic that his mission would be a success. But after the meeting, Adams was pleased to report a "far more favorable" response than he had expected, his face-to-face discussions with the Association's officers convincing him that the Association "was now wholly in earnest in wishing to give us proper help toward accrediting."[27]

The Fort Worth meeting did, in fact, approve an Executive Committee recommendation that the Association ask the American Council on Education to support a plan to organize the Association of Colleges for Negro Youth "as a standardizing agency," and also "to offer the assistance of this Association in any way, either as an organization or through the aid of individual members." "After considerable discussion," according to Horace Ivy, the Association set up a three-person committee "to act for this Association in assisting the proposed Negro standardizing agencies." Theodore H. Jack, J. Henry Highsmith (who was made secretary), and Horace Ivy (who became chairman) were appointed to the committee, which was to deal with both secondary and postsecondary institutions.[28]

While an important first step, the recommendation did not go far enough for most black educators. Leo Favrot, for example, regretted that the resolution did not commit the Association to assuming a responsibility that other regional associations had already accepted.[29] In meetings and correspondence over the following year or so with members of the Committee on the Rating of Negro Schools, Thomas Jones and other black educators, including Adams and Dean D.O.W. Holmes of Howard University, emphasized their desire that the Association take on this role. The Committee reported to the Executive Committee in 1829 that the issue "of rating Negro schools was discussed for some time" and agreement reached "that there is not now in existence any agency or organization" equipped to "handle the problem satisfactorily." From the point of view of black educators, however, it was clear that such an organization did exist. It was called the Southern Association.[30]

Thus black educators continued to press for a larger Association role in black education. In the fall of 1829, Jones asked Theodore Jack if the Executive Committee "has been able to take action regarding the question of evaluating the quality of work done by the Negro colleges in the South." In one letter, Thomas Jones told Jack that he thought "the arguments pro and con" had been "pretty well covered" in past meetings. "Needless to say," Jones reiterated, "it would mean a great deal to Fisk and other institutions if we could have a survey made by the Southern Association and a definite rating of our work determined by you." Jones also confided to Dean D.O.W. Holmes of Howard University his "hope" that the Association was "not going to ignore our plea this year."[31] Theodore Jack assured Jones that the matter would indeed be dealt with at the next annual meeting and suggested that the Fisk president attend. Jones came to Lexington, where he met the Executive Committee and "received verbal assurance from all the members that our request . . . would be acted upon favorably."[32]

At its Lexington meeting, the Association did indeed move toward becoming the accrediting body for black institutions by approving the appointment of a standing Committee on Approval of Negro Schools. This committee, chosen from the Association's membership and reporting to its Executive Committee, was to work with committees set up in each state and composed of one member each from the Higher and Secondary Commissions, along with "one or more persons selected from the Division of Negro Education in the respective states." This state committee would submit its recommendations, from which the Committee on Approval would determine which schools and colleges would be submitted to the Executive Committee for final approval. The Association's assumption of this new role was conditional on outside funding being provided to help pay for the survey of black institutions that the process would require. The General Education Board responded positively to a request from the Committee on Approval of Negro Schools with a grant of $35,000. This funding enabled the committee to employ a full-time Executive Agent to inspect the institutions seeking Association approval. The first Executive Agent was Professor Arthur D. Wright of Dartmouth College in New England, a graduate of William and Mary who had previously held the post of supervisor of Negro Rural Schools in Virginia. He was succeeded in 1931 by Fred McCuiston who served in that position until 1939 when he resigned to join the General Education Board. The field agent worked out of a central office in Nashville.[33]

The Committee began its work at the postsecondary level by writing to the 85 historically black institutions in the Association's area, explaining the committee's purpose, and inviting them to request an inspection. The inspection would "be based on a formal report to be submitted by each such institution on the regular forms of the Commission on Higher Institutions of this Association." By the time of the Committee's 1930 report, 35 of the 60 institutions that had requested the forms had submitted them. Nine of the institutions considered most likely to meet the Association's standards had been visited and approved. Of the nine, only Fisk University made an "A list" reserved for institutions that met "in full the standards set up by this Association for institutions of higher education." Six other institutions formed a "B list" of institutions that did "not yet meet in full one or more of the [Association's] standards" but whose educational work was of a sufficiently high "general quality . . . as to warrant the admission of their graduates to any institution requiring the bachelor's degree for entrance." An "Approved List of Colleges and Universities for Negro Youth" was placed in the 1930 *Proceedings*, "following the list of approved white colleges." The first twenty black high schools were approved by the Association the following year.[34]

Membership grew slowly but steadily over the coming years as the Highsmith Committee (as it became known in tribute to its secretary) continued its work. In 1934 Thomas E. Jones wrote to the Association's Executive Committee "to express the gratitude" of the ACNY "for the far-reaching and permanent service" the Association, the Highsmith Committee, and its field agents had given to black education in the South. The following year twelve four-year colleges were on the "A list" and twenty-two on the "B list," while three junior colleges made the first list and four the secondary one. By 1943, 106 secondary schools were on the Association's approved list, along with thirty four-year colleges on the "A list" and sixteen on the "B list" and five two-year colleges on the "A list" and four on the "B list." The 1930 "approved" list saw the beginning of a form of accreditation for the South's black colleges. "Approval" helped to improve standards within and artic-ulation between black institutions. It also provided the desired guidelines for Northern universities receiving applications from black Southerners.[35]

Yet inclusion on a separate "approved" list hardly brought with it the same benefits that membership and accreditation con-ferred on whites-only institutions. This inequality was compound-ed for those black institutions who only made it to the "B list" (which some black educators had been heard to suggest stood for "Berated.")[36] These separate rankings raised, in turn, the thorny problem of which standards should be applied to black institu-tions. Some educators, in the Association and in the ACNY, made the argument that was also sometimes made on behalf of some white institutions: that greater leniency was appropriate for insti-tutions laboring under serious social and economic handicaps. Rather than holding them to the highest Association standards, it would be better, in this view, to establish a more gradual path to educational improvement.

Many African-American educators strongly opposed an approach they viewed as yet another example of the separate and *un*equal treatment that they hoped Association accreditation would help to end. J.T. Cater, for example, argued that different standards for black and white schools represented "a real menace to both groups," fostering "a smug paternalism on one side, and sham and self-delusion on the other." Cater questioned the motives of those who felt otherwise, whether it was the black school principal eager "to have his school an accredited one even if manipulation of standards had to be encouraged," or the "white state officials" keen to "publish a long list of approved high schools for Negroes" as supposed evidence that they were not being discriminated against. Cater was even more critical of those who supported unequal accreditation out of genuine belief rather than blatant self-interest, criticizing "paternalistic" white educators or excuse-making black educators alike. Cater, instead, praised those white educators who offered "sympathetic understanding and cooperative help," recognizing the "troubles" and "disabilities" facing black people, yet "all the while rigidly insisting that his achievements be measured by accepted standards." Black "proponents of this school of thought," argued Cater, believed it was "the only way to maintain the self-respect required for real advancement," whereas "sham will in the long run become a serious menace to the welfare of the group."[37]

Cater's view prevailed, and it was agreed that black institutions would be measured by the same standards as other Southern colleges and schools. Writing in 1934, Thomas Jones praised studies that had "been painstaking and fair" and reported to the Association that "your ratings have generally been approved by the Negro group as helpful and just." Jones was evidently pleased with the conclusion that "At no time have you deviated from the high standards of the Southern Association to rate a Negro school, no matter how sympathetic you may have been to its appeal." Such an approach, Jones believed, "has been a service to the whole Negro race which has been much appreciated."[38]

Questions were raised, however, as to how consistently this even-handed approach was being applied. Some white educators believed that, in practice, the inspection of black schools and colleges was not being conducted in hard and fast accordance with the Association's standards. "Maybe on paper," replied T.P. Baker, when asked to recall whether the same standards were applied to black and white institutions, "but they were not being visited by

the type of committee by which they were visited after" becoming
eligible for membership or by their whites-only contemporaries. At
least as far as the secondary schools were concerned, Baker
believed that black institutions did not "meet the standards in actu-
ality."[39] As Baker suggests, even if inspectors had done their best to
treat black exactly the same as white, the inspections would still
have been unequal due to the practices and resources involved in
conducting them. Thus, at other times, recommendations that
both black and white should be treated equally, strongly implied
that this was not as yet happening. In 1943, for example, black
educators recommended that "the same methods, machinery and
standards of evaluation" used with regard to white secondary
schools should also be applied to black ones.[40] As this recommendation suggests, even if the same standards were applied, the fact
of a less stringent inspection might weaken their application in
effect. In the 1930s and 1940s, black institutions were usually visited by the Highsmith Committee's field agent, rather than by a
group of educators from an equivalent institution as was the case
with whites-only colleges. While individual agents clearly accu-
mulated a great deal of knowledge over the years, this process
could hardly have brought to bear the level of expertise and thor-
oughness provided by a larger group of inspectors drawn from
similar kinds of institutions. This remained a troubling issue over
the coming years.[41]

Progress toward greater equality of treatment could also reinforce awareness of the profound distance that remained between
black and white in Southern education. Continuing inequalities in
practice and differences in priority were evident in black educators'
creation of their own parallel organization, the Association of
Colleges and Secondary Schools for Negroes (ACSSN), formed in
1934 from a merger of the Association of Colleges for Negro
Youth and the Association of Negro High School Education.[42]
The new Association restricted membership to black institutions
that had been accredited by the Southern Association, but its leaders were adamant that, as Thomas Jones insisted, it would "not
contemplate undertaking the rating function." It was "obvious,"
Jones told the Executive Committee, "that the Southern
Association was the only 'generally recognized'" accrediting body
in the region, and that "as long as this is true, Negro, as well as

white schools, should be rated by it." Indeed, to begin their own accrediting would have been to reinforce the barriers that their efforts to engage the Association's interest in black education were designed to break down.[43]

The motivation behind the ACSSN's creation was rather the desire to preserve and expand the Southern Association's role in evaluating black institutions. One aim was to build a fund, gathered from dues-paying members, to defray the Southern Association's costs once the GEB's temporary funding of its inspection program ended. Its founders also envisioned that, like the Southern Association, the ACSSN would function as a venue for the study and debate of issues affecting black education. According to leading black educator L.S. Cozart, "the prevailing opinion" among its founders "was that an autonomous organization of colleges and secondary schools could more effectively deal with their peculiar problems." At the same time, measures designed to preserve and extend contacts with the Southern Association—such as holding their annual meeting at the same time and place as the Southern Association, distributing their *Proceedings* to members of both associations—were also instituted. Regular reciprocal attendance at each association's annual meetings were also encouraged, and J. Henry Highsmith and his committee's field agent frequently attended, and sometimes spoke, at the ACSSN's annual meeting. Thus the ACSSN was distinct from, yet linked to, the Southern Association. Its members "desired close cooperation with the Southern Association," as Jack Allen explains, "not 'dual rating machinery' and looked toward the time when cracks in the wall of segregation would allow their membership in that organization."[44]

Indicative of serious and continuing differences, the ACSSN's relation to the Southern Association also suggests the advances made by the early postwar years. Cooperation between black and white educators had contributed to the progress of black institutions in very difficult circumstances. Both black and white educators agreed that the Association's standards had provided a strong incentive for the improvement of many institutions. By 1949, H.M. Ivy could report to the Southern Association on the recent series of state-level meetings between black and white educators focused on improving black high schools and predict that the

number of institutions on the following year's "approved" list
would "far exceed" the present figure. Ivy also emphasized the
general improvement in the quality of facilities and faculty, the
increased funding from both public and private sources, as well as
the resulting improvement in the African-American student body
as a whole. Ivy reported that the number of colleges had declined
from 85 to 68, but this, too, could be read as a sign of improvement as institutions that had never really been "colleges" either
improved to that level, found their own level, amalgamated with
other institutions or, in some cases, closed their doors. Ivy also
drew attention to the "vastly improved condition" of the junior
colleges as well as to the almost annual raising of the standards
that black institutions were expected to meet. In the Committee's
view, Ivy continued, "there can be no better indication of the
development in the field of Negro education" over the previous
two decades than the rise in colleges meeting the Association's
standards from one to fifty, and of schools from eleven to 130.
Concluding with a reference to how, after the initial GEB grant
had been exhausted, the cost of inspection had been taken up by
the ACSSN and by "an annual appropriation by your Association," Ivy expressed the Committee's belief that "this appropriation has been one of your top investments."[45]

Much of the progress achieved had also stemmed from black
educators' "investment" in the hope that their persistent pushing
against the walls of segregation would find at least some white people prepared to respond positively. The Southern Association had
responded more positively than most white Southern organizations
in this period. The progress made hinted at what could be achieved
if a more wholehearted white "investment" in racial fairness and
equality could be encouraged and counted upon in the future.

The years during and immediately after the war brought further small signs of progress in the treatment of African-
Americans. In 1944 the first black journalist was admitted to a
presidential press conference. Of more practical significance,
Franklin Roosevelt had established the Fair Employment Practices
Commission during the war as a response to discrimination in
federally subsidized employment. Later Harry Truman issued his
historic Executive Order desegregating the armed forces.[46] As
always, change followed a familiar pattern of white Americans

moving because black Americans pushed them. The creation of the FEPC, for example, was prompted by the threat of black union leader A. Philip Randolph to organize a mass protest march on Washington, D.C. Nevertheless, the walls between America's and the South's parallel worlds were hardly crumbling, and to some extent these breaches in the wall of discrimination further underscored the solidity of the barriers that remained in place.

The staunch resistance of many white Americans to even minimal changes in the racial status quo also underscored how wrong the Southern Progressives had been to believe that improved education for white Southerners would encourage greater tolerance and thus pave the way for the improvement of black education and life. The virulent racism that had been such a feature of Southern life in the first half of the century showed little signs of abating in the second half. Many white politicians on the campaign trail were as keen as ever to take the low road of race-baiting and fear-mongering, any small sign of black advance only encouraging their extremism. In 1944, for example, the NAACP's long struggle against the "white primary" bore fruit when, in *Smith v. Allwright*, the Supreme Court declared this Democratic Party practice a violation of the Fifteenth Amendment.[47] Black Americans and white moderates hoped the ruling would open the way to greater black participation in Southern politics and, in turn, to white politicians being more responsive to black citizens. This did happen to some extent. But the Democratic Party often turned to other kinds of exclusionary tactics such as poll taxes, and where black participation did increase, white politicians were as likely to accuse an opponent of currying black favor as to appeal to the still small number of black voters. In 1948, South Carolina's Strom Thurmond also broke with the Democratic Party over its presidential platform which, at the urging of black Democrats and others, contained a civil rights plank of unprecedented liberality. Thurmond's illiberal reaction to this "liberal" action was to run for president on the "Dixiecrat" ticket. And so it was in many cases, as every black gain or conciliatory white action was as likely to provoke a racist backlash as it was to nurture greater tolerance.

In the face of continuing widespread white resistance, black Americans became more convinced than ever that, however welcome white help was, they themselves had to take the lead in bringing about change. Men and women like Randolph were increasingly unwilling to wait upon the goodwill of white Americans to achieve full access to the rights and duties of American citizenship. The interracial Congress of Racial Equality was established in 1942 and the older NAACP increased its membership from 50,000 to 500,000 during the war.[48] The experiences of the war years further convinced black Americans that even well-meaning white Americans could only be expected to go so far without the weight of organized black action pressing upon them. Black efforts to achieve equal rights in postwar America took many forms, from sit-ins and boycotts directed at segregated businesses to the efforts of the small, but growing, band of black elected officials around the country.

Perhaps of greatest significance to education, and to the Southern Association, were the series of court challenges, begun in the 1930s, and mounted against segregation by civil rights advocates, especially the lawyers of the NAACP, led by Charles Hamilton Houston, dean of the Howard University Law School and his assistant, Thurgood Marshall. Although they had never accepted the "separate but equal" doctrine that underpinned claims for segregation's constitutionality, the NAACP lawyers believed it would be more effective initially to challenge Southern states for their failure to live up to it. These efforts reveal the extent of the cautious and piecemeal approach that many civil rights leaders felt constrained to follow, as does the decision to focus initially on higher, especially professional education, where inequalities were most extreme and, perhaps, the interests of the majority of white Southerners less intensely concerned. Beginning with a case in Maryland, Thurgood Marshall successfully argued that paying to send Donald Gaines Murray, a black candidate for the University of Maryland law school, out of state rather than admit him at home, was not equal treatment. The following year, a similar case on behalf of Lloyd Lionel Gaines of Missouri reached the U.S. Supreme Court before resulting in a decision in support of the NAACP's position.[49]

The court decisions against separate and patently unequal educational opportunities and facilities encouraged a flurry of activity in the Southern states designed to create a greater semblance of equality while maintaining the separation of black and white. Some of these efforts reeked of bad faith, not least the separate "law school" established by the University of Texas in response to an application by Herman Sweatt of Houston. The new institution consisted of three basement rooms in Houston staffed by part-time faculty. In every conceivable respect it was a long way from the prestigious law school in the state capital of Austin. The University of Oklahoma did eventually admit an older black professor, George W. McLaurin, to its doctoral education program, but required him to sit at a desk surrounded by a railing and to occupy segregated sections of the library and cafeteria. By 1950, when the Supreme Court decided in favor of these two men, the NAACP had been joined by the Department of Justice in supporting equal education before the court. These cases were decided narrowly; the Court found in favor of the men, but did not take the opportunity to offer an opinion on the general principle underlying their particular cases. Nevertheless, these decisions were major breakthroughs.[50]

Some white politicians and educators were more sincere in their desire to make "separate but equal" something more of a reality. But they faced insuperable problems, encountering, as Charles Johnson, Thomas Jones' successor at Fisk University, explained, "the dilemma of either abandoning the dual system or committing themselves to vast sums for equalization." Running two "separate" educational systems in the nation's poorest region had always been a recipe for all-around inadequacy, even when one of them had been starved of funds. Any serious attempt to make this dual system more "equal" would be financially ruinous, even in the improbable event that the higher taxes required to pay for the transformation would meet with majority approval. Questions of funding aside, support for moves toward greater equality remained a minority position among white Southerners. Segregation and the racism that demanded it remained powerful forces in Southern society. Yet whether for reasons of financial necessity or a degree of willingness to acknowledge the unfairness of the current system, some states began to admit black students to the professional schools of their state universities. Cracks in the solid support for segregation were widening, as black appeals to the courts began to succeed where appeals to conscience had so often failed.[51]

This was the wider educational context for the Association's developing postwar relations with black colleges and high schools.

Attitudes and actions within the Association reflected and helped to shape the various positions to be found in the wider white community. Attitudes on the question of desegregating education ranged from total opposition to frank recognition of the wrongs done to black Southerners and the need to stand with black Southerners in righting those wrongs and building a better South. Some white educators implored their colleagues to recognize the historic wrongs done to black Southerners and to lead the way in righting them. John E. Ivey, Jr., director of the Board of Control for Southern Regional Education, talked to the Association in 1949 of "the fast accumulating moral and legal debt the South owes its Negro citizens." Ivey lamented the lack of "moral stamina" evident in the reluctance "to face up to the fact that nearly 10 million human beings are actually being kept from achieving the full intellectual development made possible on public funds to other citizens of this area." Ivey could find "no postulate of democracy or Christianity on which" white educators could "rest our conscience" faced with their involvement in this continuing injustice.[52]

Other educators focused on the specific actions the Association should take to help repay this historic debt. In 1949 another white educator, A.B. Beitel, president of historically black Talladega College, urged the Association to admit institutions like his to full membership. Beitel was quick to recognize the "inestimable value" of the "progressive and forward-looking step" the Association had taken twenty years earlier in extending accreditation to black colleges and secondary schools. But he argued that the time was now ripe for further action to end the disadvantages that non-membership placed on black educators and their institutions. Beitel painted a sad, ironic portrait of how exclusion denied black educators the opportunity to meet and discuss with fellow educators the philosophies and problems common to all, regardless of color. Beitel noted that in the city of Houston, where the Association was meeting, there were black educators and institutions that would benefit from, and contribute to, the conference. But with this "rich educational program at his doorstep," a leading black educator such as President Lanier of the State University for Negroes would have to travel to the ACSSN meeting in Daytona Beach the following week in order to enjoy the professional benefits and collegiality that his audience took for granted.[53]

Beitel pointed to other areas of education where black and white now worked together, including the interracial Southern Sociological Society, which drew many of its participants from member institutions of the Association. He noted how labor leaders, black and white, had recently come together in the very rooms now being used by the Association to discuss their problems. "And when the Brewers Association met not long ago in the Shamrock Hotel," Beitel also recounted, "the Negro brewers met with the white brewers to discuss the accreditation of breweries." The moral was clear. If the makers of the South's beer could get together on the basis of the issues that linked them rather than remain separated by their skin color, could the makers of the South's future leaders do less? Gently emphasizing the absurdity of the situation, Beitel felt it would be "most unfortunate if the brewers and the labor leaders move on ahead of southern educators in working together on the perplexing problems of the region." Beitel told how the leaders of black education believed it was time for the Association to "make another great step to improve education in the South by inviting the accredited schools and colleges for Negroes into full membership." "Ladies and gentlemen," Beitel ended his address, "The leaders of Negro education in the South . . . stand at the door of the Southern Association of Colleges and Secondary Schools and knock for admission." Despite Beitel's appeal, the meeting defeated a motion that the two associations unite, as well as one that suggested they meet together. It would be another seven years before the door to full membership was finally opened.[54]

The Association was clearly not ready to take the "great step" that would move them far out in front of other whites-only organizations, not to mention most of its member institutions. There were various reasons for this. While some members shared Beitel's desire for immediate black membership, others opposed the integration of the Association just as they opposed the desegregation of Southern society generally. Other members favored greater support for black institutions as part of making "separate but equal" more of a reality. In 1947, Horace Ivy, whose role in helping black education was greater than most, had understood the Association's "problem" as being how to achieve more equal forms of inspection and standardization between black and white institutions "without allowing Negroes to become members of the

Southern Association." At that time, as Jack Allen notes, many
white Southerners considered liberal on matters of race still
searched for ways to maintain racial segregation while encouraging, indeed by encouraging, greater racial equality. As Ivy's position
indicates, they were also represented within the Association.[55]

Perhaps the most widespread position was support for equality and integration, but not yet. Laurence D. Haskew remembered
supporting a recommendation calling for an end to "the second-
class citizenship that was being accorded to the predominantly
black institutions," and for their admission into the Association
"on exactly the same standards" as institutions that "were predominantly white in character." Although the recommendation
raised "a good bit of discussion," it was not accepted because, in
Haskew's view, it was "ill-timed." The view that the time had not
yet come for such a revolutionary and risky step was echoed by
Henry Hill, president at the time of Beitel's address. Hill remembered being "acutely aware of the question of timing," and supported the defeat of the ensuing motions.[56]

That the time was not "ripe" remained the majority position
within the Association. Supporters of full integration often based
this belief on their fear of the "massive resistance" it would
undoubtedly encounter from pro-segregation forces in society at
large. The inevitable opposition from other educators, both within
the Association and its member institutions, was also a strong factor in encouraging caution. Doubtless the wish not to alienate
existing colleagues and friends in the present outweighed for many
their willingness to admit new members in the future. Whether
from a desire to maintain separation or out of concern for the
negative response of those who did, the Association continued to
bring a cautious, incremental approach to the developing relations
between black and white educators and between the Southern
Association and the ACSSN.

Black Southerners found these appeals for patience less than
persuasive. Many felt that requesting the rights and status granted
by constitutional amendments passed almost a century earlier hardly represented the final word in pushiness. "No inscription on a
tombstone could be more chilling than the phrase 'the time is not
ripe' to one who is seeking avenues of progress in the field of
Southern education," insisted Charles Johnson at the ACSSN's

1953 meeting. Johnson addressed the "well-meaning people" who accepted the need to right racial wrongs but were "not convinced that the time is right." "It takes the heart out of even a stout man," Johnson lamented, "when one who has declared himself your friend and equal in educational attainments as measured by the best tests of our best institutions" responded with caution to proposals designed to advance the cause of equality. Johnson described how these friends would "agree with you that this thing ought to be done. It is a step which in fairness and justice ought to be taken. . . . It is, in fact, only a question of putting into practice principles which all right-thinking men agree upon, and which our form of government and our religion demand. BUT—just now, the time is not ripe." It appeared to Johnson "that ripeness in this kind of action is not in the fruit, but in the picker. There are things to be done which are ripe and overripe, but there is a strange greenness in the doers." Clearly suggesting the frustration of long years of listening to such reasoning, Johnson reasoned that arguing for delay on the basis of opposition from segregationists unlikely to accept change willingly was really a recipe for inaction.[57]

In the heated social and political atmosphere of the times, well-intentioned white people's caution in supporting change is in many ways understandable. Yet in practice, it often translated into passive acquiescence in the segregated status quo and a ceding of the political battleground to the vociferous and more racist elements in the white South. As President Beitel put it, "The progressive action of twenty years ago can be the reactionary position today." And as Johnson emphasized, accepting change only grudgingly could limit the potential benefits to be gained from it, since "the action seems like an ungracious yielding to pressure, rather than an assumption of initiative in behalf of fair play and democratic practice." "Too often, when the 'time is ripe,'" Johnson concluded, "it's too late." But fears regarding integration continued to be a brake on the Association's potential as an engine of greater educational and social change. Aware that it was not doing enough, uncertain as to what "more" would mean, the Association retained a clear idea of what would be too much.[58]

The widespread feeling that *now* was not the right time to act nevertheless carried with it the recognition that action would and should be taken at some point in the future. In the incremental world of Southern race relations, this in itself represented a kind of progress. Many members in the postwar period recognized that, whatever its past achievements, the Association's prevailing relation to black institutions was unsatisfactory. As Rufus Harris recalled, the fact that black institutions could be approved by the Association but could not be members of it, "involved an aspect of awkwardness, a downgrading, it was not a happy situation." And in 1949 the Executive Committee acknowledged that the Association's approved lists did not represent "adequate assumptions of responsibility for improving Negro education in the South." Indeed located between those who proposed rapid integration and those who opposed such a step, perhaps the most common response was cautious and qualified support for closer relations that would eventually lead to the ACSSN's members joining the Southern Association.[59]

So it was that even by the time Beitel spoke on behalf of one "great step," the Association had been continuing to take little steps in the direction of closer and fairer relations between the white and black institutions whose responsibility it was to accredit. Following an Executive Committee decision at the 1947 annual meeting, a liaison committee was established to meet with an ACSSN committee with the goal of helping the latter's members to "become standardized." The following year the ACSSN liaison committee committed itself to "earnestly seeking to remove barriers" to black institutions joining the Southern Association. In response to the ACSSN's continued priority of working for full membership, in 1949 the Association established another "special committee charged with studying ways to improve Negro education and the relationship between the two Associations." The liaison committees' differing approaches to this greater cooperation nevertheless also spoke to the continuing difference in the Associations' priorities: greater assistance for black institutions on the one hand, their full membership in the Southern Association on the other.[60]

Taken as a whole, however, the succession of recommendations made and committees created in the late 1940s indicate a gradual momentum toward the outcome that the majority of Association members refused to embrace immediately. In 1950, after meeting with the ACSSN liaison committee, the Special Committee declared that the Southern Association "should either indicate the desirability of full membership for black institutions and set up a time schedule for their admission or state that the idea has merit and would be continued under consideration, but is not timely." The same year the Southern Association decided that the "B list" of black institutions should be abolished after 1950-51, a move designed, according to Jack Allen, "to promote the equality of the white and black lists." The following year the Special Committee's final report called for the discontinuation of the Committee on the Approval of Negro Schools, and for applications and reports concerning black institutions to be handled by the appropriate commission of the Association.[61]

That report also included a recommendation that the ACSSN be invited to hold its annual meeting at the same time and place as the Association (and to utilize its speakers if desired), and that a standing liaison committee be appointed to meet with ACSSN counterparts after the annual meetings. The year 1952 saw the first joint meeting of the associations, at Le Moyne College, a black institution in Memphis. John F. Potts, ACSSN president, thought that "significant progress had been made toward possible membership" in the Association.[62] Thus while reflecting continuing caution, such actions and options also indicated a momentum toward eventual integration. Procedural changes brought greater contact between black and white on a more equitable basis and the gradual dismantling of the parts of the Association's organizational structure that reflected black institutions' separate and unequal status. At the same time, the segregated status quo disappeared as a long-term option as the Association's internal discussions increasingly assumed the inadequacy and inequity of the existing situation and the inevitability and desirability of eventual integration.

There were setbacks. Plans for shared meetings and events at the Association's 1953 annual meeting, also in Memphis, came unstuck due, the Association insisted, to the segregationist practices of the city and the convention hotel, rather than to any lack of enthusiasm on its part. This explanation did not placate the ACSSN's liaison committee, which lamented the "slow progress made toward closer affiliation" over the preceding year. President Stephen J. Wright bluntly reported on the "conspicuous failure" of his extensive efforts on behalf of full membership. In response, the ACSSN selected its next meeting place (Columbia, South

Carolina) without regard to the Southern Association's intended venue of Louisville, Kentucky. At a March 1954 meeting of the liaison committees, the Association representatives successfully urged their black counterparts to reconsider. At that meeting the Association also took a big step toward the "great step" by officially affirming its wish for eventual merger, going so far as to set 1960 as a target date for qualified black institutions to be admitted to the Association. But larger events were to intervene. At a meeting of ACSSN officials and the Association's Executive Committee a few months later, the Association's president, Carlyle Campbell, began by saying "Well, it seems the Supreme Court has knocked our projected deadline [of 1960] into a cocked hat." What Campbell had in mind was that year's unanimous decision in *Brown v. Board of Education of Topeka, Kansas*. Unlike previous cases that had found for the civil rights position in specific cases, *Brown* explicitly attacked the "separate but equal" doctrine set out in *Plessy v. Ferguson*. Chief Justice Earl Warren, speaking for a unanimous court, declared separate educational facilities "inherently unequal" and, therefore, unconstitutional. The *Brown* decision set in motion a series of cases that saw segregation in various public institutions and facilities declared unconstitutional. A follow-up decision in 1955 declared that integration should be carried out "with all deliberate speed."[63]

A revolutionary breakthrough, *Brown* and the efforts to enforce it inevitably provoked a white backlash which, in familiar fashion, took both official and unofficial forms. In 1956, 100 Southern members of Congress signed a "Southern Manifesto" that branded *Brown* as "a clear abuse of judicial power." By the end of the same year, half a million had joined the militantly segregationist White Citizens' Councils. Klan membership and terrorist violence aimed at black Southerners was on the rise. Nor was opposition confined to the outspokenly racist. While black Americans and white moderates hailed the decision as a great step forward, President Dwight Eisenhower privately complained that appointing Chief Justice Earl Warren had been "the biggest damn fool mistake I ever made." Opposition to school integration proved highly effective in these years. In 1956, four states in the Association's region had yet to desegregate any of its whites-only public, postsecondary institutions, and only forty-four such institutions in total had been desegregated to any extent. Change at the secondary level was even more glacial, with just over 1 percent of black elementary and secondary students (26,285 of 2,437,893), enrolled in desegregated school districts. All the Deep South states had passed legislation intended to circumvent or delay desegregation efforts. By 1960, more than 99 percent of black children remained in segregated schools.[64]

In the face of the segregationists' continuing intransigence, caution remained the watchword of more moderate white Southerners, including those in the Association. The Association moved slowly, but it did move, and did so in directions that assumed the inevitability of eventual integration. Of greatest importance was the program of inspection set in motion after the respective commissions had assumed responsibility for the inspection of black institutions. A program of visits to all relevant colleges, funded by the General Education Board, began in the early years of the decade and was completed in 1956, the year the College Commission had set for a decision regarding black membership. [65]

Black educators knew that a "one standard, one association" policy would not please everyone in their ranks. Charles Johnson frankly admitted that it would be bad news for some "weaker" institutions whose "uninspired and unchallenged mediocrity" had been preserved up to this point behind "the protective walls of segregation." Johnson perhaps overestimated the extent to which problems facing black colleges were within their own power to correct. Two chronic problems, for example, were the lack of qualified teachers and of sufficient money, both themselves consequences of past and continuing poverty and prejudice. Nevertheless Johnson could see "no good reason" why the "intelligent men and women" responsible for Southern education should continue "to try to view the problem through myopic binoculars." From Johnson's viewpoint, "A single organization would be a vast improvement and a long-deferred educational advance." Greater equality would mean greater pain in the short term—the new approach did indeed mean probation or loss of accreditation for numerous institutions—but would be for the greater good in the long run.[66]

The conduct of the inspections nevertheless also illuminated continuing differences in treatment. For one thing, only the inspection teams visiting black institutions were integrated. No

black educators participated in visits to whites-only schools and colleges. The new inspection process also reflected continuing worries
regarding real or potential opposition to changes in the Association's
ways of doing things. The College Commission, for example, avoided assigning people from the public system to integrated inspection
teams once it became clear that this program was likely a step
toward eventual admission of black institutions. On balance, however, the new inspection program provided strong evidence for a
powerful momentum toward union; sooner rather than later.[67]

In 1956 the College Commission agreed to phase out the
"approved list," and for the first time "formally approved procedures and a time schedule for admission of black institutions." The
Association's annual meeting in Dallas that year voted to admit
black colleges, beginning the following year. Characteristically,
however, it then took a cautious approach to the selection of the
institutions that would be first to join. One proposed list contained
eighteen colleges that the committee believed were eligible for
membership, while a shorter list contained those whose standards
exceeded the average of doctorate-granting white institutions. As
William McEniry recalled, the Commission's Joint Sub-Committee
on Colleges for Negro Youth "debated until 2 or 3 in the morning"
the question of whether to admit "seven that nobody could argue
with or put in eighteen that we honestly thought deserved to be in."
With the advice of Benjamin Mays and Rufus Clement (presidents,
respectively, of Morehouse College and Atlanta University), they
eventually went with the larger group and recommended the
admission of 15 colleges and 3 junior colleges from the 63
reviewed. In 1957, the same year that white Southerners screamed
"Go back to the jungle" at nine black students seeking to enter
Central High School in Little Rock, Arkansas, the Southern
Association admitted its first black colleges to full membership.
Others joined them in each of the following years, and in 1961 the
Association abolished its separate approved list for black colleges.[68]

The continuing resistance to desegregation had a constituency
within the Association. As much was assumed by the Louisville
television journalist who asked T.P. Baker whether he and his colleagues were "expecting trouble on the floor in the Business
Session" of the Louisville annual meeting. Baker "surprised" the
journalist by telling her "No, we do not anticipate any difficulty on

the floor," but later acknowledged that this may have been a "wishful," if sincerely felt, "hope." Baker's confidence may have stemmed from his knowledge of the extensive prior efforts—such as the careful selection of the first black colleges and the thorough canvassing of members' opinions—designed to limit the possibility of "trouble." Nevertheless, even for the hopeful ones like Baker, "it was a worry at that time." Hugh McEniry worried that opponents would force a debate on the floor. Although new members were voted on by the Association as a whole, there was a "gentleman's agreement" that college people would not challenge secondary recommendations and vice versa. McEniry and his colleagues worried that some secondary people were sufficiently opposed to integrating the membership that they would break with convention in order to force a confrontation. When the time came to vote, McEniry remembered voting "Aye in a void" since all around him had voted no. From this lone position, McEniry at first thought the vote close, but later learned that those around him had raised the only negative voices. Thus it was "a tense moment that [McEniry] did not need to be tense about at all," as admission was approved convincingly.[69]

Among the minority, however, some were "very bitter" about the decision. Baker recalled "one man connected with one of the leading colleges and universities in the South," who approached him afterwards, shook his hand, and told him: "I hope you realize what you have done. You have presided over a session that means the death of the Southern Association of Colleges and Schools." As far as Baker knew, the man never attended another meeting of the Association. It was also the case that some members, on returning to their communities, heard "murmuring that this was an organization to which their school should no longer belong." Asked if he recalled anything of this nature, Baker replied: "I remember it, but I never had any experience of that kind at all, yet we had a Negro college in our community. I know it helped that college, and it helped our community."[70]

Those around McEniry had been mostly from secondary schools, the area where popular resistance to desegregation was strongest since it directly affected a far larger number of white Southerners. Another six years would pass before the first black secondary schools were admitted to membership. In 1962, the

Secondary Commission decided that its Central Reviewing Committee should recommend membership for schools that met its standards and should also "go on record as favoring the eventual abolition of the list of Approved Schools." The following year, the first black secondary schools (259 of them) gained membership in the Association, and in 1966 the approved list for secondary schools was discontinued. The later admission of black secondary schools further suggests how the trajectory of integration within the Association followed that of the wider society, as resistance and caution increased, as the battleground shifted from public universities and colleges to the public schools in which far greater numbers of people had a direct interest.[71]

That the Association only admitted "black" high schools years after the Supreme Court had declared segregated public schools unconstitutional also suggests some of the limitations of the Association's approach to racial matters. Its reluctance to take a stronger lead in advocating greater racial equality in Southern education was in part the ironic consequence of its having become more diverse and democratic in many other respects. The Association had developed a membership that included the most serious flash points of racial tension and white resistance: the public schools, universities, and other public postsecondary institutions where the great majority of white Southerners received their education. The Association's continued acceptance of, or acquiescence in, the racial assumptions of the wider white community is also evident in its unwillingness to take a position on desegregation generally. As the Association insistently debated the admission of black institutions, no debates were held on the question of whether accreditation should be withdrawn from the many member institutions who did their best to defy the law of the land long after the Supreme Court's fateful *Brown* decision.

The eventual admission of black institutions, nevertheless, reveals the Southern Association's long journey away from much of the thinking, and therefore action, that had enjoyed the unchallenged status of conventional wisdom among most white Southerners throughout the early decades of the century. The years between the 1920s and the mid-1960s saw a growing disengagement from the most racist elements in Southern society. Growing distance from racism was entwined with growing contact and cooperation with black institutions. In its efforts on behalf of black education in the 1920s and 1930s, the Association had been ahead of most of the institutions that provided white Southerners with their education. When prompted and persuaded, the Association chose to respond positively and developed ties to black schools and colleges far more extensive than those to be seen in many other organizations involved in Southern education and life at that time. As civil rights and race relations took center stage in the late 1940s and 1950s, the Association shared the caution of most white moderates. But within its own precisely drawn sphere of interest, it was aligned with the more progressive forces at work in the white community. Indeed, one irony of the Association's relation to black education throughout this period is that it offered a more active and engaged approach to the challenge of racial inequality in education than did most of its member institutions acting alone.

The Association would not have moved as far and as quickly as it did without the persistent efforts of black educators to push it toward ever greater involvement in black education. This, too, reflected the dynamics of the wider society as court challenges, voter registration, and nonviolent civil disobedience eventually moved the white South much further than it would have moved of its own volition. Greater willingness to listen to black people, and to recognize white responsibility for many of their problems, was increasingly evident in the Southern Association in general, and in certain leading individual members in particular. J.T. Cater of Talladega College remembered in 1935 how, some years earlier, Theodore Jack attended a meeting of the Association of Colleges for Negro Youth. Jack announced that he had arrived "fully persuaded that the Southern Association had no responsibility in the matter of examining and accrediting Negro schools and colleges." By the time he left, however, Jack's "mind had been completely changed" and "he personally had come to the conclusion that such a responsibility did rest upon that Association." In the late 1920s, Dr. J. Henry Highsmith of the North Carolina Department of Public Instruction appeared before the Executive Committee along with two black educators from North Carolina, to make "a plea that the Southern Association adopt a plan for the improvement and approval of schools for Negroes."[72]

Black educators were quick to recognize the contribution

these exceptional individuals had made to their cause. After his death in 1953, Highsmith was remembered by a leading black colleague, L.S. Cozart, as "an example of courage to those who must face and come to grips with a greater crisis in the struggle for complete freedom for all groups of people in this country." Cozart paid tribute to Highsmith's willingness to take a minority position within his own Association by "back[ing] the judgment" of the black association, "strong voices to the contrary, notwithstanding." With "unrelenting courage" and "clarity of vision," Highsmith "labored for more than thirty-five years to improve the educational situation for Negroes in the Southern States," Cozart remembered. In doing so he had "forg[ed] a contribution which undoubtedly has become a part of our heritage." Apart from his rigorous commitment to standards, Cozart praised Highsmith for championing the equalization of salaries for black and white teachers, and for challenging the Southern Association "to assume its full duty of accrediting" black schools. The commitment of white educators like Highsmith and the "conversion experiences" of those like Theodore Jack often developed out of their contacts with the black educators who sought their cooperation. Thus, connections with individuals and institutions *excluded* from membership provided ironic support for one of the Association's founding assumptions: that contact between educators led to greater understanding of each others' situation.[73]

This recurring pattern of challenge and response, and its eventual benefits for black *and* white Southerners, is poignantly suggested by a speech made by William Hugh McEniry in 1961 before the Association of Colleges and Secondary Schools. McEniry, then dean of Stetson University and recently elected president of the Southern Association, addressed his audience with "a very real and immediate sense of gratitude." McEniry had played a central role in the new inspection and accreditation programs of the 1950s, and he now thanked those in attendance for having been "gracious and tolerant" toward a visitor who had "demanded the impossible" of them over the previous ten years. He thanked them also for being "warm in your offers of friendship even as I have given brutal occasion for you to reject me, and gentle in your instruction of another Southerner struggling, even as you, to get past the barriers of 300 years to our proper, common,

American community." "I owe you the most valuable educational experience of my life," McEniry then told the assembled educators. "Perhaps the one that has more than any other brought me my fullest realization of the possible significances of such words as *American, republic, democracy, freedom,* and *Christian love.*" After more than three decades of growing contacts between black and white educators, McEniry's words provided confirmation of a belief that had been at the heart of the Association's work from the beginning: Contact among educators increases understanding, and understanding encourages a level of cooperation at which many good and worthwhile aims can be realized.[74]

More fundamentally still, McEniry's words encapsulate a profoundly different vision of the South than the one espoused by paternalistic reformers of an earlier time, accustomed as they were to seeing black people primarily as a "problem" for a "South" defined as white. McEniry did not speak of a "Negro problem" but of interracial cooperation. He did not present himself as a superior offering assistance to an inferior. Instead, he described himself as "another Southerner," simply another part of the same community as those he addressed. McEniry came to the truth that people like him, as educators and as human beings, had a great deal more than social order and economic progress to gain from an involvement with black education. He recognized that white Southerners could also find such involvement a liberating, one might say an educational, experience.

Race and education would continue to be a volatile mix throughout the South, providing a complex context for the Association's developing and changing participation in the education of black Southerners. Nevertheless, the Association's practices and philosophies regarding race had already changed tremendously since the days when it shared the prejudiced and limiting assumptions of white Southern reformers generally. That change and its causes are to be seen in the story of the Southern Association's evolving relation with black institutions, a story that is itself a significant chapter in the broader history of race relations and educational development in the Southern states.

Endnotes

[1] See Edwin Mims, *Chancellor Kirkland of Vanderbilt* (Nashville: Vanderbilt University Press, 1940), for a short account of Kirkland's life. Paul K. Conking, *Gone With the Ivy: A Biography of Vanderbilt University* (Knoxville: University of Tennessee Press, 1985), discusses Kirkland's life and work at Vanderbilt. This assessment, furthermore, does not take into account the promising scholarly career that preceded Kirkland's careers as administrator and reformer.

[2] Spencer McCallie, "In Memoriam: J.H. Kirkland," *The Southern Association Quarterly* (hereafter *SAQ*) 4 no. 3 (Aug. 1940): 359.

[3] Ibid., 359, 360; Interview with E.B. Robert, May 24, 1973, Southern Association of Colleges and Schools Archive, Decatur, GA (hereafter SACS Archive), 48.

[4] James A. Henretta et al, *America's History, Volume 2 Since 1865*, 2nd edition (New York: Worth Publishers, 1993), 844. Due largely to medical advances such as penicillin, the death *rate* was actually half that of World War I.

[5] Ibid., 825, 823; James T. Patterson, *America Since 1941: A History* (Fort Worth, TX: Hartcourt Brace College Publishers, 1994), 23-4. The gross national product rose from just under $100 million in 1940 to $211 million by war's end.

[6] See "Editorial Notes: The Schools in Wartime," *SAQ* 9:3 (August 1945): 416; James H. Stiltner, "The Commission on Secondary Schools in Transition," (doctoral dissertation, Georgia State University, Atlanta, 1982), 110-11. These circumstances created the oddity of G.D. Humphrey of Mississippi State College (later president of the University of Wyoming) becoming the Association's longest-serving president, yet never having the opportunity to preside over an annual meeting.

[7] J. Henry Highsmith, "North Carolina Schools in Wartime," *SAQ* 9 (February 1945): 3; Stiltner, 109-10.

[8] "Notice," *Proceedings* 53 (1948).

[9] See Patterson, 28.

[10] Ibid., 38; Rosalind Rosenberg, *Divided Lives: American Women in the Twentieth Century* (New York: Hill and Wang, 1992), 143; Hugh Hawkins, *Banding Together: The Rise of National Associations in American Higher Education, 1887-1950* (Baltimore: The Johns Hopkins University Press, 1992), 165-66, n. 268. Hawkins notes that many of the GI Bill's "effects on educational institutions were reenforced [sic] by the more generous provisions in Public Law 16, 78th Cong., passed in 1943 for the vocational rehabilitation of disabled veterans enrolled in college." According to Hawkins, this law "accounted for under 10 percent of World War II veterans enrolled in college." On discussion of these events within the Association see, for example, Lieutenant M.A.F. Ritchie, USNR, "The Veteran as a Postwar Student," *SAQ* 9:3 (August 1945): 295-305.

[11] Hawkins, 165-66.

[12] Booker T. Washington, "Atlanta Exposition Address," reprinted in Louis R. Harlan, ed., The Booker T. Washington Papers, Vol. 3, 1889-95 (Urbana: University of Illinois Press, 1974). As historian John Hope Franklin notes, however, ultimately the differences between Washington and most white reformers were profound. His policy represented a strategic decision based on the *circumstances* that black people presently found themselves, and which he hoped that policy would gradually end. Washington hoped for far more egalitarian outcomes than even the moderate white reformers had in mind. For its part, most white approval for Washington's educational approach was based on the assumption that such an education suited the *nature* of a "naturally" inferior people. And as Franklin also points out, few if any of the white reformers who praised his approach to race relations knew that he was "financing some of the earliest court cases against segregation." John Hope Franklin, *From Slavery To Freedom: A History of Negro Americans* 3rd ed. (New York: Vintage Books, 1969), 392-93. See also Edward L. Ayers, *The Promise of the New South: Life After Reconstruction* (New York: Oxford University Press, 1992), 322ff.

[13] George Donelson Moss, *America in the Twentieth Century* (Upper Saddle River, NJ: Prentice Hall, 1993), 18, 57.

[14] Franklin, 391. W.E.B. Du Bois quoted in Franklin, 393. See also Moss, 57.

[15] See Ayers, 17-18, and 144ff for discussion of the *Plessy v. Ferguson* case. In 1892, Homer Plessy, a black man in Louisiana was arrested for sitting in the whites only carriage of the train between New Orleans and Covington. Plessy argued that his Fourteenth Amendment guarantee of equal protection made separate cars illegal. The Supreme Court disagreed, arguing that separate facilities, if equal, met the requirements of the 1875 Civil Rights Act. See John B. Boles, *The South Through Time* (Englewood Cliffs, NJ: Prentice Hall, 1995), 471.

[16] C. Vann Woodward, *The Strange Career of Jim Crow* (New York: Oxford University Press, 1966 2nd Revised Edition), 67-9.

[17] Ayers, 144. That segregation itself was not only "modern" but considered "progressive" by many white Americans, South and North, is well illustrated by the efforts of Woodrow Wilson, in many ways the embodiment of the term "progressive," to segregate the federal government during his presidency.

[18] Franklin, 387, 382.

[19] Ibid., 308, 391.

[20] Whatever the foundations' motives, both black and white Southerners, as John Hope Franklin concludes, "benefited substantially from their generosity." Franklin, 386, and 382ff generally. As Franklin also points out, it was "an age of philanthropy," much of it directed toward education generally. Vanderbilt in 1873 and Johns Hopkins in 1876 are two examples of institutions founded with such assistance. Peabody was a merchant and financier, Slater a textile manufacturer from Norwich, Connecticut, and Jeanes the daughter of a Quaker merchant family of Philadelphia. Franklin surveys the specific and varying interests of each of these funds and others.

[21] Franklin, 387; James H. Kirkland, Abstract of address on "Southern Education and Southern Thought," delivered Feb. 27, 1914, in James H. Kirkland Papers, Vanderbilt University Library, Nashville, TN. Quoted in Grantham, *Southern Progressivism: The Reconciliation of Progress and Tradition* (Knoxville: University of Tennessee Press, 1983), 27. Grantham, 31, discusses educational reformers' attitudes regarding race relations and their desire to get away from it as a dominant issue and to focus instead on white education as the means to other desirable, long-term ends. See also Hamilton Wright Mabie, "The New North," *South Atlantic Quarterly* 4 (April 1905): 109-14.

[22] Tucker and *New York World* quoted in Raymond B. Fosdick, *Adventure in Giving: The Story of the General Education Board, A Foundation Established by John D. Rockefeller* (New York: Harper & Row, Publishers, 1962), 7. See also Jack Temple Kirby, *Darkness at the Dawning: Race and Reform in the Progressive South* (Philadelphia: J.B. Lippincott Company, 1972), 101-02 and Grantham, 27. "By and large," Grantham notes, "the Northern press was extraordinarily tolerant of Southern white social practices; seldom was there a strident note in their criticisms, or for that matter, any genuinely radical proposal for reform. " According to Kirby, 101-02: "The Southern Education Board had its beginnings in the Conference for Education in the South, which began in 1898 in Capon Springs, West Virginia. Here gathered the New York-based directorate of Northern philanthropy to black 'industrial' schools," the financier and Wanamaker store manager Robert C. Ogden became president of the board; members of the board included the famed financier, George Foster Peabody, and the railroader William H. Baldwin, Jr. They were joined by transplanted Southerners: Jabez L.M. Curry, an aged educational uplifter originally from Alabama; and Walter Hines Page, the North Carolina-born publisher who in 1897 had delivered the famous address, "The Forgotten Man" on the plight of the Southern illiterate masses. Curry and Page subscribed to the paternalism of their fellow members and, as diplomats to the suspicious white South, promoted the expansion of the board to include other white Southerners—Alderman, McIver, and Charles W. Dabney, another dynamic Carolina school man who had become president of the University of Tennessee; and Edgar Gardner Murphy, whose 1900 race conference had attracted the admiration of Ogden and company."

[23] William Preston Few, "Southern Public Opinion," *South Atlantic Quarterly* 4 (Jan. 1905): 5. Cited in Grantham, 31. Grantham argues that these attitudes fit within a broader desire to bring "culture" to the masses; and with the elitist view that under their leadership, the ignorance of the white masses could be dispelled, paving the way for, among other goals, the amelioration of the problems facing the black population. Grantham, 29, also notes that the liberal group at Trinity associated with the *South Atlantic Quarterly* insisted "upon the central importance of Southern industrialization, education, and the gospel of work," and "were convinced that the most serious obstacle to progress lay in the ignorance and misconceptions of the mass of the Southern people, which sustained the demagogue."

[24] Grantham, 105. "To their credit," Grantham also writes, "Aycock and the Southern white reformers vigorously fought attempts to destroy the black schools

outright, and they despised James K. Vardaman and similar leaders for inflaming white extremism and frightening the North. Their middle way—the way of appeasing Yankees with rhetoric, while maintaining local control at home—was preferable (103-04)."

25 *Proceedings* (1920), quoted in Stiltner, "Commission on Secondary Schools in Transition," 129.

26 George Jackson Allen, Jr., "A History of the Commission on Colleges of the Southern Association of Colleges and Schools, 1949-1975" (doctoral dissertation, Georgia State University, Atlanta, 1978), 129; Interview with H.M. Ivy, May 19, 1972, SACS Archive (hereafter Ivy interview), 24; M.W. Adams to Constituent Members of ACNY, Dec. 19, 1928, T.E. Jones Papers, Fisk University, Nashville, TN (hereafter Fisk).

27 M.W. Adams to Constituent Members of ACNY, Dec. 19 1928, T.E. Jones Papers, Fisk.

28 Report of Executive Committee, *Proceedings* 33 (1928), 42; Ivy interview, 24. See also Allen, 139, and Guy E. Snavely, *A Short History of the Southern Association of Colleges and Secondary Schools*, [Reprint from the *Southern Association Quarterly* (hereafter *SAQ*) 9 (Nov. 1945)], 65. Snavely notes that 12 years after 1929, three more educators were added to the committee: R.L. Cousins, Jr., the Georgia State Agent for Negro Schools, D.B. Taylor of the Texas State Dept. of Education, and S.D. Williams, principal of the University of Kentucky Training School. A further two members were added in 1943: David M. Key of Birmingham-Southern College, and C.L. Barrow, Baton Rouge Parish superintendent.

29 Leo M. Favrot to R.L. Marquis, Jan. 3 1929, T.E. Jones Papers, Fisk. Marquis was the Association's president at the time.

30 Report of Executive Committee, *Proceedings* 34 (1929), 35-36.

31 Thomas E. Jones to Theodore Jack, Nov. 13, 1929, Thomas E. Jones to D.O.W. Holmes, Nov. 23, 1929, T.E. Jones Papers, Fisk. Holmes wrote to Jack two days later, mentioning the earlier request that the Association "appoint a commission to rate the Negro colleges in strict accordance with your standards." D.O.W. Holmes to Theodore Jack, Nov. 25, 1929, T.E. Jones Papers, Fisk.

32 Theodore Jack to Thomas E. Jones, Nov. 23, 1929, Thomas E. Jones to Dean J.T. Cater, Talladega College, Dec. 30, 1929, T.E. Jones Papers, Fisk.

33 Report of Executive Committee, *Proceedings* 34 (1929), 35-36; Allen, 130; Donald C. Agnew, *Seventy-Five Years of Educational Leadership* (Atlanta, GA: Southern Association of Colleges and Schools, 1970), 29. Snavely, 65ff, discusses the large contributions made by the Jeanes and Slater Funds to historically black colleges and universities. These funds were later combined with others to become the Southern Education Foundation, headquartered in Washington, D.C. Arthur Wright, first executive agent of the Association's Committee on Negro Schools, succeeded J.H. Dillard as head of these funds. Dillard had been dean at Tulane and active in early founding of the Association. Fred McCuiston was the second

executive agent (1931-1939), based in Nashville. McCuiston went on to become a staff member of the General Education Board of the Rockefeller Foundation.

[34] Report of Committee on Approval of Negro Schools, *Proceedings* 35 (1930), 41-2; Report of Executive Committee, *Proceedings* 34 (1929), 36. The first six institutions on the "B List" were Johnson C. Smith University in Charlotte, North Carolina, Morehouse and Spelman Colleges in Atlanta, Talladega College in Alabama, and Virginia State College in Petersburg and Virginia Union University. Report of Committee on Approval of Negro Schools, *Proceedings* 35 (1930), 41-2. Of the original nine, there was no place on either list for Shaw University and Winston-Salem Teachers College, both in North Carolina. The 1929 report had "expected that the survey will give information for the classification of Negro Schools into at least three groups, A, B, and C," but in the end only two categories were used. See Report of Executive Committee, *Proceedings* 34 (1929), 36.

[35] Thomas E. Jones to the Executive Committee of the SACSS in session in Atlanta, Georgia, Dec. 1 to 7, 1934, n.d. for letter, T.E. Jones Papers, Fisk; Allen, 130; Minutes of the Executive Committee, *SAQ* 9 (1945): 189-94.

[36] Allen, 130.

[37] J.T. Cater, "What Adjustment or Adaptation, If Any, Should Be Made in the Application of Standards to Negro Schools?" *Proceedings of the Association of Colleges and Secondary Schools for Negroes* (hereafter ACSSN *Proceedings*) 2 (1935), 67, 65-66.

[38] Thomas E. Jones to the Executive Committee of the SACSS in session in Atlanta, Georgia, Dec. 1 to 7, 1934, T.E. Jones Papers, Fisk.

[39] Interview with T.P. Baker, May 20, 1973, SACS Archive (hereafter Baker interview), 17; Allen. 132. Baker was Association president when the first black institutions were finally admitted.

[40] ACSSN *Proceedings* 10 (1943): 30. Cited in Allen, 133. The same recommendation called for changes in the method of inspecting colleges, suggesting the creation of a committee appointed by the Executive Committee of ACSSN and the Southern Association's Committee on Approval of Negro Schools. From this twenty-two member committee, comprised of one black and one white educator from each of the eleven member states, three-person inspection teams would be chosen to visit black colleges. The inspection team should include one black educator and one member of the Committee on Approval of Negro Schools.

[41] Allen, 131ff.

[42] T.E. Jones to Fred McCuiston, Jan. 26 1934, T.E. Jones Papers, Fisk. Jones refers to a recent meeting in St. Louis with President McCrory of Johnson C. Smith, Dean Cater of Talladega, and Theodore Jack, by then President of Randolph-Macon Women's College, in which the relationship of the ACNY to the Association was discussed.

[43] Thomas E. Jones to the Executive Committee of the SACSS in session in Atlanta, Georgia, Dec. 1 to 7, 1934, T.E. Jones Papers, Fisk.

44.L.S. Cozart, Foreword to ACSSN *Proceedings* 2 (1935), 3; Allen, 131. The new Association was "prepared to make a substantial contribution toward expenses involved in such rating," up to the amount of $2,000. See Thomas E. Jones to the Executive Committee of the SACSS in session in Atlanta, Georgia, Dec. 1 to 7, 1934, T.E. Jones Papers, Fisk. As well as an academic career that included the presidency of Barber-Scotia College, Cozart was Secretary-Treasurer of the ACSSN throughout its history and also its historian. See L.S. Cozart, *A History of the Association of Colleges and Secondary Schools*, 1934-1965 (Charlotte, NC: Heritage Printers, 1967), which includes a detailed account of his and his colleagues' dealings with the Southern Association.

45 H.M. Ivy, "The Southern Association Committee on Approval of Negro Colleges and Secondary Schools," *Proceedings* 54 (1949): 89-90. Of the 68, only four (two two-year and two four-year) had no accredited status, while 50 of the remaining 57 four-year colleges, and three of the seven two-year colleges were on the "A list," and the remainder on the "B list." There were 146 approved secondary institutions (125 public and 21 private), 130 of which met "full requirements," according to Ivy, "for a Southern Association approved high school." Ivy noted that the "B list" for secondary schools would continue for only two more years, after which schools would have to "meet the full requirements in order to have accreditation recognition."

46 Patterson, *America Since 1941*, 25.

47 Boles, *South Through Time*, 473.

48 Patterson, 27.

49 Boles, 471.

50 Ibid., 471-2.

51 Charles S. Johnson, "Next Steps in Education in the South," ACSSN *Proceedings* 20 (1953): 71-2. Johnson noted how, in the years since 1948, "the process of desegregation has been moving at an increased pace in the Southern institutions of higher learning, until there are now some 20 or more institutions admitting Negro students with no noticeable adverse results."

52 John E. Ivey, Jr., "Building A Better Region Through Higher Education," *Proceedings* 54 (1949): 213.

53 A.B. Beitel, "Knocking At The Door," *Proceedings* 54 (1949): 214.

54 Ibid., 214-15. See also Allen, 136.

55 SACSS, Minutes of the Executive Committee, Dec 1, 1947. Quoted in Allen, 133.

56 Interview with Laurence D. Haskew, May 21, 1973, SACS Archive, 7; Interview with Henry Hill, July 18, 1972, SACS Archive, 18-19.

57 Charles S. Johnson, "Next Steps," 79-81. Speaking by the time that some desegregation had already taken place, Johnson asked how the time could be ripe

for black students in the public and private schools of Texas, but not in those of Georgia or South Carolina, or "for Negro nurses studying under unsegregated conditions in New Orleans, but not ripe in Florida, an air hour away?"

[58] Beitel, "Knocking At The Door," 214; Johnson, "Next Steps," 80.

[59] Interview with Rufus Harris, Dec. 10 1973, SACS Archive, 9; SACSS Minutes of the Executive Committee, Oct. 4, 1949. Cited in Allen, 134.

[60] Allen, 133-36. Allen notes that the Executive Committee also approved, at the urging of the Commission on Institutions of Higher Education, a study of graduate education in black and white institutions

[61] Ibid., 137; *Proceedings* 56 (1951): 70-1. Cited in Allen, 138. See also Stiltner, "Commission on Secondary Schools in Transition," 131-32. Members of the committee included Doak Campbell, H.M. Ivy, Harmon Caldwell, W.E. Turner, Ralph B. Draughton, and Clyde A. Erwin.

[62] ACSSN *Proceedings* 19 (1952): 28. Cited in Allen, 141.

[63] ACSSN *Proceedings* 20 (1953): 38, 25. Cited in Allen, 141-42; Henretta et al., *America's History*, 946-47.

[64] Henretta et al, 946-47; Allen, 146.

[65] Allen, 143.

[66] Johnson, "Next Steps," 75-6; Allen 139ff.

[67] Interview with William Hugh McEniry, Dec 11, 1973, SACS Archive (hereafter McEniry interview), 15. See also Allen, 145.

[68] McEniry interview, 15; Allen, 144-47; *Proceedings* 61 (1956): 140. Mays, a "great man" in the estimation of McEniry, would go on to become the first black member of the Commission on Colleges. It is a curiosity of the civil rights era and its relation to the Southern Association that neither the most significant court case nor what was for many the most horrifying example of resistance to its implementation took place within the Association's jurisdiction. Both Little Rock and Topeka were in the North Central Association's region. The fact that the Board of Education in the *Brown* case was in Topeka, Kansas, also illustrates, of course, that racism and segregation were hardly the preserve of the South.

[69] Baker interview, 16-17; McEniry interview, Dec 11. 1973, 16.

[70] Baker interview, 16-18.

[71] Agnew, 31.

[72] Snavely, *A Short History of the Southern Association* 65. See also Stiltner, 129.

[73] L.S. Cozart, "Citation for J. Henry Highsmith," *ACSSN Proceedings* 20 (1953): 110-11.

[74] William Hugh McEniry, "Educational Progress in the Southern States," *Proceedings* 28 (1961): 53.

Chapter Four

North Carolina Speaker Ban and Other Controversies

The interconnections between social change, political conflict, and the world of education has been a central theme of the Southern Association's history over the past century. While the Association's ongoing involvement in black education offers perhaps the most striking evidence for this, questions of civil rights and race relations have not been the only issues to involve the Southern Association in matters far beyond the world of educational standards and institutional accreditation. Throughout its history, the Association has also become embroiled in controversies arising from politicians' efforts to influence the running of various institutions holding membership in the Association. This chapter will briefly sketch early instances of the Association's involvement in such controversies before paying fuller attention to its participation in a major conflict of this kind in the 1960s; a conflict that revolved around the legislative efforts to ban certain kinds of speakers from the campuses of North Carolina's public institutions of higher education. The Association's involvement in this "Speaker Ban" controversy proved to be a highly illuminating and defining moment in the modern history of the Southern Association.

At the heart of these controversies lay the question of when elected officials' involvement in educational affairs constituted the legitimate stewardship of the public interest and when it became an unjustifiable threat to academic freedom and institutional autonomy. For institutions that enjoyed accredited status, how this question was answered had great significance. If, in the Association's view, political involvement did amount to an infringement of an institution's autonomy, it brought with it the possibility of suspension from the Association. As early as the 1920s, as the conflicts and complaints of that era illustrate, educators and administrators were well aware of the negative public perception that could accompany an institution's exclusion or expulsion from the Association. The dangers of exclusion only increased with the Association's transformation into an accrediting agency and as the steady growth in its membership made an institution's non-membership all the more noticeable. Furthermore, lack, or loss, of accreditation had an increasingly damaging impact on an institution's status, not just in relation to public opinion but in the eyes of other public bodies and educational agencies. This has been increasingly true of higher educational institutions in the period since World War II, in large part because of the federal government's unprecedented levels of participation in education over the last fifty years. As the range and expense of that participation has grown, so too has the reliance of federal agencies on the evaluations of regional accrediting agencies in making judgments as to which institutions and students should be eligible for federal funding. Thus, to follow the Association's participation in these affairs is, in part, to trace not only its growing influence on education in the South, but also the increasingly complex causes of that influence.

These separate moments of controversy and conflict, their differences and similarities, also tell a great deal about the complex nature of the Association's place in Southern society, especially as its influence grew in the years after mid-century. With growing power and prominence came growing public awareness and scrutiny. Inevitably, this scrutiny has been both positive and negative. Some welcomed the Association's presence as a force for academic independence. Others resented its unwarranted and intrusive presence in affairs not rightly any of its business. Sometimes the Association has been seen as adding weight to efforts to resist the "outside interference" of politicians and others in the running of schools and colleges. At other times the Association has been viewed as an external threat to local autonomy, the supporter of outside interests and the bearer of alien values. This mixed reception is suggestive of the ongoing tensions in Southern education as traditional commitments to local control came up against increasing levels of state and federal government involvement and direction. It points also to the ambiguous role of the Association in Southern education and society. Neither an arm of government nor an organization rooted in a specific locality, the Association has developed in the space (sometimes meeting-ground, sometimes battleground) between local autonomy and central power. This chapter focuses on how these themes of the Association's history are revealed in its connections to wider conflicts between politicians and educators from Mississippi to North Carolina.

Most of the Association's dealings with state politicians and education departments were conducted without controversy and were, especially for the Secondary Commission, essential to its everyday work. There were, however, moments of conflict and controversy which, although not the norm, do reveal much about the Association's general approach to the relations between the political and educational realms. The most important early incident of this kind took place in Mississippi in 1930. Governor Theodore Bilbo replaced 179 employees, including presidents, administrators and teachers, at four of his state's institutions of higher learning. No charges were made against them, nor were they afforded any opportunity to appeal their dismissal. When Bilbo then filled some of the positions with friends and political supporters, including some retiring members of the Mississippi legislature, he provoked outraged protest against what many viewed as an unacceptable attack on academic and institutional freedom. Some of those protests took the form of complaints to the Southern Association and requests for the Association to respond to actions that seemed to threaten the autonomy of some of its member institutions.[1]

The Association responded by sending an investigating committee appointed from the Executive Committee. The committee consisted of James Kirkland, and Guy Snavely of Birmingham-Southern College and, at the time, secretary-treasurer of the Association.[2] The resulting report "condemn[ed] with all possible emphasis the ruthless manner" in which the Board of Trustees had followed Bilbo's orders by getting rid of "scores of officers and teachers without warning, without charges, and without the opportunity of defense, and without action by the administrative head of the institution." These actions, in the report's view, had placed the Board of Trustees "outside the category of educational bodies." This was highly significant for the Southern Association, since it was "organized to deal only with educational boards." So with contact impossible between the Association and the Mississippi institutions as currently operated, the committee recommended that the four institutions in question "be suspended from membership in this Association until time shall prove the existence of an educational and non-political administration." A "stormy" debate brought forth vigorous defenses of the Mississippi institutions, from Chancellor J.N. Powers of the University of Mississippi among others, but an amendment calling for probation rather than suspension went down to defeat. The Executive Committee's recommendation passed by a large majority and the suspension took effect on September 1, 1931.[3]

The Association's decision further fueled the controversy consuming higher education in Mississippi. The loss of accreditation entailed by suspension placed great pressure on the Mississippi system, contributing to a significant decline in enrollment (from 1,254 in 1929-30 to 778 in 1931-32). Despite this, little public anger seemed to be directed at the Association. Instead, much of the public's anger at this blow to their institutions was directed at those who had precipitated the crisis in the first place. Theodore Bilbo was defeated in the next gubernatorial election in 1931, a campaign which saw all candidates promise to do something to rectify the state's educational crisis. Mike Conner, the new governor, attended the Association's annual meeting in 1931 and conferred with both Snavely and Kirkland. Legislation was eventually passed that greatly reduced the possibility of future dictatorial action by the governor, and new administrative heads were chosen for all four institutions. Satisfied that the changes met its objections, the Association restored the Mississippi institutions to full membership in 1932. The Mississippi case suggests the Association's effective but relatively uncontroversial intervention in a situation in which its actions reinforced rather than ran counter to a public mood that generally shared the Association's view of Bilbo's behavior as an unwarranted overstepping of his legitimate powers.[4]

The Association's next conflict with overweening gubernatorial power came two years later and one state to the West. Louisiana's legendary governor, Huey Long, had "encouraged" Louisiana State University to award a Bachelor of Laws degree to a state senator whose legislative duties had unfortunately prevented him from meeting all the requirements normally considered appropriate prior to the receipt of a diploma. The dean of the Law School refused, but the Board of Trustees decided that the senator should graduate with his class. Undue political interference in the affairs of the Louisiana State Normal College, as well as in the public school system, had also been reported. In 1935, a Special Session of the state legislature passed the School Budget Control Law which gave the State Budget Committee the power to hire and fire, at any time, the state's public school teachers. The governor also had the power to appoint the members of school boards in some of the state's parishes.[5]

As in Mississippi, complaints within Louisiana about flagrant abuses of political power included appeals to the Southern Association to come and investigate. The Higher Commission appointed a special committee, consisting of President James R. McCain of Agnes Scott College and President Alexander Guerry of the University of the South, to look into the claims of political interference in the higher institutions. Along with the chairman of the Secondary Commission, S.B. Hathorn, this special committee also looked into political abuse of the public school system. Its report recommended that Louisiana State University "be placed on probation" until its Board of Supervisors passed by-laws or resolutions in accordance with the Association's priority of preserving from outside influence institutional decisions on such things as the awarding of degrees and the appointment of faculty and staff. According to Guy Snavely, the Association may have taken a more lenient approach in Louisiana out of deference to influential Association leaders—like C.A. Ives—who hailed from that state. With the adoption in 1935 of resolutions designed to meet these concerns, LSU avoided being placed on probation. As in Mississippi, the Association's intervention in the state's educational and political affairs brought little if any criticism from the people of Louisiana, reflecting again the way in which the public's view of the Association depended on its view of the political actions the Association opposed.[6]

This pattern was extended further, into Georgia, in 1941 when yet another governor aroused controversy when he tried to influence matters of finance and personnel in the University of Georgia system. Much of the controversy revolved around Governor Eugene Talmadge's attempts to pressure the Board of Regents into firing Walter D. Cocking, the dean of the College of Education. Cocking's "crime," which he later denied, had been to offer the opinion that white and black students would one day be admitted to the University of Georgia on an equal basis. The board refused to fire Cocking and a subsequent five-hour "trial" found him not guilty of any of the charges against him by a vote of 8 to 7. Cocking was appointed for another year. Talmadge then sought to change the composition of the board, eventually encouraging three members to resign. With his hand-picked replacements in place, the governor called for a retrial after which Cocking was fired (along with President Marvin Pittman of Statesboro). More faculty firings followed at various institutions throughout the University of Georgia system.[7]

Following its standard practice, the Association formed a committee to investigate the situation. Made up of Alexander Guerry, John J. Tigert, and O.C. Carmichael, the committee held hearings at the Ansley Hotel in Atlanta in November of 1941. Other interested groups were invited to participate and representatives of the American Bar Association and the American Association of Teachers' Colleges, among others, did so. Along with President S.H. Whitley of the Association and M.C. Huntley of the CIHE, they heard from various interested individuals and groups, including representatives of the Board of Regents, Chancellor Sanford of UGA, several presidents from the Georgia system, as well as alumni and students from the University of Georgia. In its report, the committee was unequivocal in viewing the investigation preceding the firings as a "mockery of democratic procedure," and declared itself "convinced that the charges" were either "spurious or entirely unsupported by the evidence." The report also found fault with state statutes that gave the governor the power "to modify in any way he sees fit" the Board of Regents' budget, and therefore the ability to influence or "nullify" board actions through control of their funding. "Arbitrary power of this kind in the hands of any individual or agency," the committee declared, "is a threat to sound procedure in the operation of an educational system." The committee was "forced to conclude," therefore, "that the University System of Georgia has been the victim of unprecedented and unjustifiable political interference," and that the governor had "violated not only sound educational policy, but proper democratic procedure" in engineering changes in the Board of Regents for the purposes of pursuing his own political aims. The committee recommended that all ten of the Georgia system's institutions of higher education be suspended as of September 1, 1942. Other organizations such as the American Bar Association, the American Association of Law Schools, and the American Association of Teachers' Colleges also opted for suspension.[8]

Governor Talmadge responded by dismissing the threat of suspension and the loss of accreditation that came with it. "We credit our own schools down here," he is said to have boasted, also railing against the Southern Association in his weekly newspaper,

The Statesman.[9] Talmadge was neither the first nor the last Southern politician somewhat slow to recognize the importance that accreditation had assumed in the educational life of the nation. In this regard, it seems Talmadge misjudged the mood of his constituents who, perhaps with children going through the educational system, understood better than the governor the diminished value of an unaccredited education. As with Bilbo in Mississippi, public opinion laid most of the blame for the crisis at the governor's door. Talmadge failed to win re-election, and in 1942, Ellis Arnall, an alumnus of the University of Georgia, became governor. Appearing before the Association's meeting that year in Memphis, Arnall promised new legislation to remove, or at least greatly diminish, any governor's ability to exert control over university trustees. Such legislation was passed. The Executive Committee of the Higher Commission subsequently deemed it acceptable and recommended that Georgia's institutions be restored to full membership.[10] Once again, the Association had made a significant contribution to resolving a conflict of power and jurisdiction between a state's politicians and its educators. Again the threat of lost accreditation had been the key to this influence. All three events help to chart the growing role of accreditation, and therefore the Southern Association, in Southern life and education in the years before World War II.

In all three of these cases, a further key to the Association's effectiveness was the state of public opinion. The public's perceptions of the Association's involvement were shaped by its prior perceptions of the political actions that precipitated the involvement. In Mississippi and Georgia especially, public unhappiness with the actions of the governor encouraged a generally favorable view of the Association's opposition to those actions. Hence Talmadge's largely unsuccessful attempt to play what might be called the "outside interference" card. Yet Talmadge's failure did not mean that such appeals might not succeed on other occasions, especially when the politicians were seen to be reflecting rather than flouting the desires and values of the majority of their constituents. The North Carolina Speaker Ban controversy of the 1960s was such a case. On June 25, 1963, the North Carolina General Assembly passed House Bill 1395, "An Act to Regulate Visiting Speakers at State Supported Colleges and Universities."

This legislation quickly became known as the Speaker Ban Law. The speakers the legislators had in mind to ban were "known member[s] of the Communist Party," people "known to advocate the overthrow of the Constitution of the United States," or to have "pleaded the Fifth Amendment . . . with respect to Communist or subversive connections or activities." The ban they had in mind would stop people in these categories from speaking on the campuses of state-funded colleges and universities.[11]

The Southern Association was gradually drawn into the controversy that developed in the wake of this legislation. This time, however, it would find itself in a more ambiguous position, caught in the middle of a conflict between, on the one hand, politicians who carried substantial public support and, on the other, academics and administrators from the state's institutions of higher education. Largely aligned with the latter grouping, the Association faced a far more hostile reception from the public than had been the case in Mississippi or Georgia. In this case, the Association would be perceived by a large proportion of the public as part of the external assault on local interests and values, not as a force to be enlisted on their behalf.

The Speaker Ban Law was passed in controversial circumstances, pushed through on the final day of the 1963 legislative session. There were no prior public hearings nor were there any consultations with the educators from institutions to be affected by the ban. Its passage provoked an immediate barrage of vociferous opposition. If its opponents complained of a lack of publicity before the Bill's passage, no such assessment could be made of the aftermath as the pros and cons of the Speaker Ban were argued across North Carolina and beyond. The controversy dragged on for several years, with the Southern Association eventually drawn into the fray. But where the pre-war cases had been settled, at least to the Association's satisfaction, with relative speed, the Speaker Ban dispute proved more contentious and long lasting.[12]

There were several reasons for this. The ongoing debate over the Speaker Ban reflected very different circumstances than the earlier disputes in which the Association had become involved. While broader social issues certainly impinged on events in the earlier cases (Professor Cocking's supposed endorsement of integrated education, for example), they were largely the raw power plays of politicians accustomed to having their own way when it came to questions of political patronage and power. Also they largely revolved around the executive actions of the executive branch of state government, the governor. The Speaker Ban controversy was squarely focused on legislation passed by a majority of the state's representatives and senators. And while many of the pre-war governors' actions had been legally as well as ethically dubious, no one disputed the North Carolina politicians' right to pass legislation relating to public education. Crucially, and again unlike the earlier cases, the legislation attracted broad public support among North Carolinians, who saw it not only as reflecting their values, but as an important weapon in struggle to protect those values in the politically and culturally charged social circumstances of the 1960s. While the ban had wide popular support, it aroused strong criticism among academics and opinion makers. Most of the state's major newspapers editorialized against it, while it drew strong and persistent opposition from academics, administrators and students throughout the UNC system and beyond. As the ban gained national attention, both sides drew support from individuals and organizations across the country. The opposing sides of the Speaker Ban issue thus consisted of groups likely to be opposed to each other on many other political and social questions.

To some extent, then, differences over the Speaker Ban reflected the deep-seated mutual suspicion of mass and elite that had long been an important feature of American life. One strand of this cultural conflict has been an anti-intellectualism that often found its targets among the "ivory towers" of the nation's universities and colleges. John Hope Franklin, a member of the ACSSN who would go on to become one of the great American historians of this century, discussed this chronic public suspicion directed toward the educational system in a 1952 speech on "The Current Crisis in Education and Freedom." Franklin addressed the ambiguous, sometimes precarious position of education in a strongly materialistic culture. He described the ridicule heaped on ivory-tower academics branded as ineffectual dreamers by a society that prided itself on its supposedly unique capacity for "common sense" thought and "practical" action. This traditional suspicion of intellectual or cultural elites clearly played a part in support for the Speaker Ban, support that seemed to grow stronger the more academics and editorialists spoke against it.

But the legislation struck a responsive nerve with many "ordinary" white North Carolinians because it crystallized their sense of dissatisfaction with the contemporary state of the nation's culture and with education's role in encouraging developments they viewed as destructive, even un-American. In the postwar context of the Cold War, the Korean War, and, later the Vietnam War, traditional anti-intellectualism increasingly coincided with a powerful current of anti-Communism aimed at perceived enemies, foreign and domestic. The Bill's focus on Communism and college campuses suggests this link. Opposition to Communism abroad had long been linked to a persistent concern, elevated by some to the level of hysterical obsession, with Communism and subversion at home. It was an article of the anti-Communist faith that a Communist was, by definition, someone committed to the overthrow of freedom and democracy. It was also assumed that such people would take every available opportunity of the freedoms afforded by the American system to undermine or overthrow that system. It followed that to give Communists a platform was to give subversion a platform.[13] From this perspective, it was especially galling that property paid for and maintained by patriotic taxpayers might be used as a platform for subversion.

Some opponents of the Speaker Ban focused their efforts on challenging this anti-Communist reasoning, especially the view that the best way to defend against subversion was to limit rights to free speech. Among the groups represented at the public hearings that were eventually held, no group pursued this approach more forcefully than the American Association of University Professors. The AAUP had been among the first to respond to the new law, dashing off a telegram of concern to the North Carolina state house in Raleigh as the legislation was being enacted.[14] At the public hearings in Raleigh, Professor John P. Dawson, first vice president of the AAUP and a member of the Harvard Law School faculty, set his organization's opposition to a "highly undesirable" law that he believed surpassed any other state law in America in "drastically" interfering with both "the autonomy and the academic freedom of educational institutions." Of these two areas of concern, however, the AAUP emphasized its belief that the legislation "violate[d] academic freedom."[15]

Defining "academic freedom" largely as freedom of speech, Dawson and his colleagues focused on several points. One was the vagueness of the statute. How, they asked, were words like "known" and "Communist"—terms notoriously susceptible to imprecision and abuse—to be defined?[16] As one witness pointed out, there were some groups in America so reactionary that they "knew" President Eisenhower had been a "Communist."[17] A further area of vagueness was whether admitted "known Communists"—the Soviet ambassador, for example, or a physicist from a Communist country—were to be banned, even if they were invited to speak on matters solely related to their fields of professional expertise. The vagueness of the statute, opponents argued, would encourage administrators to play it very safe, banning many speakers who were not Communists or who, although Communist, might contribute greatly to the education rather than the subversion of North Carolina's students.

The defenders of free speech also insisted that speakers who were known Communists should be allowed to speak on campuses, even if their purpose was to promote their political creed. Here their main argument was that anti-Communist censorship was itself anti-Democratic, and therefore far more damaging to the American social and political fabric than any damage a tiny band of American subversives was capable of inflicting on the nation. Banning speakers represented a "long step" in the direction of "thought control," according to John P. Dawson, while his AAUP colleague and Duke faculty member, Frances Brown, went so far as to suggest that it "follow[ed] the methods of totalitarian countries as demonstrated in the Nazi and Communist countries."[18] Furthermore, opponents insisted, free speech was a powerful weapon against the spread of Communist ideas and the encouragement of subversive activity. "The surest way of demonstrating how threadbare and also harmful these ideas are," the AAUP's Dawson insisted, "is for their proponents to speak out and expose themselves," rather than for them to be imbued with "some mysterious added attraction by leaving them to work underground." On the nation's campuses, opponents of the ban argued, inoculation rather than quarantine was the best way to protect students from potentially subversive influences.[19]

The proponents of free speech remained adamant, then, that

their defense of Communists' right to speak should in no way be interpreted as sympathy for Communism. Indeed, while differing with the ban's supporters on Communism's ability to indoctrinate the nation's students, they did agree with them as to Communism's subversive intent. Consequently, they accepted that some limits could legitimately be placed on *what* they could say. Dawson agreed with Committee-member and State Representative A.A. Zollicoffer of Vance County that the AAUP had "no quibble" with North Carolina's 1941 law making it illegal to advocate the violent overthrow of the government. Indeed Speaker Ban opponents pointed to the 1941 legislation as another reason why the new legislation was not only ill-advised, but unnecessary. In doing so they insisted on a distinction between different kinds of speech: a distinction, in Dawson's words, between the "discussion of ideas" and the "advocacy of action." So when asked by Zollicoffer whether academic freedom should allow for a discussion of the subversion of the government, Dawson was adamant that it should not. At the heart of the limited defense of free speech championed by the AAUP and others lay an effort to distinguish between *who* was allowed to speak and *what* they were allowed to say.[20]

Thus even the most outspoken defenses of free speech made at the Speaker Ban Hearings contained significant qualifications. Indeed the AAUP's entire argument actually shared the central premise underpinning the ban: that Communist subversion was a threat to legitimate government and had to be countered. Yet if the AAUP could agree, indeed insist, upon limitations to free speech, why could the elected representatives of North Carolina not do the same? As its defenders were quick to point out, the Speaker Ban did not prevent people from airing subversive views, only from doing so on state-funded campuses. Representative Phil Godwin, for example, was surprised by the opposition to a law that he insisted did not restrict free speech, merely its location.[21] Was this limitation not every bit as reasonable as those suggested by the AAUP and others? Given the strength of anti-Communist feeling and the AAUP's somewhat less than comprehensive definition of free speech, it is hardly surprising that these particular arguments failed to sway supporters of the ban. After all, they had heard most of them long before the ban, never mind the hearings. Resistance to such arguments was further strengthened for many by their suspicion of the kinds of people who usually made them: Harvard professors, for example. Such people often were seen as sources of, or at least sympathetic to, many modern ideas and movements also considered suspect.

Academics who set out the free speech argument at the hearings and elsewhere did so firmly assured that their campuses were not nearly as susceptible to subversion as the Speaker Ban?s proponents feared, and equally confident that educators like themselves were up to the task of guiding students through the few potential hazards that might exist. Implicit in these assumptions were two broader premises. One was that both opponents and supporters of the legislation agreed about ends even if they disagreed about means. The second was that the end of legislation like the Speaker Ban was to protect campuses from undesirable *outside* influences. Whether from a desire to downplay differences or out of real ignorance as to the sources of popular and political discontent, proponents of free speech on campus failed to acknowledge that much of the impetus behind the ban came from the belief that many campuses were *already* hotbeds of subversion. In this regard, they did not address the problem John Hope Franklin had identified some years earlier, namely that to the familiar anti-intellectual "ridicule by the practical-minded" had been added, in a time of ideological (and later military) warfare against Communism, "exploitation by the super patriots" and "violent attacks by the demagogues." Franklin described "an 'open season'" on "articulate scholars" and "energetic and progressive administrators," a sustained attack that identified campuses as places where significant numbers of students *and* professors already thought and behaved in ways inimical to the wider community.22

For their part, opponents of the ban questioned the motives of its proponents. Arguing that the subversive intent of academics and students was greatly exaggerated, and pointing to the smallness of the threat actually posed by Communism and to the existing, and far more comprehensive, anti-subversion legislation already in place, they looked for other motives behind the ban's introduction. The rhetoric of anti-Communism was indeed frequently employed in debates covering a wide range of political views and cultural developments that owed nothing to Communism. At least since the New Deal era, for example, many had decried the "creeping socialism" they saw in the expansion of the federal government. Groups and institutions as disparate as Holly-wood moviemakers, state department officials, and military leaders had found themselves huddling together under the blanket accusations of Communism made by Senator Joe McCarthy of Wisconsin and others during the 1940s and 1950s.

In the South of this period, it was inevitable that the charge of anti-Communism would be made against those who wished to "subvert" the existing racial order of the region. Southern politicians like Strom Thurmond of South Carolina fueled this belief by insistently pairing racial liberalism with political radicalism, and arguing that any step toward racial integration represented a triumph for those whose long-term goal was the undermining of Americans' way of life at home, and their political and military power abroad. In the specific context of North Carolina, some of this suspicion was directed against the University of North Carolina-Chapel Hill, the campus of which was widely perceived as an island of support for black civil rights in an otherwise solid sea of white opposition. This was the era of sit-ins at whites-only lunch counters and other businesses, a phase in the nonviolent protest movement that had started with the Montgomery Bus Boycott of 1957. The lunch-counter sit-ins began in Greensboro, North Carolina, and quickly spread across the South, aimed in part at raising the economic cost of segregation for the region's businesses. Many black students in Raleigh, most from the city's Shaw University, participated in sit-ins. Targeted businesses included the Sir Walter Hotel, a favorite meeting-place for legislators.[23]

For some opponents of the ban, the connection was clear. "The wrath of the legislators," in the opinion of Louis R. Wilson, librarian at UNC, "boils down to the fact that the Negroes of America have at long last determined to claim the rights and privileges which were promised them 100 years ago but have been studiously denied them through various means by our forebears and ourselves." Of immediate relevance was their having "had the nerve to demonstrate in Raleigh and in the new legislative building" alongside, it was widely believed, students from UNC-Chapel Hill. "That," concluded Wilson, "was the last straw." The bill's sponsors denied any connection. Representative Phil Godwin, for example, testified before the committee that neither the civil rights demonstrations nor "personal animosity" toward the Chapel Hill campus had fueled his support for the law. Yet given the politicians' anger at the Sir Walter sit-in and the growing sentiment against a Chapel Hill campus seen as supportive of such civil disobedience, the passage of the Speaker Ban shortly afterwards continued to strike many observers as something less than a coincidence.

Whatever their denials, legislators like Godwin could not have been unaware that at least some of the public sentiment behind the bill was fueled by a belief in a treasonous triad of Communism, civil rights, and campus radicalism. Mrs. Ada Davis of Cherryville, North Carolina, told William Friday, president of the University of North Carolina-Chapel Hill, that she was "surprised and shocked" by his opposition to the bill, insisting that "surely our students can get a rounded out education without being exposed to brainwashing by Communist students." Davis also hoped that the ban on subversive speakers being "allowed to enter our halls of learning," would include "enemies in the colored race such as Martin Luther King." Davis thought that Friday could surely recognize King "as an enemy of our efforts to create good race relations," and as someone who "poisons the minds of Negro students, and we fear some whites else why do they assist negros [sic] in demonstrating." Davis' great "fear" of "Negro domination" was tied to her "lost faith" in government, especially in President John F. Kennedy and his advisers who she worried were "striv[ing] to lead us into socialism, a polite word for Communism." "Surely," Davis insisted, Friday could "see the trend and realize all I have written is true." Many white North Carolinians would have disagreed with Davis' somewhat apocalyptic assessment of how far Communism had already advanced in America, and of how much President Kennedy had contributed to the process. But her basic assumption that radicalism and racial change were inextricably linked was widely shared. So, too, was her belief that both radicalism and racial change should be resisted if further erosion of the existing social order was to be prevented. In this respect, Davis was representative of the majority of white North Carolinians who supported the Speaker Ban Bill as one means to that end. However many white North Carolinians would have agreed with Davis' specific views, it was clear that in her general support for the bill she spoke for the majority.[24]

John Hope Franklin had warned of an emerging "crisis not only in education, but in the tradition of freedom as we have known and cherish it in this land," a crisis that was "endangering our free institutions." A decade later, as the Cold War turned hot in Southeast Asia, the crisis was full blown. Many of the nation's college campuses had become centers of opposition to war abroad and of support for radical cultural and political change at home. Many more Americans had turned against educational institutions they no longer saw as representatives of local communities and American expectations, but rather as promoters of outside forces and alien values. The Speaker Ban was, in part, a reflection of times and circumstances in which many Americans made college campuses a major focus of their discontents and desires regarding the state of the nation. In this environment the Speaker Ban became a rallying point for a variety of more general concerns regarding society, politics and culture.[25]

With so many North Carolinians convinced that the bill reflected rather than threatened their most cherished values, it is not surprising that principled statements on behalf of free speech or strong calls for the bill's outright repeal did not get very far. Opponents of the bill within North Carolina understood all too well, as William Friday put it, the "widespread and disturbing public support" the new law enjoyed among North Carolinians. Indeed, with support for overturning the legislation far from solid even among the university's Board of Trustees, it soon became clear to Friday that repealing the bill would be "an almost impossible task," with a compromise amendment probably the best its opponents could hope for.[26] Opponents of the bill, led by William Friday, consequently adopted a different course of action, one that stressed amendment over repeal. They also adopted a different debating strategy, one that emphasized the autonomy of the institution to govern rather than the freedom of the individual to speak. In other words, a strategy that sought to shift the debate from the question "Who should speak?" to "Who should *decide* who speaks?"

Efforts to shift the grounds of debate did not necessarily reflect a lack of concern for the principle of academic freedom understood as freedom of speech. Friday was not unconcerned about freedom of speech. In replying to Ada Davis, for example, he defended the need to preserve free speech, not least because it offered the best means to defeat subversive speech.[27] But the principled defense of free speech did not play a major part in efforts to reach a compromise with the ban's supporters. Instead, opponents of the bill advanced an argument for academic freedom that emphasized the importance of the university system's governors, trustees and administrators being able to run their institutions free from excessive political involvement.

In making this argument, they sought, as the free speech proponents had done, to convince supporters of the ban that their disagreements did not reflect a conflict of values but rather alternative views of how best to advance those values. Friday, who understood the complex context for the Speaker Ban controversy as well as anyone, worked to convince supporters of the ban that, whatever a minority of students and a relatively small group of faculty were getting up to, the administration of the system remained safe in the hands of people fully aware of majority opinion and of their own responsibility to take account of that opinion. Friday was at pains to insist on his and the university's support for the spirit as well as the letter of the 1941 law making it illegal to advocate the violent overthrow of the government. He was also quick to point out how few Communists had ever actually been to the Chapel Hill campus, a tradition that he and his colleagues had no intention of changing. Friday and others were adamant that lifting or amending the ban would not precipitate a flood of radicals onto North Carolina's campuses. The outcome intended by the legislation, in other words, could be achieved without the legislation, since those in charge could be trusted to heed its general intentions.[28]

If opponents sought to reassure the ban's supporters that it could safely be amended, they also tried to persuade them of the irreparable damage that leaving it unchanged would do to the quality and reputation of the state's educational system. Where appeals to first amendment principle had failed, it was hoped that matters of economic practicality and state pride might sway the lawmakers and their constituents. In turn, such issues inevitably involved the question of whether or not the legislature's intervention in the affairs of the state's universities and colleges would, as in Mississippi and Georgia, precipitate a loss of those institutions' accredited status. Thus, as debate over these questions increasingly moved to the center of discussion, so too the Southern Association came to occupy a more visible and significant place in the Speaker Ban controversy, becoming the focus both of intense public criticism and of efforts to reach a satisfactory compromise.

Whatever its eventual prominence, the Association had initially kept a deliberately low profile in the crowded and complex proceedings surrounding the Speaker Ban. The legislation only came to the official attention of the Association in early March of 1964, in the course of a visit to the Chapel Hill campus conducted by a thirteen-person committee as part of a scheduled Institutional Self-Study and Periodic Visitation Program. During the visit, faculty and administrators spoke "freely" of their concerns about the new law. The committee also received various documents relating to the ban, including a resolution of the Faculty Council, statements by William Friday and Chancellor Aycock to the Board of Trustees, and materials from other affected institutions in the Carolina system. These documents challenged the Speaker Ban "as a violation of the principle of intellectual freedom and an abridgment of the authority of the governing board of the university." The visiting committee also received a copy of a Board of Trustees resolution of October 28, 1963, that criticized the Speaker Ban as a "departure from tradition."[29] From the Association's perspective, the Speaker Ban was potentially in conflict with its *Standards for Colleges,* Standard Two of which stated that an institution's "governing board should not be subject to undue pressures from state officials or other outside political or religious groups; furthermore the governing board should protect the administration from outside pressures." In its final report, the visiting committee declared itself "in accord with the position taken by the university faculty and administration," expressed its concern, and applauded the "steps aimed at corrective action" taken by the trustees and others.[30]

The Association did not, however, take any public action at this early stage of its involvement. This cautious approach was dictated by several factors. Important among these was the influence of William Friday. Friday encouraged a careful approach lest the Association's efforts undermine ongoing efforts to resolve the crisis within North Carolina. He worried, for example, that hopes for the more moderate candidate to emerge victorious from the

1964 Democratic gubernatorial primary might be harmed should the Association make any public statement on such a volatile political issue prior to the primary.[31] He called A.D. Holt, president of the University of Tennessee, to express the hope that the Association's Executive Council would not take any action "until such time and in such manner" as he recommended, a suggestion with which Holt "heartily concur[red]" as he passed it on to Emmett Fields at Vanderbilt. Both Fields and Executive Secretary Gordon Sweet, reflecting Executive Council opinion, agreed that it was "clear," as Fields told Friday, that the Council "should take no action until you feel that such might be helpful." This caution stemmed in part from respect for Friday and for his judgment regarding political and educational affairs in his home state. It also reflected the procedural reality that several institutional steps remained to be taken before any official decision was taken, as well as the Association's awareness of a public opinion already showing hostility toward the Association's involvement.[32]

On a more philosophical level, the Association's accommodation of William Friday's wishes indicates how closely they identified with the university administration's position. As with earlier episodes of conflict between educators and politicians, the Association lined up squarely on the side of the former, and did so with a shared sense of priority: the restoration of administrative autonomy. As in Mississippi, Louisiana and Georgia, the Association's concern was focused less on the wider principle of free speech than on the more specific question of whether politicians—in this case through passage of the Speaker Ban—had so restricted the autonomy of the affected institutions that it cast doubt on their membership in the Association and, therefore, on their status as an accredited institution. Restoration of that autonomy, for the Association as well as for Friday and his colleagues, was the key to defusing what Emmett Fields would later call this "bitter spectacle." A variety of factors, then, encouraged the Association to approach the Speaker Ban with its customary caution, reinforced by contemporary circumstances.[33]

Gordon Sweet and Emmett Fields, nevertheless, quietly took steps to prepare for action should events in North Carolina fail to resolve the problem. These included appointing a special committee that would familiarize itself with the situation, "confer" with

William Friday, and "design a statement" of public response should one be required.[34] When Emmett Fields contacted Friday in November for an update prior to the following month's Executive Council meeting, Friday could report little or no progress toward the "amicable" resolution to the "gag law" controversy that he hoped for. Believing there was still "some reason to hope for an amendment" that would "return the jurisdiction of this area of university life to the control of the Board of Trustees," Friday felt there was still no "helpful" step that the Executive Council could take at that time. He told Fields that he would get back to him when he knew what course of action was to be followed in the 1965 legislative session.[35]

The Association's continued willingness to avoid any public intervention in the affair did not, however, prevent rumors from circulating in North Carolina that it planned to get involved. When a reporter from the *Charlotte News and Observer* contacted Gordon Sweet about "a rumor that the Association was going to chastise the legislature," Sweet informed him that the Association did not accredit legislatures, and felt he had been successful in not giving the reporter anything.[36] The rumors were perhaps fueled by the fact that, while it remained silent publicly, the Association's representatives had been involved in private discussions with Governor Dan K. Moore and his representatives as well as with Friday and his allies. Emmett Fields and Gordon Sweet traveled to Raleigh in May of 1965 to meet Moore (in his capacity as chairman *ex officio* of the Board of Trustees of the Consolidated University of North Carolina), and to tell him of the Executive Council's "deep and urgent concern." The governor told them of the moves underway to improve the situation. Fields told the governor that he had no way of knowing, prior to any changes, how the College Commission or its Executive Council might respond to them. Despite these talks and many others, as well as amendments offered during the 1965 legislative session, the search for a compromise was making little if any progress.[37]

Perhaps prompted by this lack of progress, after meeting with Governor Moore on May 16, Emmett Fields called a special session of the Executive Council of the Commission on Colleges. Meeting on May 19, the Council unanimously approved a statement to be issued to the chairmen of the governing boards and the

chief executive officers of the affected institutions. It focused mostly on the precise aspects of the new law that brought it in conflict
with the existing requirements of the College Delegate Assembly's
standards. The statement declared that to the extent that "the act
removes from governing boards . . . their traditional authority to
handle such matters [as campus speakers] with administrative discretion it raises an issue of interference with the necessary authority of the boards." The statement further noted that "the
established principles and standards of the college delegate assembly . . . recognize this necessity and authorize the Commission to
protest in the name of academic integrity when the educational
effort is hampered by political interference or is in any way men-
aced by those who would subvert the search for truth." The
Council found "that such interference has occurred with detrimental effect on the state supported institutions of higher learning
in North Carolina," and gave "notice" that the Commission's next
meeting would "determine the status of these institutions with
respect to continued accreditation." The Association's continued
caution was evident in its decision not to issue a press release
about the statement "except as requested in confirmation of a
release issued by others."[38] Nevertheless the statement marked the
Association's first official and public intervention in the Speaker
Ban controversy.

The statement dramatically enlarged the Association's role in
the controversy and its public profile in North Carolina. From that
point on, the Association would play a prominent role in discussions as to how the situation might be resolved. In turn, a measure
of attention was focused on the Association by friend and foe
alike, its motives praised and damned, its influence played up or
played down. Responses to the Association's involvement were
often critical, sometimes extreme. State Senator Thad Eure likened
the Association to the Ku Klux Klan because of their supposedly
"sinister" methods, but most critical comparisons leaned to the
left. Writing to praise William Friday in the mistaken belief that
he supported the ban, A.B. Gilliland, coordinator of industrial
cooperative training at Greenville High School in Tennessee, wondered if the Association itself was "Communist." He expressed
the hope that Friday would "tell them to ——— and publicize the
fact that you are more than meeting the requirements set up by

this board and because they lean toward Communism they threaten you."[39] Gilliland was not alone. "Perhaps it is time," Martha McKinney of Jacksonville, Florida, told Governor Moore, "to find out just who is running the Southern Association of Schools and Colleges [sic]." McKinney described how "this body" had come to Jacksonville "and made trouble for our public schools." She felt it was now time "to do away with this un-American body and get an Association of Schools and Colleges which are 100 percent American." McKinney linked the Association's subversive tendencies to a wider web of "professors, foundations, preachers" and so on, who stood only for "chaos in education, chaos in government, chaos in America and in the souls of all men." It was "high time," McKinney urged, for "cleaning up these evil schemers, without force if possible but with force if NECESSARY FOR THIS NATION TO REMAIN FREE." That the Association's leaders and members could be confused with "Communists" provides inadvertent support for the argument that such terms were hopelessly susceptible to vagueness and abuse. Opinions such as these further reflect the rapidity and willingness with which many white Southerners could link unwelcome local or regional change to the catchall threat of Communism.[40]

More influential public voices were also raised inside North Carolina, fomenting and reinforcing a perception of the sense of the Association as not only beyond the boundaries of North Carolina, but also beyond the values of the majority of its people. Jesse Helms, later a Republican senator in Washington but at the time an editorialist on WRAL-TV in Raleigh, was one such leading voice. He slammed the Association for "inviting itself into the controversy" and making a "bald threat" to North Carolina's legislature. Helms agreed that it was now time "for the legislatures of all states whose taxpayers help finance the Association" to devote some time to how it functioned. Helms had also heard from an educator in another state suggesting that the legislators "look into this Association," obtaining, for example, "the names and backgrounds of the members of the executive council of the Association who sent the threat to North Carolina." The irony could not have been lost on the likes of Fields and Sweet. Drawn reluctantly into the debate by their concern to resist unacceptable "outside interference" in the affairs of the University of North Carolina, the Association now found itself viewed as an unacceptable and alien intrusion into the affairs of the people of North Carolina.[41]

Whatever the dismissive tone of the Association's strongest critics, other supporters of the ban recognized that the possible loss of institutional accreditation had to be taken seriously. It became a priority, therefore, to ascertain the Association's future course of action should the Speaker Ban remain the law. The main venue for this inquiry would be what came to be popularly known as the Speaker Ban Hearings. The Association's caution and their cooperation with Friday had not prevented Judge Dan K. Moore, a supporter of the Speaker Ban, from winning the gubernatorial race, thus effectively ending any lingering hope of the bill's repeal. But in the midst of the apparently unending controversy, Moore did appear amenable to a compromise if it could satisfy the bill's opponents without alienating its many supporters. Moore's efforts to find a compromise were spurred in part by his grasp of the possible consequences should accreditation be lost.[42] Many private meetings and contacts took place in pursuit of a way forward, including those between Governor Moore and representatives of the College Commission. Efforts to resolve the conflict also produced a nine-person "Commission to Study the Statutes Relating to Visiting Speakers at State Supported Educational Institutions," created by the North Carolina General Assembly at the urging of Governor Moore. The committee was chaired by State Representative David M. Britt and consisted of a mix of representatives, senators and members of the community, including a newspaperwoman and a representative of the North Carolina Bar. Held at the legislature in Raleigh, the televised hearings attracted a great deal of media and public attention throughout North Carolina and in the nation beyond.[43]

In an effort, as Chairman Britt put it, to get "straight, direct information," and to clarify some of the "conflicting statements" that had been circulating about it, the Association was invited to send representatives to the Raleigh hearings. On the morning of August 11, Gordon Sweet and Emmett Fields were the first witnesses to appear before the first two-day session of the hearings. Aware of the wider public atmosphere, in introducing them Chairman Britt made a point of clarifying that the Association's representatives had been "invited" to attend. Emmett Fields did most of the talking. His general tone and approach was clearly dictated by two main priorities: not saying anything that might either overstep the policies or preempt the procedures of his own Association, or fuel existing criticisms that the Association represented an external, and therefore illegitimate, challenge to the authority of North Carolina's elected representatives. These priorities inevitably dictated a cautious approach, evident in both Fields' opening statement and in both men's responses to later questions. Fields began with a prepared statement devoted to outlining the history and organization of the Southern Association. He particularly emphasized the "voluntary" nature of the organization and the representative character of the procedures for formulating and enforcing the Association's standards. He explained the Association's relation to other regional accrediting bodies as well as the Association's policies and procedures insofar as they had relevance to the Speaker Ban, and set out the general practices and philosophies of the accreditation process.[44]

Fields was also at pains to insist that nothing in its aims and responsibilities led the Association to question "the right of the General Assembly of North Carolina to pass, amend, or repeal any law it wishes, including the one which is the basis of the present controversy." "At no time," furthermore, had "the Executive Council addressed itself to the General Assembly of North Carolina." Rather, Fields explained, the Association's "authority" extended only to its member institutions. Where evidence existed that a member institution was "failing to comply with one or more of the Standards" it became the Commission's responsibility to determine the future membership status of that institution, "whether or not," Fields stressed, the failure arose "from causes within the control of the officers." Fields assured the committee that the procedures for doing so, established by the membership and allowing for the institution in question to be heard, had been followed in the present case. The Association's initial public statement of May 19 had, then, been a "first step" in a longer process whose next step would be decided upon by the Commission on Colleges when it heard the case at the next annual meeting.[45]

Fields' answers to subsequent questions reflected the same caution that characterized his introductory statement, and indeed the Association's entire participation in the affair to date. Yet despite Fields' careful clarification of the Association's aims, methods and limited jurisdictional claims, the questioning that followed did not always go smoothly. Albeit in more measured tones than sometimes adopted by the public and the pundits, some Commission members voiced their suspicions that the Association was being intrusive and inconsistent. Some members wanted to know why the Association had chosen to act in this case, but seemed uninterested in others. Senator Russell Kirby pointed to Fields' home state of Tennessee, which still had a law on the books banning the teaching of evolution. Asked if that did not "infringe upon your academic freedom," Fields frankly responded, "You bet your life it does." But when asked why the Association had not taken action in that case, Fields could only "admit I hadn't thought about this question until this morning, and I feel a little reluctant to think about it now, I must admit." In this and other ways, the Association's emphasis on academic integrity was probed for inconsistencies and contradictions. To the extent that Fields and Sweet were unable to provide satisfactory explanations of inconsistency, the hearings reinforced the belief that North Carolina was being unfairly singled out by the Association.[46]

Yet the Association had become involved, and what they would do now that they were involved became a topic of discussion in North Carolina. Public opinion could be scathing on these questions, too, as suspicion regarding the Association's involvement was matched by a scornful confidence that both the stature of the organization and the significance of accreditation had been overstated. Tom White, a state senator from Kinston and strong supporter of the ban, thought that UNC should go ahead and withdraw from an association that was "unworthy of being privileged to 'accredit' any kind of educational institution." "A lot of people strongly feel that loss of accreditation would not mean too much," claimed Carson Gregory, state representative from Harnett County, and in any case, "would be far more preferable than subjecting our young people to the influence of Communist speakers." The educator who had suggested to Jesse Helms that the Association be investigated also thought the state's legislators should "find out whether the Southern Association would amount to a hoot without the membership of North Carolina institutions." Others, too, wondered whether the Association would be the loser should it part ways with one of the more prestigious systems of higher education within its jurisdiction. This view, in turn, encouraged the belief that the Association lacked the resolve to withdraw accreditation even if the Speaker Ban did remain in place. Jesse Helms, for one, mocked the "hysterical fear" being fueled by some educators and newspapers, clearly suggesting that they were exaggerating the threat represented by lost accreditation.[47]

Questions regarding the potential consequences of withdrawn accreditation were also raised in a milder, more probing, form during the hearings. As usual, Fields was cautious, emphasizing, for example, that it was not certain that other institutions would refuse admission to students transferring from North Carolina institutions that had lost their accredited status.[48] Lacy Thornburg, a state representative from Jackson County, told Fields that he had "heard discussed the possibility of the various institutions of higher learning pulling out from the Southern Association and forming their own accrediting association." Asked if such a course of action would "have any detrimental effect" on the Association or the new grouping (provided "they adopted the same or similar standards"), Fields replied: "This is a request for me to comment on a set of facts which don't exist and I think I'd better not try. I'd be making speculation, Mr. Thornburg." And having bluntly asked Fields whether the law presented "any real threat" to the continued accreditation of the state's institutions, Thornburg was far from satisfied with Fields' response that the May 19 statement "speaks for itself," and that he did not wish to make a guess as to the College Commission's eventual decision. Nor, despite further questions pressing him to do so, would Fields comment on what action he would personally recommend. "That least of all," he insisted. [49]

Fields' unwillingness either to speculate on what action the Association might take or to state unequivocally the negative consequences of expulsion reflected his consistent wish not to throw fuel on the fire of public resentment. Sensible as Fields' approach may have been if the aim was to limit public and political opposition to the Southern Association, it did little to rally public and political opposition to the Speaker Ban. Indeed, it may have undermined the efforts of those who wished to make the disastrous consequences of lost accreditation the centerpiece of their argument for amending the Speaker Ban legislation by inadvertently reinforcing the view that even if the Association had the resolve to act, the loss of accreditation would do little damage to education in North Carolina. Rightly resisting any effort to predict the outcome of this particular investigation, Fields could nevertheless have provided a more forceful general account of the likely consequences for *any* institution of losing their accreditation.

Perhaps Fields' caution was encouraged in part by his awareness that there were other individuals and organizations who were far from reluctant to defend the Association's resolve, to insist upon its influence, and to make the case for retaining accreditation at all costs. At the second round of hearings, Watts Hill, chairman of the Board of Higher Education of North Carolina, took up this challenge. Hill refuted claims that the Association had precipitously transgressed on territory where it did not belong, emphasizing that the ban, not the Southern Association, was the source of the current controversy. Given that the Association was only acting as its standards required it to do, Hill insisted that "we cannot afford to let the mistaken impression persist—as it now appears to in certain quarters—that the Southern Association lacks the courage to act." To those who, like Jesse Helms, suggested that the Association would not dare to expel such a prestigious member institution, Hill suggested another possibility, wondering, "now that the controversy has become a matter of national concern," whether the Association would have "any alternative" but to act if the ban remained in force. Could the Association "retain any future effectiveness if it fails to act?" Hill asked. "Would not its failure to act be interpreted as a lack of courage to act?" His own answers to these questions left Hill convinced that "the Association will act" if the authority and responsibility of the Boards of Trustees were not restored.[50]

Hill, as well as other speakers at the hearings, were also at pains to bring home to the ban's supporters what the consequences would be if the Association's actions included suspension or removal of the UNC system's accredited status. In making this case, they also provided a lesson on the increasingly influential role of accreditation in postwar American education. A major reason for this new influence was the corresponding growth in influence of the federal government, whose unprecedented involvement in postwar education had transformed the lives of

institutions and individual students alike. As this growing involvement relates to the Association and the Speaker Ban, one issue
was paramount. The federal government needed to evaluate the
institutions to which it now awarded research grants or to whose
students to whom it made loans. Yet with neither the authority nor
the means to do so itself, the federal government depended on the
evaluation of other bodies as to the educational legitimacy of
receiving institutions. The stamp of approval most often looked for
by the government was the institution's accredited status. The
chance of receiving all kinds of government funding, from student loans to research grants, depended on an institution's prior
accreditation by organizations like the Southern Association.
Conversely, the chance of receiving that funding without accreditation grew ever more unlikely.

These new realities of higher education were set out for the
Commission, and the public beyond, by various witnesses at the
Hearings. Hill, for one, described the "vicious circle" of departing
faculty, lost revenues, declining quality, and suffering students he
believed the loss of accreditation would set in motion. Other witnesses before the Commission also proved eager to spell out the
detrimental consequences of lost accreditation. The AAUP representatives also predicted an exodus of faculty, especially of those
best qualified and, therefore, best able to find positions elsewhere.
The exodus might not be massive nor immediate, but it would
alter faculty members' attitudes toward their institutions, and
therefore become an important factor in any future career choices.
The departure of existing faculty would also damage morale
among those remaining, while making it difficult to recruit new
faculty of high quality. How long could an institution survive
when no professor capable of winning a government grant would
want to teach there, or no student eligible for a student loan could
afford to attend it? Dr. Howard Boozer, acting director of North
Carolina's Department of Higher Education, had, at Chairman
Britt's request, prepared a report that sought to provide specific
answers to these kinds of questions. In his testimony before the
Commission, Boozer provided a detailed estimate of the financial
cost to the UNC system of lost accreditation. His report fully
revealed the extensive connections between accreditation and the
vast, various and increasing levels of federal and foundation funding

now pursued by postsecondary students and institutions. The relative importance that different agencies and programs placed on accreditation varied, but the unmistakable conclusion of Boozer's extensive research was that the financial blows would be heavy and would quickly start landing if accreditation was withdrawn.[51]

Various witnesses at the hearings drew a convincing picture of a higher education environment in which to institutions' longstanding desire to enjoy the prestige and practical help that came with membership had been added a major, and growing, financial incentive to gain accreditation. Conversely, losing accreditation, once gained, could be a disaster, even threatening an institution's very existence. In this new educational world, the place of accreditation had been greatly enlarged. In turn, the power of regional accreditors like the Southern Association had grown significantly. As we shall see, the Association was far from uniformly pleased by this new proxy power, or with other aspects of its expanding and complicated relation to federal politicians and agencies. Nevertheless this was the implied power it brought to the Speaker Ban controversy.

For their part, Commission members seemed willing to accept the importance of accreditation, at least for the purposes of their inquiry, and proved keen to gain an understanding of the Association's likely response if the law was not changed. They were also keen to elicit a sense of what kind of changes the Association might find acceptable. Nevertheless, members continued to be frustrated by Fields' cautious responses to various hypothetical questions designed to garner that information. Hoping to head off some of these questions, Fields had concluded his opening statement with the hope that the panel would "understand" his unwillingness to "trespass" upon the College Commission's independence "by entering in advance into speculation as to the nature of the determination it will make." It did not work. Numerous hypothetical questions were put, designed to get a sense of what would not be in conflict with the Association's standards should future amendments to the law be considered. Elizabeth Swindell, editor and publisher of the *Wilson Daily Times* and immediate past president of the North Carolina Press Association, asked whether, "if the law were amended to permit non-political speeches by so-called Communists," it would "still threaten the accreditation of tax-supported colleges?" While a "good question," Fields again declined to comment "on a set of facts which do not exist," again referring to the statement of May 19. Swindell had no better luck when she asked Fields how the Association would view such a distinction being made as part of a set of guidelines drawn up by the Board of Trustees.[52]

Fields' cautious responses generated increasing frustration among the Commission members as the hearings progressed. Once the Association had been accepted as a major voice among those who could not accept the "gag law," Fields' efforts to be precise and to avoid speculation did not sit well with those Committee members who clearly felt the point of his being there was to provide guidance as to what the Association *would* accept. Senator Gordon Hanes was not being complimentary when he described one answer as "a remarkable performance." One observer, an opponent of the ban, found Fields' presentation "embarrassing." One person's precision, it seemed, could be another person's prevarication.[53]

Yet Fields' performance was also praised and defended. Watts Hill considered the Association's refusal to give a "simple 'yes' or 'no' answer" to questions quite "understandable." *The Greensboro Daily News* felt he "faltered only once or twice," "fielded the toughest questions with relative ease," and generally made "an eloquent and affable spokesman for the cause of trustee autonomy." Jay Jenkins of the *Charlotte Observer* also considered the "evasive label" unjustified, agreeing with the men from the Association that it would have been "impertinent and presumptuous" for Fields to predict his colleagues' actions.[54] In retrospect, it is far from clear what alternative approach Fields could have adopted that would not have generated just as much, if not more, criticism. He was surely right neither to preempt or predict a course of action to be decided later, especially since Fields would be presiding at the relevant Commission and delegate assembly meetings. Furthermore, as he pointed out to Elizabeth Swindell, the Association's refusal to rush to recommendation was partly out of "deference to the fact that this study commission is in session," just as their actions all along had been designed not to disrupt efforts within North Carolina to reach a solution. Nor, of course, could Fields' unwillingness to speculate be judged apart from the prevailing public suspicion regarding outside influence in the affairs of North Carolina, the very atmosphere that had fueled passage of the Speaker Ban in the first place. With the Association already being widely, and wildly, criticized, it was somewhat disingenuous of the Commission panelists to demand a frankness they surely knew that many would immediately reinterpret as arrogant assertion. Both the panel's frustration and Fields' caution are illustrated by one exchange. After Senator Hanes had asked a series of questions intended to ascertain how and from whom the panel could get a definitive answer to what the Association would accept, the frustrated legislator insisted, "We've got to have somebody to go to and say what do you want us to do." "Well, what would you say if I told you what I want you to do?" Fields replied. Although Hanes replied, "Then we would know," he did not address the issue implicit in Fields' question: Would the demanded forthrightness not be interpreted as further evidence for the Association's supposed arrogance? Jay Jenkins, however, did accept this point, suggesting that if, for example, Fields were to say that he favored removing accreditation, he would immediately be accused of bias.[55]

The Association's caution reflected more than modesty, commitment to procedural timetables, or an acute sensitivity to public opinion. It was also a symptom of the Association's chosen emphasis on the Speaker Ban's threat to institutional autonomy, rather than to freedom of speech. Like most opponents of the bill, the Association was happy to accept existing legislation curtailing certain kinds of speech. Regarding the distinction between existing laws banning certain kinds of speech and the new one banning certain kinds of speakers, Fields was asked why such laws did not also infringe on the traditional authority of governors and trustees. The Southern Association had "never seen any issue that infringed upon the standards for membership in the Association" in North Carolina's 1941 legislation, and Fields assumed that "the governing boards of the institutions have themselves not seen any infringement of their responsibilities." Here Fields reflected the Association's main concern with institutional autonomy rather than the protection of free speech.[56]

This sense of priority is further clarified by contrasting the Association's position with that of the AAUP. The latter organization took the position that the ban would still be unacceptable even if imposed by academic trustees or administrators rather than

state lawmakers. Committee member Hanes contrasted this position with the testimony of Fields, from which he "got the feeling" that the Association's representatives "felt that we should rely
entirely on the Trustees and if this were done, that their objections would be more or less satisfied." Hanes' interpretation finds
support in an exchange between Emmett Fields and Commission
member William Joyner. Noting that the words "Communist" or
"Communism" had not appeared anywhere in Fields' testimony,
Joyner asked if it was Fields' "sole position" that North Carolina's
legislators had "wrongfully invaded the province of the trustees of
North Carolina . . . in enacting this statute and permitting it to
remain on the books?" "That's correct," Fields replied.[57] Fields
further agreed with Representative Zollicoffer that, had the regulations been adopted by the trustees rather than mandated by the
legislature, they would not be faced by the same "problem." While
Fields did consistently maintain that he did not know whether the
regulations might still have raised questions about accreditation,
he further reinforced the impression that institutional integrity was
the Association's key concern in response to Zollicoffer's questioning. Asked if there were "any specific phrases of this law,"
such as Communists or those who had taken the Fifth
Amendment not being allowed to speak, "that affect accreditation," Fields replied that "None of these is as significant as the fact
that the governing boards" had been "deprived of their traditional
authority to set policy over visiting speakers." In this and other
answers, Fields clearly reflects the priorities of the Association,
which he represented in Raleigh with such consistent caution and
circumspection.[58] The limited scope of the Association's opposition to the ban, in turn, shaped its understanding of what an
acceptable compromise might look like. Inevitably, it would fall
short of satisfying those for who freedom of speech rather than
institutional autonomy had been the central question. Such a compromise was eventually finalized in the fall of 1965. Developing
out of negotiations between the various parties and the recommendations of the Britt Commission, in essence, it was agreed
that the Speaker Ban Law should be amended in order to return
control of campus speakers to the trustees and administration. In
return, the university people gave certain assurances as to how
speakers' visits would be arranged and conducted. Among the

conditions, as historian William Link describes them, were "that speakers who advocated ideologies or forms of government 'wholly alien to our basic democratic institutions' should be 'infrequent,' only tolerated when it served some clear educational purpose." According to Link, "the key provision of the speaker policy was that the trustees and administrators would exert 'reasonable and proper care' in supervising speakers so as to balance the considerations of anti-Communism and free speech."[59] Like most political compromises, this one allowed the different parties to view the final result as sufficiently close to their own starting position than their opponents liked to think. In the coming years, the new policy would prove more fragile than its creators hoped. It would face serious challenges, especially from students at Chapel Hill who invited left-wing speakers, then protested when they were not allowed to speak, and who eventually challenged the Speaker Ban's constitutionality in court. In the short term, however, the issue at the center of the Association's concern—its member institutions' freedom from unacceptable political influence over its internal affairs—had been sufficiently resolved to please the Southern Association and to remove the threat of the UNC system being placed on probation or losing accreditation.

The Southern Association played an important role in North Carolina's Speaker Ban controversy. Its participation strengthened the bargaining position and credibility of the ban's opponents. It did so, in part, by enabling them to shift the terrain of debate from "free speech for the enemies of society" to the potential consequences for state pride and pedagogy if this self-inflicted wound to one of North Carolina's most nationally respected institutions was not healed. Once the public debate was in progress, furthermore, the power of the Association became evident, albeit less through the actual words and actions of its own representatives than through other educators' strong statements of accreditation's indispensability in the modern educational world. Whatever the skepticism regarding the Association's willingness to suspend some of its most prominent institutions, the possibility of lost accreditation contributed to the willingness of ban supporters such as Governor Moore to seek a negotiated compromise with its opponents.

In following the Association's involvement in the Speaker Ban controversy, we see also something of its growing engagement and influence in Southern education and society. Often its consistent involvement over time, especially in the form of accreditation, had brought higher standards and greater prestige to local institutions. At times of particular crisis, as in Mississippi and Georgia, the Association's intervention on the side of member institutions was not only welcomed by many in those institutions, but also met little resistance from the general public. At other times, its involvement in controversies, from Centre, Kentucky, to Chapel Hill, North Carolina, revealed a different response to the Association's power and influence: an opposition to "outside interference" grounded in a powerful sense of "localism." The Association's leaders were not always successful in arguing that, rather than an unrepresentative outside force, their organization was attached to each locality through the participation and influence of its local colleges or schools. This difficulty was compounded in a period of social tension and cultural conflict, such as the 1960s, when an institution like UNC-Chapel Hill might be viewed as an alien institution in the sense that it was claimed to nurture views and behavior at odds with the majority of the people the educational system served.

These ambivalent attitudes toward the Association's involvement in the communities of the South were perhaps inevitable given the Association's location between the local communities in which its member institutions were located and the state and federal governments that occupied an increasingly influential role in the development of those institutions. In some ways, the Association had grown up in the void created by a legal and cultural context in which the central government had little or no say in educational matters. Generally agreeing on the need for some system of standards and inspection in an ever-expanding educational system, many Southerners recognized the importance of some form of accreditation. In the absence of a federal role in school and college inspection, accrediting bodies like the Southern Association had gradually assumed a great deal of power. Yet reluctant to grant such power to government, it is not surprising that both institutions and communities alike at times resented the exercise of that power.

The Association was often unhappy with the impact that federal dependence on accreditation had both on the Association's public image as well as its accrediting activities and practices, especially at the postsecondary level. If federal dependence on accreditation as a guide to an institution's worth enhanced the Association's influence, it also brought with it increased governmental demands on its time and activities. The Association's efforts to be responsive to the demands of individual institutions and local sensibilities, while at the same time negotiating its increasing labyrinthine relationship not only to the federal government but to other governmental and accrediting bodies, proved to be crucial elements of another major theme of the Association's life and work in modern times: the transformation of the philosophy and practice of accreditation. It is to that chapter of the Association's history that we now turn.

Endnotes

[1] Guy E. Snavely, *A Short History of the Southern Association of Colleges and Secondary Schools,* [Reprint from the *Southern Association Quarterly* (hereafter *SAQ*) 9 (Nov. 1945)], 48; George Jackson Allen, Jr., "A History of the Commission on Colleges of the Southern Association of Colleges and Schools, 1949-1975" (doctoral dissertation, Georgia State University, Atlanta, 1978), 168. The institutions involved were the University of Mississippi, the Mississippi Agricultural and Mechanical College, the Mississippi State College for Women, and the Mississippi State College for Teachers at Hattiesburg, the first three of which all shared the same Board of Trustees.

[2] Snavely, 48-9. President Dinwiddie of Tulane was also appointed to the inspection team but was unable to take part in the visit.

[3] *Proceedings* 35 (1930): 35-7. Cited in Snavely, 23, 49-51. The recent events, the report stated, "indicated not only the control but the active management of these Mississippi institutions was taken over by the Governor and a small group of his appointees, with which group this Association has little in common and can make no arrangements." According to Snavely, the report was largely the work of James Kirkland.

[4] Allen, 168-69; Snavely, 51. See also Jack Kirby, *Darkness at the Dawning: Race and Reform in the Progressive South* (Philadelphia: J.B. Lippincott Company, 1972), 28-29. Kirby discusses the "rambunctious" Bilbo, who was both "heir" to the race-baiting James K. Vardaman and the promoter of "remarkable" reforms in areas such as taxation, health, and education. According to Kirby, Bilbo was "no less a racial extremist but was a more successful governor. When 'The Man' left office, however, Mississippi's public services still lagged hopelessly behind other states. And insofar as he could control his reforms, he left blacks out entirely from his programs." Kirby nevertheless considers Bilbo "by far the most effective Southern mass leader before Huey P. Long."

[5] Snavely, 51-7.

[6] Ibid.

[7] "Report on University System of Georgia," *SAQ* 6 (Feb. 1942): 71-3. Quoted in Snavely, 58-9. For a fuller account of these events see Snavely, 57ff, and Allen, 170-71.

[8] Snavely, 58-60.

[9] Quoted in Allen, 171.

[10] Ibid., 171-72; Snavely, 61; *SAQ* 7 (Feb. 1943), 177.

[11] Quoted in William D. Snider, *Light on the Hill: A History of the University of North Carolina at Chapel Hill* (Chapel Hill: University of North Carolina Press, 1992), 271.

[12] Snider, 271, notes that the North Carolina law had been modeled on legislation proposed not long before in Ohio. However, Professor William Van Alstyne of Duke Law School pointed out to the Speaker Ban Hearings that the Ohio bill had been extensively debated in both houses of the legislature and "finally adopted after drastic modification" that removed much that was most objectionable to the defenders of free speech and institutional autonomy. William Van Alstyne, Testimony before the Speaker Ban Study Commission (hereafter Speaker Ban Hearings), Aug. 12, 1965, William C. Friday Records, University Archives, University of North Carolina, Chapel Hill (hereafter cited as UNC), 66. The Friday Records contain a full transcript of the questions asked and testimony offered at the hearings.

[13] Not all anti-Communists of the right were in favor of speaker bans as a way to combat the enemy. Barry Goldwater, senator from Arizona and Republican candidate for president in 1964, not normally a man to be mistaken for a "bleeding heart" liberal, told an audience at Ohio State in 1961 that he thought "that schools make a mistake when they deny their students the right to hear all sides [including the Communist side]." Quoted by William Van Alstyne, Aug. 12, 1965, Speaker Ban Hearings, UNC, 68.

[14] John P. Dawson, Aug. 12, 1965, Speaker Ban Hearings, UNC, 5.

[15] Ibid., 4-5.

[16] Some observers mockingly noted that the statute would have barred Robert E. Lee from speaking on campus. A university archivist also alerted William Friday to the historical curiosity that were a particular Ku Klux Klansman who had "taken the fifth" during Reconstruction, somehow to return to Chapel Hill, he would be barred from speaking in the campus building that was subsequently named for him. James Patton to William C. Friday, Jan. 5, 1965, William C. Friday Records, UNC.

[17] John P. Dawson, Aug. 12, 1965, Speaker Ban Hearings, UNC, 10.

[18] John P. Dawson and Frances Brown, Aug. 12, 1965, Speaker Ban Hearings, UNC, 6, 87.

[19] John P. Dawson, Aug. 12, 1965, Speaker Ban Hearings, UNC, 8, 9. Such a

view was premised not only on a dim view of the ideas involved, but also on an optimistic assessment of the students who would be exposed to them. In this regard, Dawson believed that the Bill underestimated the intelligence and maturity of students, and their ability to emerge from encounters with opposing arguments strengthened rather than weakened in their own beliefs and principles.

[20] Ibid., 26.

[21] Louis R. Wilson to I.C. Wright, July 3, 1963, William C. Friday Papers, UNC. Godwin quoted in William A. Link, *William Friday: Power, Purpose, and American Higher Education* (Chapel Hill: University of North Carolina Press, 1995), 123.

[22] John Hope Franklin, "The Current Crisis in Education and Freedom," *Proceedings of the Association of Colleges and Secondary Schools for Negroes* (hereafter *ACSSN Proceedings*) 19 (1952): 71-3. Franklin regretted "The proliferation of local and national organizations devoted to the destructive criticism of the nation's schools and colleges" that had "been one of the most significant educational (or anti-educational) developments of recent years." Organizations like the Minute Women of the USA, the Friends of the Public Schools, and the Conference of American Small Business Organizations, had sought to establish an "intellectual vigilantism over schools, textbooks, teachers, and administrators" in their efforts to guard against what they viewed as "collectivist doctrines" or "anti-patriotic indoctrination."

[23] Link, 111ff. Link argues that "the real reason for the growing public criticism of Chapel Hill lay elsewhere: anxiety about the mass uprising, during the spring of 1963, of black North Carolinians." William Snider, *Light on the Hill*, historian of UNC-Chapel Hill and, as the title of his book suggests, a strong supporter of the institution and opponent of the Ban, argues that while "anti-Communist hysteria combined with civil rights furor," to fuel support for the ban, "enactment of the law had more to do with racial policy than with political doctrine (271)."

[24] Ada Davis to William C. Friday, June 30, 1963, William C. Friday Records, UNC. The letters to legislators and newspapers alike ran heavily in favor of the Speaker Ban. Many of the newspapers themselves opposed the legislation.

[25] John Hope Franklin, "Current Crisis," 71-3; Link, 112ff.

[26] Quoted in Link, 118. Link provides an excellent and full account of the events preceding and during the controversy.

[27] William C. Friday to Ada Davis, July 4, 1963, William C. Friday Papers, UNC.

[28] See Link, 119ff.

[29] Emmett B. Fields, Aug. 11, 1965, Speaker Ban Hearings, UNC, 12-13.

[30] Cited in ibid.

[31] Snider, 273. Friday was hoping for the victory of Judge L. Richardson Preyer, preferred successor of outgoing governor of North Carolina, Terry Sanford, who was also chairman of the Board of Trustees. The more liberal Sanford knew that

the Speaker Ban could be a damaging issue for his favored successor, Judge L. Richardson Preyer, against the more conservative (and racially moderate) Judge Dan K. Moore and Professor Beverly Lake, a segregationist. Some people, according to Snider, believed that Sanford "delayed action on fighting the bill until after the Democratic primary in the spring of 1964." It was not until October of 1964 that Sanford appointed a special study committee, chaired by William Medford. The final report of the Medford committee also reflected the likelihood that some form of compromise was the most likely course. In April of 1965 the committee noted its "clear preference for outright repeal" of the bill but concluded that seeking its amendment was "a more practical objective to pursue."

32 A.D. Holt to Emmett B. Fields, June 26, 1964; Emmett B. Fields to William Friday, June 30, 1964. See also William Friday to A.D. Holt, June 30, 1964, and Emmett B. Fields to A.D. Holt, June 30, 1964, Gordon W. Sweet to A.D. Holt, June 29, 1964. All in William C. Friday Papers, UNC.

33 Emmett B. Fields, Aug. 11, 1965, Speaker Ban Hearings, UNC, 22.

34 Executive Council Minute, quoted in Gordon W. Sweet to A.D. Holt, June 29, 1964; Emmett Fields to William C. Friday, June 30, 1964, William C. Friday Papers, UNC.

35 William C. Friday to Emmett Fields, Nov. 4, 1964, William C. Friday Papers, UNC.

36 Message from Gordon Sweet to William C. Friday's office, Jan. 27, 1965, William C. Friday Papers, UNC.

37 Emmett B. Fields introductory statement, Speaker Ban Hearings, UNC, 16-17. Fields and Sweet had also met with representatives of the governor on April 26, at which time the governor was ill.

38 Emmett B. Fields to William C. Friday, May 20, 1965, Western Union Telegram containing text of the statement, William C. Friday Papers, UNC; William C. Friday, Sept. 8, 1965, Speaker Ban Hearings, UNC, 17.

39 A.B. Gilliland to William Friday, October 4, 1965, William C. Friday Papers, UNC.

40 Martha McKinney to Dan K. Moore, July 22, 1965, copy in William C. Friday Papers, UNC.

41 Jesse Helms, WRAL-TV "Viewpoint", May 25, 1965, Southern Association of Colleges and Schools Archives, Decatur, Georgia (hereafter SACS Archives).

42 Link, *William Friday*, 122.

43 Five of the members were nominated by the governor, two by the president of the Senate and two by the speaker of the house. As part of their efforts, the Commission conducted public hearings in August and September of 1965.

44 David M. Britt, Aug. 11, 1965, Speaker Ban Hearings, UNC, 7-8; Emmett B. Fields, Aug. 11, 1965, Speaker Ban Hearings, UNC. Fields described the participation of the 411-member institutions that constituted the College Delegate

Assembly in formulating the eleven major standards to which they agreed to conform. He also distinguished between the Assembly and the 54-member Commission on Colleges, elected by the Association and representing all eleven states covered by the Association, which had "the primary responsibility for determining compliance" with the standards.

[45] Emmett B. Fields, Aug. 11, 1965, Speaker Ban Hearings, UNC, 18-19, 22.

[46] Ibid., 71. This line of questioning was pursued with other organizations. Colonel William T. Joyner, for example, told AAUP General Secretary William Fiddler that he was "interested in ascertaining . . . whether the explosion [of opposition to the Speaker Ban] in North Carolina was spontaneous in North Carolina or whether it was stirred up from Washington." Joyner's choice of "stirred up" perhaps suggests the way his suspicions leaned. William T. Joyner, Aug. 12, 1965, Speaker Ban Hearings, UNC, 53.

[47] White quoted in Link, 121-22; Jesse Helms, WRAL-TV "Viewpoint," May 25, 1965, SACS Archive; Gregory quoted in Snider, 273.

[48] Emmett B. Fields, Aug. 11, 1965, Speaker Ban Hearings, UNC, 49-51. Asked by Colonel William T. Joyner, a member of the Raleigh bar, whether this should be interpreted as meaning that a member institution accepting such a student would not necessarily incur the Association's "disfavor," Fields answered: "Well, the answer may or may not be 'yes' to that." But he did later agree that it was "correct" that "irrespective of accreditation, a member university of your organization would be fully free to appraise each applicant on his own merits."

[49] Emmett B. Fields, Aug. 11, 1965, Speaker Ban Hearings. UNC, 55, 60-61.

[50] Watts Hill, Sept. 8, 1965, Speaker Ban Hearings, UNC, 4-6.

[51] Ibid., and Howard Boozer, Aug. 11, 1965, Speaker Ban Hearings, UNC, 23ff. Among the striking pieces of evidence presented by Boozer was the fact that of the approximately $750 million granted by the Ford Foundation to higher education institutions over the preceding several years, "in no case has any of this money gone to a college or university that was not regionally accredited (39)." John P. Dawson, Aug. 12, 1965, Speaker Ban Hearings, UNC, 18, offered anecdotal evidence from Ohio State that three departments had lost half their faculty in the wake of that state's speaker ban controversy. His colleague William Fiddler also mentioned a report that about 175 faculty members at Chapel Hill had signed a letter declaring their intent to leave should it lose its accreditation. Fiddler also pointed out that students would be the largest group to suffer, including those seeking to transfer credits or to enter graduate school. Fiddler also noted that teachers at non-accredited institutions could not join the AAUP, although existing members whose institution lost its accreditation could remain members (58-9).

[52] Emmett B. Fields, Aug. 11, 1965, Speaker Ban Hearings, UNC, 60-61.

[53] Gordon Hanes, Aug. 11, 1965, Speaker Ban Hearings, UNC, 78; Link, William Friday, 122.

[54] Watts Hill, Sept. 8, 1965, Speaker Ban Hearings, UNC, 4-6; "Speaker Ban:

Study in Contrasts," *Greensboro Daily News,* Aug 13, 1965, p. 8 Sec. A; Jay Jenkins, "You Can't Blame Dr. Fields for Evading Direct Answers," *Charlotte Observer,* Aug. 15, 1965. Copies of articles in SACS Archives.

[55] Emmett B. Fields, Aug. 11, 1965, Speaker Ban Hearings, UNC, 57-8, 60, 78.

[56] Ibid., 67-8.

[57] John P. Dawson, Aug. 12, 1965, Speaker Ban Hearings, UNC, 12-13, 20; Emmett B. Fields, Speaker Ban Hearings, 52.

[58] Emmett B. Fields, Speaker Ban Hearings, 66-7.

[59] Link, 126-27.

Chapter Five

The Increasing Importance of Accreditation

The previous chapters addressed the postwar era's impact on the Association's ongoing role in matters of race and politics in the South, especially its relation to black institutions and to state governments. This chapter explores organizational developments within the Association during this era, linking them to wider debates regarding the future of education and the place in it for regional accreditors such as the Southern Association. The Association's engagement with wider changes in educational practice and philosophy is reflected during this period by the increasing momentum in the commissions' rethinking of their role and methods in encouraging educational improvement in the region's schools and colleges. It can also be seen in its growing participation in cooperative efforts not only to rethink the role of accreditation, but also to deal with challenges—especially the proliferation of accrediting bodies—which, since national in scope, encouraged nationally organized responses. These changes in organizational structure and accrediting aims and methods must also be understood in relation to ongoing conflicts within the Association as to how it could best meet its various education goals. In particular, the perennial debates over how centralized the Association should be or how autonomous the commissions should remain proved a major focus of Association attention in the postwar years. In looking at the specific events and challenges of this period, this chapter nevertheless illuminates two of the broad, recurring themes of the Association's history. One is the impact on the Association's activities of wider educational and social events and pressures. The other is the way in which change, and debates about change, in the Association's organizational structure reflect persisting differences of philosophy and perspective within the Association and its members, as well as the continuing efforts to resolve those differences to an extent sufficient to ensure the continued viability of both the commissions and the Association.

In 1955, Edwin Mims addressed the Southern Association's sixtieth annual gathering in Miami Beach, Florida. Mims was the last surviving participant in the Association's first meeting in Atlanta, and he spoke of the "Six Decades of Southern Education" to which he and the Association had contributed. Mims described watching the Association grow "from an infant crying in the night and with no language but a cry, to a mature

man, with increasing resources and functions, even to a giant, slay-
ing educational, ecclesiastical, and political demagogue" alike.
Now, sixty years on, it had reached the status of "a most powerful
educational association" with significant impact on "the economic and social development of the South." Mims' delight at the
Association's development from infant to giant was not without its
ironies. Its eventual rapid growth after a slow start had been due in
significant part to its admitting the *kinds* of institution that had
hardly been of chief interest to the founders. Of the College
Commission's 281 members in 1955, for example, more than one-
third (95) were junior colleges, while the ranks of the four-year colleges included many of the land grant universities and teacher
training colleges that many of the liberal arts traditionalists had
long viewed with indifference or disdain. An Association that
included no secondary schools at its creation, and mostly private
ones in its early years, now contained a large Secondary
Commission—the majority of whose more than 1,700 members
consisted of public schools. Mims had worried about the
Association's slow growth in its early years and had been more
open than many of his colleagues to enlarging and strengthening
the Association through the development of a more diverse membership. To address hundreds of representatives drawn from more
than 2,000-member institutions must surely have seemed an especially fulfilling experience for this one remaining witness to the
first infant steps of the original six.[1]

In other respects, Mims might well have been struck by how
little had changed over the years. He would no doubt have been
pleased to see that the Association remained, as its founders had
intended, an important forum for the energetic debate of the central questions facing Southern education. Perhaps he would have
been surprised by the extent to which, in their general outlines,
those questions (and the debates they prompted) had remained
unchanged from those which preoccupied the Association in its
early years. Indeed, many of these debates—focused on issues
such as curriculum reform and teacher training—had developed
their modern form around the time of the Association's creation.
Writing in 1955 on the "sharpening educational controversies" of
the postwar era, Lawrence Cremin found it "increasingly clear
that several of the most hotly debated issues in recent educational

discussion stem directly from decisions made during that momen-
tous era" running from the 1890s to 1920. Thus the broad questions of philosophy and practice—regarding such areas as
curricula and pedagogical methods—that dominated education as
the Association began its first half century continued to do so as it
began its second.[2]

Debates among educators also continued to be shaped by the
educational system's relation to the wider society in which it was
embedded. Here again, ideas with their roots in the previous century continued to have a profound impact as America moved into
the second half of the twentieth century. Chief among them was
the belief that education should occupy a central role in preparing
individuals for useful and fulfilling lives in a complex industrial
democracy. Increasingly the "democratizing" corollary of this
belief was that all citizens should have access to a worthwhile
education. Consistently influential throughout the century, faith in
education as an engine of social and democratic progress intensified in the period following World War II, as public expectations
regarding education's potential and responsibility to serve social
and individual ends reached unprecedented levels.

The war had helped to fuel these demands. War had been
hard but America, along with its allies, had proved its strength and
resolve by winning it. Furthermore, America had risen from economic depression to reach ever higher stages of the consumer revolution begun earlier in the century, as new prosperity, new forms
of consumption, and new forms of encouraging consumption
(especially television) took hold on middle America. No force
played a larger role in seeking to meet these rising demands than
the federal government. Thanks in significant part to the GI Bill,
the growing democratization of education (understood as increased
access for increased numbers) apparent throughout most of the
century took a quantitative leap forward in the postwar era. As we
have seen, educational progress was surely, if slowly, being made
by African-Americans. Millions of other American men and
women also emerged from war with their educational expectations
transformed and enlarged. The quantitative increase in postwar
enrollments was so great as to, in effect, bring about a qualitative
transformation of postsecondary education. When the century
began, 239,837 students had participated in higher education. By

mid-century, this number had increased by more than 1,000 percent
to 2,456,841. At the secondary level, the increase over the corresponding period had been almost as rapid. Enrolled secondary students increased in number from 736,000 to 6,533,000. Supply
expanded rapidly to meet this demand. As the Association's Henry
Hill reported in 1950, 75 colleges had been created in the previous
two or three years alone, many of them junior colleges.[3] Thus
many more students than ever before filled the schools, colleges
and universities of America. As a consequence, many more
Americans, not just students, but also parents and family members,
took a closer interest in the educational affairs that loomed larger in
their private lives. It really did seem an era, in Henry Hill's phrase,
of "Higher Education Unlimited."

The GI Bill offered only the most striking evidence for a
major transformation in American life: the expanding role of the
federal government in the nation's education to an extent that
would have been unimaginable to those who labored on behalf of
the Association for most of its first half century. This expanded
role had wider aims than the satisfaction of domestic desire. As
Edwin Mims spoke, the United States had experienced a generation of sustained crisis: from the Great Depression through global
conflict and into a Cold War that few could see ending. The experiences of the preceding decades had shown just the fundamental
importance of economic strength and scientific and technological
progress to social stability and improvement. As domestic
demands grew alongside global tensions, America's leaders
increasingly looked to education to serve a variety of national
interests, from boosting productivity at home to winning technological races in space. Thus the greater expectations and deeper
anxieties of a new age of super powers with nuclear power fueled
the ongoing expansion of Americans' participation in education as
both? consumers? and citizens. From increased parental concern
to foreign policy considerations, from vastly increased student
numbers to the spreading influence of federal power and money,
most signs pointed to how education was being drawn further
toward the center of the nation's public life.

The Southern Association's growing involvement in all levels
of education, in turn, brought it closer to the center of Southern
life. Of the many significant themes and issues of this period, this

chapter will focus on two. The first is the evolution of accreditation, a process that did not begin in the postwar period, but did receive a major impetus in the kind of social environment sketched above. The second, and related, issue is the Association's growing, often troubled, relation to central government as federal politicians and agencies increasingly sought to shape education in ways that brought them into contact and conflict with regional accrediting bodies. The federal government's expanded role in education would create an entire new field of activity and concern for those who did the Association's work in the next half century.

With the greater expectations of politicians and pubic alike came greater scrutiny of those within education charged with meeting them. In 1949, for example, John E. Ivey, director of the Board of Control for the Southern Regional Education Board, began his address to the Association's annual meeting by telling the assembled educators something they doubtless already knew. Ivey reported that Americans had recently been "turning a more critical eye toward their institutions of higher learning," anxious to know what kind of education their children were receiving as well as "what their dollars are buying in the way of creating more competent citizens." Suggesting the widespread nature of these concerns, Ivey noted how recent issues of mass circulation publications like *Time* and *Life* had addressed questions of education's future and its obligations to Americans as individuals and as a society.[4]

Educators breathed in the national atmosphere of anxiety and optimism just as deeply as did their fellow Americans. Ivey, like many others, emphasized the dangerous possibilities of a bewildering new world in which "men, machines and ideas are weaving a crazy quilt" of different cultures "into a new international culture." Continuing concerns and changing circumstances generated a sense of challenge, even crisis, within educational circles. Yet despite their awareness of what Ivey called "the sobering forces play[ing] across our daily lives," many educators remained optimistic that they could meet these challenges and make the improvements in the relations between education and society upon which progress depended. Ivey looked to "a new union" between professional educators and a public ready "to join hands with us if we can help show the way." Indeed the more educators shared their fellow citizens' concerns, the more they seemed strengthened in their convictions that the closer blending of social and educational goals was the key to national advance. For many educators it followed that if education and society were inextricably linked, they themselves should assume more of the responsibilities of social leadership. "Our institutions must become dynamos of democracy," Ivey insisted to his annual meeting audience, adding that the "needed leadership in education" could only come from "those in this room" and their counterparts across the nation. Many Association members listening to Ivey's appeal that day would have agreed that educators should be front and center in the crusade for a better educational system and, it followed, a better society.[5]

For the Association, the general goal of improving education was pursued through the specific inquiry into how the accreditation process might play a larger, more positive role in the broader project. Continuing debate and experimentation over the coming years would eventually bring about a transformation in the accrediting philosophy and practices of the Association. As with most other changes in the Association, however, it resulted from a slow, often cautious, process, as the need to overcome differences and build consensus among diverse constituencies inevitably took time. Changes within were also in part a response to criticisms from without, and these too must be taken into account in charting the evolution of accreditation over the past half century. Thus the eventual transformation was the result of much debate, varied research and numerous piecemeal changes stretching back over many years. The final shape of this transformation, as radical in its own way as the shift to accreditation had been in the 1910s, will be described in the concluding chapter. But first we must look at the pivotal postwar period.

Discussion of how to improve accreditation had been a continuing part of Association life almost as long as accreditation had been. Nevertheless, it was often at its most intense during periods when accreditation was not just under scrutiny from its friends, but under attack from its enemies. Educators committed to accreditation had always been well aware of the skepticism, sometimes outright antagonism, felt toward the whole concept of accreditation. Critics in the educational world and beyond consistently questioned accreditation's current practices as well as its likely contribution to future reforms. This created something of an unwelcome irony for the Southern Association in the period of its rise to regional prominence. The same years that saw the Association steadily increase in size and influence also brought a rising chorus of demands that its activities be reformed, even abolished. At a time when unprecedented demands were being made on educators to take the lead in society, the debate as to whether accrediting associations should have any place in that leadership reached its peak. Inevitably, external (and internal) criticism generated a great deal of anxiety as to the future of accreditation and, in turn, a flurry of activity designed to identify its current problems and to chart a course toward greater effectiveness and significance in the future. Although hardly new, it was in the 1950s that this inspection of the inspectors, as it might be called, helped to precipitate the changes that would eventually lead to the transformation of the Association's philosophy and practice of accreditation. Thus, to understand the Association's activities in this period, it is first necessary to get a sense of the criticisms leveled at accrediting.

Like the educational debates that produced it, the critique of accreditation had been around for some time. In one sense, it began the first time an Association representative or report told an institution something that its administrators or academics did not wish to hear. Inevitable tensions arose when "outsiders" sought to dictate standards to individuals and institutions accustomed to significant autonomy and power. Of course, the people who complained about undue influence and unfair standards had often, voluntarily, helped to expand that influence and develop those standards through their participation in the Association. But as, for example, the furor aroused by the Higher Commission's 1921 approved list suggests, this did not always dampen their lively sense of injustice in their own particular cases. Arguably endemic to any standard-enforcing or law-making endeavor, some level of frustration and resentment was, and continues to be, a perennial feature of relations among the Association, its commissions, individual members and prospective members. It simply comes with the accrediting territory.

Whatever the validity of specific complaints, their persistence suggests something more than just the self-interested grumbling of particular institutions. In total, they point to deeper conflicts and debates regarding educational theory and practice. At the center of concern was the nature and purpose of the standards employed by organizations like the Southern Association. The argument against standards went something like this: Standards were too "quantitative," too focused on the counting of books owned, salaries paid, endowments raised. By making a priority of such things, uniform standards bred "standardized" sameness and a stifling conformity, results that clearly ran counter to the goals of nurturing individuality and creativity that many reformers considered a priority, not only for individual students, but also for institutions. Just as classroom regimentation stifled student development, so too, it was argued, the quantitative standards intrinsic to accreditation did the same to institutions. Thus traditional complaints, heard even before John White butted heads with James Kirkland in 1921, blended with concerns raised about the educational system's ability to respond to the pressures and demands of the atomic age. A changing social context and growing acceptance of new philosophies of education in some ways strengthened what had been a long-standing criticism of accrediting procedures: that they were too tied to quantitative measurement. Criticisms of any effort to formulate or enforce common standards intensified in a social context increasingly obsessed with individualism and an educational ethos in which the personal development of each unique student became an increasingly central goal.

Making matters worse, from the critics' viewpoint, current inspection procedures reinforced the negative consequences of quantitative standards in several ways. Charges of bias against certain kinds of institution, or of favoritism toward members over prospective members, were not uncommon. At the postsecondary level, for example, some members and would-be members felt that the Association operated a de facto double standard. Prospective members were held to the strict letter of the law during a lengthy application and probationary period. Those already "in" frequently received more sympathetic treatment when it came to violations of standards and seldom seemed to face probation, much less expulsion, as a consequence of their failings. Although methods changed somewhat over the years, the inspection procedures at the postsecondary level also reflected a difference in treatment. A prospective member faced several demanding steps. As required in the wake of the 1949 Standards, for example, after its initial application a college would undergo inspection and evaluation by a visiting committee. If it met all the standards, it would then go through a two-year period of provisional membership, during which it would continue to be reviewed through follow-up studies.[6] This arduous membership process contrasted with the relative lack of scrutiny that could be expected once membership had been achieved. Once admitted, an institution still had to submit reports every year on whether it was meeting the standards, but was unlikely to receive further inspection visits *unless* a failure or violation had been revealed.

Considered by some to be unfair to prospective members, a larger problem for many critics was that existing inspection practices provided little incentive for institutions to improve once they had attained accredited status. Despite the best intentions and frequent exhortations of the accreditors, the prevailing inspection regime encouraged institutions to see membership as an end rather than a beginning. Many believed that the absence of consistent scrutiny after admission implicitly encouraged an institution to relax once it had achieved membership. This tendency was strengthened by the Association's policy of not making qualitative distinctions between members, meaning that the prestige of membership was bestowed equally, irrespective of an institution's enthusiasm or indifference regarding further improvement.[7]

Accreditation, then, actively hampered progressive educational change by encouraging conformity by its focus on the materialistic and the quantitative at the expense of the individual and the particular. The inspection processes employed compounded the shortcomings of the standards themselves by giving institutions little incentive to continue improving. Thus mediocrity and conformity were too often the interrelated and unintended consequences of a system intended to promote excellence and encourage improvement in the region's schools and colleges. Accreditation, it seemed, was no longer part of the solution, but a major part of the problem. Thus, demands that education should change in order to serve society better fueled related demands that accreditation should change to serve education better.[8]

Some critics were so convinced of accreditation's malign impact on education that they believed that organizations like the Southern Association could best serve society by immediately disbanding and vowing never to darken a schoolhouse door again.

Needless to say, such views elicited something less than unanimous agreement among accreditors, or indeed among the many educators who appreciated accreditation's benefits. Yet accreditors were neither unaware of the complaints, nor, in many cases, unsympathetic to them. Indeed, often the most searching analyses came from committed accreditors who also accepted the need for reform in order to remain relevant to changing educational aims and ideas. This was true in all regions of the nation. In 1935, for example, the North Central Association (NCA) had become so convinced that the critique of standards was valid that it stopped calling them "standards" as part of wider changes that, according to historian of the NCA, Mark Newman, "transformed accrediting" in that region.[9]

It would be another quarter of a century before similar steps began to transform the aims and practices of the Southern Association. Yet the transformation's character, if not its timing, would be similarly focused on the central issues of standards and inspection. The eventual transformation of the Association's philosophy and practice with regard to these two interrelated priorities would bring more qualitative, individually oriented criteria for assessing each institution's value and progress. It would also bring the adoption of new methods of assessment, the most important of which would be the introduction of continuing self-studies by institutions and periodic visits by Association committees. Taken together, these broad sets of interrelated changes "implied assessment of schools and colleges on how well they met their own objectives," rather than on how well they measured up to a set of universal standards. They also assumed the value of accreditation, adopting methods that encouraged members to make continuous progress rather than to rest, safely accredited, on their laurels.[10]

The Southern Association did not initiate these major changes in the 1930s, but it was involved in the efforts of that period to address the intermingled priorities of improving education and accreditation alike. Like its peers elsewhere, for example, the Association's debates frequently linked questions of accreditation's future to ongoing discussion of curriculum reform where, as Doak Campbell put it in 1937, there existed a "widespread belief" that present programs were "inadequate in a number of respects," especially at the secondary level.[11]

Anyone reading the Association's *Proceedings* for this period would gain sense of the prominence given to the issues of accrediting and curricular reform. The most institutional manifestation of their related significance was the creation in 1935 of the Commission on Curricular Problems and Research. Created in part through the leading efforts of Dean K.J. Hoke of the College of William and Mary and supported financially by the General Education Board of the Rockefeller Foundation, the new commission emerged from the constitutional and organizational changes of the mid-1930s as well as in response to the era's educational debates. It met for the first time in February of 1936 in Atlanta. The commission's purpose was to study "the accrediting policies of this and similar associations," to report on "notable procedures in administering programs of study," and to "stimulate experimentation and report . . . significant trends in either secondary or higher education."[12] The new commission pursued many different inquiries into different areas of educational life, including the administrative costs of junior colleges, college admission policies, high school programs for advanced standing, system-wide evaluation and curriculum development. Among the consequences of these activities was the involvement of many new people in the Association's work and the adoption of new programs by the other commissions.[13] More generally, the new commission's priorities and activities indicate the growing acceptance that the Association should take a more active role in researching how schools and colleges worked, and that it needed to initiate stronger, more consistent, connections with its member institutions.[14]

The new commission also reflected the Association's continued focus on "articulation" between secondary and postsecondary education, a concern also at the center of the new commission's first major project: a "Cooperative Study Between High Schools and Colleges Designed to Develop an Educational Program That Will More Adequately Meet the Needs of Our Adolescent Group." The Southern Study, as it came to be known, was "an experimental project . . . created to explore ways for improving education at the secondary and higher levels" across the region.[15] The Southern Study also reflected the view that the Association needed to take a more active role in educational research, experimentation and reform if it was to maintain its prominent place in educational life. In its introduction, for example, the study's authors acknowledged the criticisms directed at the accrediting process, "especially at the high school level," and also noted the "sporadic efforts" over recent years to improve accreditation. They located the Southern Study among more recent and more comprehensive efforts to pursue the dual priorities of improving education and accreditation.[16]

The philosophies and expectations underpinning the study did indeed share a great deal with wider national trends. Those who conducted the study shared the view that educational advance should be compatible with the needs of America's evolving democracy. As the study's foreword made clear, its method "was accepted on philosophical grounds, as being compatible with our best knowledge of how to solve educational problems . . . consistent with democratic theory."[17] This democratic sensibility is suggested by the words of Doak Campbell in a 1937 discussion of the study's underlying aims and assumptions regarding the improvement of secondary education. According to Campbell, it was "assumed *that the secondary school is obligated to provide educational experiences appropriate to the needs of young people of secondary school age.*" Campbell considered it unacceptable for schools to insist on the adequacy of existing curricula while maintaining "that students who cannot or will not demonstrate achievement according to present standards should be denied the privileges of further work in a secondary school." The underlying message of Campbell's words was that the improvement of secondary education in a democratizing society had to be toward the goal of satisfying the needs and potential of all students, not just those bound for college.[18]

The study reflected the belief that a curriculum capable of meeting the diverse needs of high school students could be arrived at, in Campbell's words, "through a planned program of experimentation and demonstration." The report also recognized what would become a central tenet of almost all subsequent reform efforts: That institutions themselves should take a leading role in their own improvement and, therefore, that "a considerable amount of freedom" should be enjoyed by the participating schools. A related requirement would be that the Association provide "only such supervision and guidance" as was necessary to provide "general direction" and to "make the results usable."

Campbell was adamant that "in no sense is a pre-conceived type of curriculum to be imposed." In terms of the institutions' responsibilities, the experiment presupposed a willingness on their part to take the initiative in both the diagnosis and remedy of their particular problems.[19]

A first step was the selection of a group of secondary schools, through the state committees of the Secondary Commission, willing to conduct experiments with their teachers and students. It was also necessary to gain assurances from the region's colleges that they would accept the graduates of the test schools "without the usual restrictions." This approach was similar to that taken by other groups across the nation. The Eight-Year Study of the Progressive Education Association, for example, begun in 1932, asked "How Can the High School Improve its Service to American Youth?" It also encouraged a group of thirty schools (none from the South) to conduct diverse experiments while asking colleges to waive the usual entrance requirements for their graduates. Applicants needed to meet various requirements beyond a general openness to self-study and experimentation. As well as being Association members, they had to have adequate facilities and a reasonably good record of graduates going on to do well in college. The "understanding and support" of the local community was required, while the chosen schools also had to be "representative of a fairly large group of schools within the region." From 78 applicants, 33 were eventually chosen, representing all states in the Association's area.[20]

Whatever the autonomy of each participating school, general guidance was considered desirable, and the Executive Committee appointed Frank C. Jenkins director of the study in July of 1937. A staff was then put together consisting of people who provided a breadth and depth of relevant experience with Southern institutions and education. After a preparatory period, the active phase of the study began in the spring and summer of 1938. The study ran until 1942, expanding, as it progressed, to include various cooperative studies and workshops devoted to improving teacher education. Thousands of school and college teachers participated in a total of thirty conferences held at colleges and universities across the South and at twenty-four conferences conducted with the cooperation of sixteen county school systems in seven states. Meetings with the state committees of the Secondary Commission sought ways to disseminate as widely as possible the resources and reports generated by the study. The study helped to familiarize participating schools with new methods for identifying areas needing improvement and illuminating the specific ways in which that might be done. All of these efforts fit within the broader aims of achieving extensive institutional and individual participation in the study, and the widest possible subsequent dissemination of any findings that might contribute to the cause of educational improvement in the South.[21] Like studies and research being conducted elsewhere in the nation at this time, the Southern Study reflected the growing influence of a new philosophy of accreditation that demanded more "scientific" research into educational problems, greater recognition of institutional distinctiveness, a more active approach to self-examination on the part of these institutions, and a greater degree of continuing and cooperative contact between institutions and their accreditors.

Also like these other reform efforts, the Southern Study could not be sustained as wartime mobilization absorbed ever greater levels of social and educational energy. The motives and assumptions embodied by the study, nevertheless, remained central to the reform efforts and organizational changes that continued to dominate the Association's activities in the years after the war's end. Change affected all areas of Association life. Within a general consensus that the Association should be open to change, as in the past, there were important differences between individuals and commissions as to how, and how far, change should be pursued. These differences, like others, were often linked to long-standing conflicts of interest and philosophy between secondary and college commissions, and within the college commission, between liberal arts and teachers' college groupings. Members' enthusiasm for innovation also depended on other factors, including their estimation of how much effective change had already occurred and their understanding of the future priorities for education and accreditation.

In general, support for greater change in standards was strongest among those concerned with secondary education or with postsecondary institutions whose priority was vocational, technical or teacher training. When Frank C. Jenkins spoke in 1955 on the "Future Program of the Commission on Secondary Schools," he began by looking back to past periods of radical reconstruction in secondary education. Jenkins recalled the part that the Association and the Secondary Commission had already played in improving the region's secondary education. "This progress" had in turn "helped to pave the way" for "important educational undertakings" that had "placed emphasis on school improvement" and "helped to broaden the concept of accreditation." Jenkins had in mind efforts like the Association's own Southern Study, as well as others conducted at the national level.[22]

Events within the Secondary Commission bear out the importance of national involvement and influences in shaping its approach to the study and introduction of new standards. The most important of these wider studies was the 1933 Cooperative Study of Secondary School Standards. At the time, the authors of the Southern Study had recognized the Cooperative Study's path-breaking importance as the beginning of "a concentrated attack on the problem" of accreditation reform. The Cooperative Study developed from the efforts of the regional associations. As early as 1928, Commission Secretary Joseph Roemer had discussed with colleagues in the rest of the country the possibility of developing new methods of evaluation that placed reduced emphasis on quantitative measurement. Their idea of a cooperative study was well-received by the regional associations who also agreed to give it financial backing, although it was another five years before the study was set up, with representatives from all the regional associations participating. The Southern Association was represented by Roemer, W.R. Smithey, S.B. Tinsley, a school principal from Louisville, Kentucky, and G.R. Wilcox, headmaster of the Darlington School in Rome, Georgia.[23]

A period of testing and revision eventually produced what came to be called the *Evaluative Criteria*, standards that many participants hoped would provide the basis for new accrediting standards for secondary schools. The regional associations proved reluctant to replace their existing standards with the new guidelines, but were more open to using them to assist in evaluating schools' effectiveness. The Secondary Commission of the Association shared this reluctance, but it did establish a plan for using the criteria in evaluating schools. Published shortly before the Southern Study began its work, the *Evaluative Criteria* exerted a strong influence on the Secondary Commission's work long after the study had ended.[24]

Responses to the new criteria were mixed. Despite their creators' willingness to revise the *Criteria* to improve their usefulness to schools, by 1947 their adoption was still less than had been hoped. Two regional associations did not adopt the materials produced by the Cooperative Study at all, while in the other regions their use was recommended rather than mandated. The *Evaluative Criteria* did receive a warmer welcome in the South than in most other areas of the nation. The only association with more schools than the Southern Association using the criteria was the Middle States Association. But even there the figure was only just more than 50 percent by 1947. Use of the criteria was also mixed within the South: good in Virginia, Tennessee and Texas, but limited in the Deep South states of Georgia, Alabama and Louisiana. Commission members' response to the *Evaluative Criteria* indicates that they were not yet prepared to translate their willingness to address problems and consider changes in accreditation into a full-scale rewriting of existing standards and practices.[25]

Yet the Commission was committed to the *Evaluative Criteria* from the beginning. In 1940 it established a Committee on the Use of the *Evaluative Criteria* to study their adoption and use, suggesting the belief that the new evaluation program could at least be an important complement to accreditation. This commitment persisted throughout the decade. In 1947, for example, the Committee on the Use of the *Evaluative Criteria* recommended that all member schools be evaluated by a visiting committee. The same year, the Commission's Committee on Standards reinforced this commitment to ongoing evaluation when it included "low standing as indicated by evaluation using the criteria of the Cooperative Study of Secondary School Standards" among the bases upon which a member could be warned or expelled. As James Stiltner explains, this "amendment effectively tied the evaluation process to the accrediting procedure." As a result, the Southern region became the major consumer of the *Evaluative Criteria*. With the evaluative program "well-established in all Southern states" by 1951, the Committee on the Use of the *Evaluative Criteria* was dissolved in 1953.[26]

The 1950s saw the continuation for the Secondary Commission of an extended period of growth, both in terms of type and number of institution claiming membership. In 1955, it had more than 1,700 members, almost 600 more than twenty years earlier. A

tied evaluation process to accrediting procedure

significant number were private schools and a smaller group was from Latin America, but the great majority of member institutions were drawn from the public school system. Increased membership had not only expanded the size of the Commission but also its visibility and influence within the Association. Its expanded role in the institutional life of the region's schools involved a greater place for research and reform in the interests of better educational methods alongside more traditional accrediting priorities.[27]

The Secondary Commission's support for reform initiatives such as the *Evaluative Criteria* suggests, among other things, its willingness to look across regional boundaries in the search for ideas and allies.[28] If the Commission took a nationwide approach to exploring ways to improve its standards and practices, it also remained resolutely committed to a localized approach to accreditation, leaving a great deal of the responsibility for the formulation, implementation and inspection of standards to individual states, school systems and schools. This commitment to localism had several sources. One was a simple question of numbers. With so many schools in the region, the more centralized inspection processes favored by the Commission on Colleges was not feasible. The Commission's devolved structure also fit with deep-seated commitments to states rights and local control in various areas of social and political life, and the consequent suspicion of outside involvement not firmly in step with local circumstances and values. Another source, in some ways combining practical and philosophical considerations, was the assumption that those most closely involved in a school's life were best placed to identify its problems and its priorities. Thus, a great deal of secondary work was conducted by the state committees and other volunteers at the state and local level, while consistent efforts were made over time to increase local involvement in the work of accreditation and to encourage as much local decision-making as possible. Over the years the Secondary Commission and its state committees have deployed a voluntary army of accreditors willing to give their time, thought and energies to improving the schools of their state and region as well as their own local institutions.

This commitment to localism did not always sit easily with the need to maintain some level of uniformity in the application and measurement of standards. An equally powerful assumption of regional accreditation was, after all, that some broad level of uniformity, if not conformity, was a valuable and necessary means to further the interests of all educational institutions, whatever their particular local circumstances. Thus the search for an acceptable balance between local control and innovation on the one hand and a fair and constructive region-wide framework of standards and inspections, and the tensions sometimes arising from those efforts, on the other hand, have been persistent aspects of the Commission's work over the years.

The persistence of these themes is evident in the changing role of the Commission's Central Reviewing Committees (CRC). Originally there was one CRC. Created in 1928 and made a standing committee in 1931, the CRC was composed of a representative from each of the eleven state committees. The representatives' role on the reviewing committees was to present and, if necessary, defend the accrediting reports prepared in their respective states. As James Stiltner explains, this task "almost dictated" that the state representative to the CRC and "the person who prepared the reports" (usually the chair or executive secretary of the state committee) be the same person. In 1935, for example, nine of the public CRC members were chairmen of their state committee while the other two were representatives of their state's department of education. Yet as members of the CRC, it was also the representatives' responsibility to review the reports from the states and to ensure that they were applying the Commission's standards properly and consistently.[29]

The CRC's pivotal role in the inspection process quickly made it the Commission's most powerful committee. Such was its power that private school members were soon concerned that, as only 15 percent of the total membership, they could be outvoted without difficulty by the dominant public school group. To meet this concern, the Central Reviewing Committee for Private Secondary Schools was created in 1936, after which time the Secondary Commission had two CRCs.[30] By the 1950s, the Commission was also ready to act on concerns that the committees exercised too much power in relation to the state committees; and in 1955 a committee was formed to examine the role and function of the Central Reviewing Committees. The committee's report endorsed an expanded role for the Central Reviewing

Committees in some areas. One of its main conclusions was that the committees should become more than review boards focused on existing standards but also venues for the consideration of possible new standards.[31]

In other respects, the report called for a diminution of the CRCs' role, in particular recommending that the state committees take on "much of the primary regulatory and accreditation function" previously the preserve of the CRCs. Along with this, it called on state committees to involve more people in the work of accreditation and to enlarge their committees on an unofficial basis if that would help to achieve this end. Many state committees did this, increasing the numbers of people involved in the Association's work and to some extent creating a training ground for people who would later become official members of the committees.

Concern for expanding the states' autonomy, nevertheless, existed alongside the wish to preserve some level of regional uniformity in standards. This was evident in the requirement that the newly empowered state committees cooperate with the CRCs to develop "operational procedures" that would assure "conformity" with the Association's "philosophy." Members of the Secondary Commission recognized that whatever its benefits, a devolved state-based accrediting process could make it difficult to apply standards uniformly and fairly across the region.[32] These changes, it was hoped, would go some way to mitigating this problem and maintaining the appropriate influence of the Secondary Commission with state committees. Collectively, it was hoped that these changes would encourage a more informed process for the development of new standards, greater consistency in their application, and a better appreciation of the needs and the interests of the schools themselves.

But concerns persisted that the strong emphasis on the autonomy of the state committees, while advantageous in some respects, meant too much of a diminution of the collective role and influence of the Commission. "By 1970," according to James Stiltner, "the Central Reviewing Committee had practically abdicated their right to question the [accrediting] decisions of state committees." Compounding this concern was the widespread view that in some cases state committees' judgments tended toward an unacceptable leniency when local sympathies won out over the rigorous application of the Commission's standards. The potential for arbitrary or inconsistent application of regionally agreed accrediting standards thus remained a persistent concern. Efforts to balance the interests of the local and the regional, the unique circumstance with the general standard, were inevitably part of the Association's work generally, but took on particular significance in the Commission most committed to local control as well as regional standards. It would continue to be an inevitable characteristic of a Commission respectful of state and local control, yet nevertheless committed to region-wide educational evaluation and improvement.[33]

This period also saw the Association's interests expand geographically as well as philosophically, as contacts with educational institutions in Latin America also developed. In the wake of the 1959 study, a new "at-large" position was created on the Secondary Commission to accommodate a representative from the Latin American Relations Committee. This committee had responsibility for the Commission's role in accrediting various "American" schools throughout Latin America. The Association's contacts with institutions beyond its own region began in 1930 when it accredited the American School Foundation in Mexico City. Over time, increased cooperation and coordination among regional accreditors in the United States clearly assigned particular areas of overseas education with relevance to America to different associations, with the Southern Association eventually counting several dozen "American schools" in Latin American countries such as Mexico and Argentina among its members. The new position for the first time gave representatives of the Latin American institutions a vote in its affairs. This organizational move also reflected, according to its historian, the Secondary Commission's "growing commitment" to its overseas members.[34]

The Commission on Colleges became involved in "extraterritorial" accreditation in the 1940s, but several decades later, and despite various efforts to encourage as well as evaluate educational improvement within the Commission's sphere of Latin American influence, its membership had not increased beyond the two Mexican institutions initially admitted to membership. Methods of financing and administering these institutions proved especially difficult to reconcile with the Commission's standards.

Thus, despite significant enthusiasm among some Commission leaders, especially Gordon Sweet, for greater contacts with Latin American institutions and educators, the Commission's impact on Latin American education remained minimal.[35]

Many other areas of the Commission on Colleges' postwar activities experienced far more significant growth and change. In particular, piecemeal changes in methods and standards took place in a context of intensifying debate on the question of whether a more radical re-ordering of priorities and practices was required. Opinion within the Commission on Colleges was mixed on the need for change along the lines advocated by prevailing views on how accreditation should develop. Many, especially those from a liberal arts background, were cautious, if not skeptical, regarding the claimed benefits of further development toward more qualitative, institution-based, methods of measuring educational improvement.

Resistance to certain changes was rooted in the belief that they were based on criticisms of existing practices that were largely invalid. Many in the Commission acknowledged that, historically, the Commission's standards had a quantitative focus and, indeed, that they still did. But they also insisted that critics neglected certain key reasons why this had been so. One reason, as M.C. Huntley explained in 1955, was that the chaotic and impoverished circumstances of the Association's early work made it "imperative" that, "when patterns of excellence were being set," the Association's emphasis be placed on encouraging basic improvements in faculty, facilities and funding.[36] Thus it was inappropriate to draw a simplistic line between quantitative and qualitative standards. It was more accurate to view quantitative standards as one means by which progress toward qualitative goals could be measured and encouraged. Indeed the very success of "quantitative" standards in bringing institutions to a minimum level of material achievement had contributed significantly to the circumstances in which so many critics could confidently argue that such standards had outlived their usefulness and now presented a barrier to further progress. The irony, it can be assumed, did not escape people like Huntley.

Defenders of existing practices also argued that the critics took insufficient account of how existing practices did allow for the kinds of informal, individual forms of encouragement that

critics argued were lacking. A familiar argument, it was made by
L.H. Hubbard, chairman of the College Commission, in 1949
when he suggested that complaints about the Commission's leniency toward members rested in part on ignorance of its preference for
quieter methods of persuasion—such as warning letters—which,
Hubbard insisted, often proved sufficient to secure the necessary
improvement.[37] M.C. Huntley also argued that critics who carica-
tured the hard-line conformist nature of the standards forgot some
important factors in the accrediting process that mitigated somewhat its generally quantitative emphasis. One was the standard,
admittedly "truly somewhat vague," that directed the Commission
to take account of "the spirit and tone of an institution." Another
was the extensive contacts, informal as well as formal, that the
Commission's officers and volunteers had "with administration,
faculty, students, alumni, and friends" of member institutions.
Through such encounters, he argued, the Commission's representatives were able to "secure an overall understanding that cannot be
reflected in quantitative Standards or written reports." "Judgments
so secured," he insisted, "are as important as measurement of a
college through application of the Standards."[38]

Another source of caution was the sense that many reforms
proposed in the name of progress threatened the position of the
liberal arts tradition in the educational system and, therefore, of its
defenders within the Association. Many advocates of change were
indeed frankly antagonistic to what they saw as an elitist tradition
increasingly irrelevant to modern social and economic circumstances. Even moderate demands that education be made more
"democratic" or more "relevant" at the very least called for a significant re-ordering of academic priorities that would greatly
reduce the role of liberal arts subjects and institutions at both the
secondary and postsecondary levels. Defenders of the liberal arts
tradition within the College Commission shared, therefore, the
caution and resistance of predecessors who had been reluctant to
relinquish the primacy of liberal arts in education or the dominance of its representatives within the Association.

Yet those predecessors had also been prepared to change and
compromise when circumstances demanded. Thus, Commission
members could counter calls for more change by pointing to how
much significant change had already taken place over the preceding

years in response to the nation's changing educational demands. As he looked to the future in 1955, M.C. Huntley saw the College Commission as evolving out of a progressive past in which standards had "been kept fluid, and in accord with the times."[39] The preceding decades had indeed seen incremental, sometimes significant, change in standards. The years between the 1930s and the 1950s were punctuated by debate and revision of the two sets of standards established in 1925 for colleges and teacher training colleges on the one hand, and for junior colleges on the other. In 1939, for example, the standard specifying the number of departments a college should have was eliminated and several others were changed and consolidated. The following year saw similar alterations to the junior college standards, while a new standard relating to extension and correspondence courses was introduced in 1942.[40] In 1949 a special committee formed to revise all the standards, taking into account the advice of other committees of the Commission, recommended further changes in the Standards for Colleges of Arts and Sciences and Teacher Training Colleges that were approved the following year.

The Commission's developing role in research and accreditation also brought a greater willingness to allow institutional experimentation. For example, new standards were devised in the 1950s for off-campus education offered at locations such as military bases. Symptomatic of the new age, part of the research in this regard concerned the usefulness of television as an educational tool. More significant, after much debate and no little conflict, a compromise agreement on new standards for graduate education was eventually reached early in the decade. These standards allowed institutions with experience in graduate instruction to conduct, with prior Executive Council approval, experimental programs not necessarily in accord with the standards. In 1957 the standards for junior colleges, whose enrollments and budgets had greatly increased, also underwent significant upgrading in the areas of enrollment, financial support and expenditures on libraries and instruction.[41]

Some of the changes of these years did reflect an uneasiness with the prevailing emphasis on quantitative standards, and some willingness to move toward more qualitative measurements. In 1949, for example, the specification of the minimum number of volumes an institution's library had to contain was removed from the new standard on libraries, to be replaced by a judgment as to whether the holdings were large enough to meet the needs of the institution's particular programs. Yet the removal of this quantitative measurement was accompanied by the addition of another new standard, which specified a minimum level of annual expenditure on books that institutions had to meet. This example nicely illustrates the cautious blend of willingness to change and attachment to familiar practices that characterized much of the Commission's attitude toward its standards.[42] As the 1950s began, commitment to existing kinds of standards still outweighed support for a more qualitative approach.[43] While Huntley was correct to point to the important changes of the preceding years, the development of the Commission's aims and methods had not been quite as fluid as he suggested, at least when it came to the philosophical over the procedural. Instead, change had taken the form of the "piecemeal" revision of postsecondary standards, more in response to specific changes in circumstance (the expansion of programs, for example) than in obedience to a comprehensive commitment to rethinking the Commission's mission or overhauling its practices. By and large, as Jack Allen concludes, the standards of the 1950s "remained philosophically unchanged" from those of the 1920s.[44]

Nevertheless, the 1950s did see the beginnings of a transformation in the entire Association's approach to accrediting. In a pattern common to other major issues in the Association's history generally, growing acceptance of eventual change co-existed with persisting resistance to change taking place immediately. Increasingly, however, debate was no longer focused on *whether* fundamental reform was necessary, but on *when* it should happen. M.C. Huntley, for example, acknowledged the "increasing pressure" for new methods of evaluation, especially from the land grant colleges, while studies of these matters requested by the Committees on Junior Colleges and on Standards and Reports were approved.[45] These sources of "pressure" perhaps suggest some of the traditional distinctions between the liberal arts group and the representatives of other postsecondary institutions when it came to enthusiasm for change. Yet even those who defended the value of quantitative standards had grown more amenable to the

222

idea of more significant future changes in the aims and practices of accreditation. M.C. Huntley, for one, allowed that there might be some truth to the complaints that "undue emphasis" had been placed on quantitative standards, and thought it "possible" that "qualitative criteria" might be developed in the future, and that the adoption of periodic visits and an "institution-wide approach" to accrediting might prove to "be the best plan for coordinating all accreditation, both academic and professional."[46]

This view proved increasingly influential in shaping the Commission's policies and practices. In 1956, for example, Donald Agnew, executive secretary at the time, proposed a system in which each institution would provide a full report every five years and receive an inspection visit every ten, the timing to be based on the year the institution became a member. Where appropriate, these visits would take place in conjunction with visits from professional accrediting bodies, thereby streamlining the accrediting process and mitigating complaints that the accrediting process had become an unacceptable imposition on institutions' time and energies. Agnew's suggestions helped to prompt the Commission's authorization of new accrediting procedures that included periodic visitations. In 1958, Dean Elford Morgan of Converse College, the Higher Commission's chair, resigned that post to become the director of the Self-Study and Periodic Visitation Program.[47]

As part of this new program, seven invited institutions conducted self-studies in 1958, guided by a Brief Manual of Suggestions for Institutional Evaluation produced the previous year by sub-committees of the Committee on Standards and Reports. After submitting the findings of these self-studies to the Higher Commission, the participating institutions received a visit from an evaluating committee made up of administrators and faculty from other member institutions. The committee's report provided the basis for deciding whether accreditation should be continued. The proposed changes aroused enthusiasm among member institutions, perhaps indicating their dissatisfaction with earlier standards and methods of inspection. The number of volunteers for the 1958 self-study had been many more than could be accepted; and by the time the first studies had been completed in 1959, thirty more colleges and universities had begun a similar examination. [48]

The success of the pilot study and the enthusiasm of those

seeking to participate in it convinced the Commission's leaders of its importance. Executive Secretary Gordon Sweet acknowledged its potentially great importance, and Commission Chairman Henry King Stanford also hailed the "increasing vitality" he found in the work of the Commission. Stanford supported the new program as a necessary break with past ways of doing things. "Skeletons in administrative closets from the Potomac to the Rio Grande are rattling in a lively dance macabre," as he vividly described its consequences, with "musical accompaniment" provided by "the sound of [the] splitting ice of faculty complacency" as the re-evaluation of their programs and practices required academics and administrators alike to find a "better justification for existing procedures than that they have always done it this way." Slowly but surely momentum was building toward new methods of accrediting that emphasized more qualitative standards, greater self-study on the part of each institution and periodic visits conducted by the Commission.[49]

Much of the momentum for change grew out of the experiences of members and from their inquiries into the benefits and drawbacks of applying new ideas to Southern education that went on within the Association. As in other periods of fundamental change, however, events beyond the Association and beyond the South also proved significant in building a consensus in favor of fundamental change. Perhaps the most crucial national impetus behind the Association's growing willingness to change its methods and expand its role as an accrediting body was the proliferation of other accrediting bodies. The diversity of educational options and institutions, especially in the postwar period, had brought forth a plethora of accrediting organizations. Charles Friley, president of Iowa State College, described how the accreditation "movement" had "spread so rapidly" that it now included bodies for all kinds of groups, from doctors and dentists to social workers and journalists; indeed "just about every major field in higher education is included, except agriculture and home economics," and in Friley's opinion, "it is not at all clear that they will remain immune." Friley acknowledged the "high-minded" motives of creators of these bodies, as well as what he believed were the "reasonably satisfactory results" often achieved by the expansion of accreditation.[50]

Yet Friley also recognized the "gathering storm of criticism" surrounding many of these new bodies. Like many others, he attributed this growing disaffection to "the conviction of college people that control of their institutions is being surrendered to these outside bodies." Large institutions especially, with numerous programs and several professional schools, could feel besieged by the diverse platoons of inspectors that seemed to have become a permanent, and demanding, feature of institutional life. Thus the conflict and resentment inherent in any system of inspection was multiplied. A nationwide problem, proliferation brought forth nationally organized efforts to deal with it. In 1949 the National Commission on Accrediting was created to represent the interests of college and university presidents. There was widespread agreement within the Southern Association on the need to cut back this kudzu-like growth of accrediting agencies. "No one can quarrel with the idea of reducing the number of national accrediting or quasi-accrediting agencies in this country," Felix Robb stated in 1952, assuming unanimous assent for the view that "200 is too many." In general Association members worried that proliferation, if unchecked, would generate the kinds of disorder and lack of articulation that accreditation was originally intended to end.[51]

There was no unanimity on what was to be done about the situation. Opinions differed on which of the new bodies were useful and which were superfluous. Many agreed, for example, on the desirability of separate accrediting bodies for professional schools such as law and medicine. A body such as the American Association of Colleges for Teacher Education aroused more mixed feelings. Felix Robb, for example, welcomed the presence of an accrediting body that, from his "teachers' college" perspective, filled some of the gaps left by the College Commission's emphasis on the liberal arts component of institutions such as state universities or teachers' colleges. Some of the steps taken by others to resolve the problem could also arouse suspicion. Many members, for example, were skeptical regarding the motives of the National Commission on Accrediting. The new organization disavowed any desire to become an overarching accrediting body in its own right. In fact its program called for the regional associations to expand their accrediting role to include professional schools and special purpose institutions. But many shared Felix Robb's skepticism, expressed at the 1952 annual meeting, regarding the new organization's denial of any desire to become a super-accrediting body. This somewhat cautious, turf-conscious response to the National Commission's initiative did not diminish the sense that reform was necessary, and both sentiments were evident in the resolution passed at the Association's 1952 meeting. The resolution commended "the stated purposes" of the new organization, "especially the policy of looking to the regional associations to bear the major burden of accrediting." As one might expect, the Association also welcomed the new body's "avowed intention . . . not to act as a super-accrediting body with concentrated control of accrediting at the national level."[52]

Whatever the skepticism regarding the National Commission, there was growing acceptance of the logic of its appeal. Simply put, its underlying assumption was that if the regional associations did not expand their responsibilities into developing educational areas, other bodies would step into the vacuum. In 1950, for example, Chairman of the Higher Commission L.H. Hubbard had warned that if the Association could not "develop an adequate means of evaluating graduate work, some other agency or agencies will do so."[53] The accreditation of graduate programs proved to be a highly contentious issue, bringing out many differences between the "liberal arts" and the "teachers' college" groups before it was settled. But this internal conflict, nevertheless, took place in the context of a shared concern about preserving the Association's accrediting preeminence, a concern that proved to be a factor in encouraging those involved to reach a compromise on that divisive issue.[54]

The proliferation of accrediting bodies also encouraged an increasingly sympathetic response to the growing number of vocational and technical institutions requesting that the Association take responsibility for their accreditation. The concern that someone else would take on the task if the Association did not again proved a spur to action, as did the concern that if other accrediting bodies did step in there was no guarantee they would share the Commission's strong emphasis on the liberal arts.[55] More generally, as other agencies took responsibility for accrediting what were becoming large and important areas of the region's education, many of the Association's members feared that not only would its

influence over many individual institutions be lost, but its ability to
shape the values and priorities of Southern education in general
would be significantly diminished.

The nationwide problems facing accreditation strengthened
the general feeling that significant change had to come. At the
same time, however, the national scope of the challenge encouraged caution, as many doubted that reform could be effective
unless it was the product of careful planning and coordination at
the national level. The 1952 resolution, for example, qualified the
Association's willingness to work toward change with the hope
that "the time schedules for effectuating final arrangements can be
kept flexible so that maximum cooperation can ensue."[56] Time
was needed for several reasons. For one, it was necessary, as the
resolution also made clear, to gain the cooperation of the national
professional accrediting agencies whose legitimacy and usefulness
most regional accreditors recognized. Conversely, it would take
time to build the levels of cooperation and resolve required to
exclude bodies considered superfluous to a simpler, more coherent
accrediting system. The Commission on Colleges' desire for
greater cooperation with its counterparts in the rest of the country
is reflected in its participation in the National Committee of
Regional Accrediting Agencies (NCRAA), formed in 1949 by the
regional Higher Commissions.[57]

Association members' awareness of wider problems such as
the proliferation of accrediting agencies and their willingness to
cooperate in national efforts to deal with them meshed with
debates and experiments aimed at improving their own accrediting
aims and methods. The aims of both the NCRAA and the
National Commission on Accrediting reflected the growing commitment of the nation's accreditors to more qualitative standards
as well as to new forms of institutional evaluation. The NCRAA's
statement of principle read like a summary of the latest thinking
on accreditation, endorsing the introduction of qualitative standards, institutional self-studies and periodic visits, all to the end of
stimulating institutions' continuous improvement in seeking to fulfill their particular missions.[58] These aims continued to win support and encourage action within the Southern Association.

Despite the not insignificant changes of this period, neither
the Association in general nor the commissions in particular could

be said to have undergone a radical transformation. Change
remained piecemeal. Growing acceptance of the need for change,
even agreement as to what change should consist of, had not yet
brought about a full-scale re-directing of accrediting aims and
energies. Acceptance of change did not eradicate anxieties about
its eventual consequences, nor did it always alleviate concerns
about the persistence of the problems that prompted calls for
change in the first place. In particular, the feeling that the fundamental question of the Association's role in the future development of an increasingly diverse and complicated educational
world remained to be settled. The commissions and the
Association were changing, but perhaps doing so too much in
response to wider circumstances, not enough in ways that would
establish regional accreditation as a force in deciding the pace and
path of future reforms. Not surprisingly, this contributed to a sense
of drift and indirection in the 1950s that had in some ways deepened in the years since the end of the war.

Given the combined impetus of the times—practical, philosophical, social and organizational—it was perhaps not surprising
that the Association decided to perform its own self-study as part of
its effort to deal with wider change. Calls for such a study had been
building for several years and for various reasons. Despite the
changes that had taken place in policies and procedures, a sense of
"discouragement," as the study's eventual report put it, had lingered
"in the air" as members faced "many loose ends" in their work.
The persistence of "unsettled matters needing study and decision"
had been, it was explained, "severely restrictive of the usefulness
and vitality of the Association." And as Rufus Harris remembered
in 1960, the Association had also felt the widespread "anxiety"
engendered by the intensity of national debates regarding education
and society. Harris had received "ceaseless entreaty from every part
of the South to lead our associational activities to wider endeavor
and to more effective organization." This "resounding demand"
that the Association "re-examine its operational areas and re-fash-
ion its procedures," Harris believed, "was an inevitable sequel to
changing conditions, which brought into bold outline the imbal-
ances in our political, educational, and economic systems." Harris
thus linked change within the Association to changes in the South's
social circumstances, as well as to altered attitudes regarding the

aims of accreditation. Thus, despite the significant growth and
change of the period since World War II, these various developments and events in the wider world of American education and
society had encouraged a certain sense of drift, of anxiety regarding the Association's future direction. It was hoped that a full self-
study would address and resolve many of these concerns. As
president in 1958, Harris had received approval for a committee to
be formed to that end, under the chairmanship of James M.
Godard. In 1959 another committee, led by Hugh McEniry of
Stetson University, was formed to translate the recommendations
of the Godard committee's report into a new Constitution. Sent to
the members in 1960, discussed in 1961, the new Constitution was
approved in 1962.[59]

The lack of a definite sense of organizational direction and
purpose, and the resulting calls for a major self-study, was also
rooted in internal conflicts and concerns that also need to be
explored. The focal point of much of this internal debate and disagreement was the question of whether the Association should
develop a more centralized organizational structure, or whether it
should remain more of an "umbrella" organization that linked
the commissions in matters of mutual concern while leaving them
largely autonomous in the conduct of their own affairs: especially
accreditation itself. This was not a new debate. As the Association
had grown over the decades, so too had calls for it to develop a
more centralized organizational structure, calls made for both
practical and philosophical reasons. Toward this end, the idea of
establishing a central office had been raised in the late 1930s but
not pursued, partly for financial reasons and partly because the
developing international crisis seemed an inappropriate context in
which to make such major decisions. The proposal was made
again after the war and eventually acted upon. Approved in 1948,
the office was opened in July of the following year with Secretary-
Treasurer A.J. Geiger and one secretary sharing a small office
space in downtown Atlanta.[60]

Approval for a central office was not unanimous. A significant
degree of skepticism existed within both the Secondary and
College commissions as to its necessity. Resistance was partly a
consequence of the commissions' own quite limited organizational
structures. The College Commission did not employ its first paid

full-time executive secretary until 1930. M.C. Huntley, who occupied the position from then until 1949, operated from an office on the campuses of Birmingham-Southern and, later, the University of Alabama. The College Commission funded this full-time position from its own income, derived largely from institutional dues. In the immediate postwar period, the Commission on Colleges moved its office from Birmingham to Atlanta, coinciding with the election of James Godard to succeed Huntley as executive secretary. The Secondary Commission had historically taken a very decentralized approach to the theory and practice of secondary accreditation. It did not establish an executive secretary position until almost a quarter of a century after the College Commission. Prior to that time, the secretary's position was filled on a voluntary basis. A prodigious amount of the work was done by just two educators: Joseph Roemer from 1921-1935 and Frank C. Jenkins from 1936-1954. Roemer had bases at the University of Florida and later George Peabody College, while Jenkins began his service at the Mississippi State Department of Education before moving to Millsaps College in Mississippi. In this period the Secondary Commission disbursed an amount similar to the College Commission's expenditure on its full-time position among the various state committees.

Educators like Roemer and Jenkins were among the more visible examples of the widespread voluntarism that characterized most of the work done by both commissions. Raymond G. Wilson, the Secondary Commission's first full-time executive secretary, described his commission's tradition of "dedicated service" on the part of volunteers, "heavy reliance" on state committees and a "strong commitment to the grassroots approach" when it came to making decisions. This tradition partly explains why the Secondary Commission was "much slower" than the Commission on Colleges to appoint an executive secretary. It eventually did so, however, appointing Wilson in 1954. Despite this important acknowledgment of expanding responsibilities and workloads, the Secondary Commission's commitment to localism and decentralization remained strong, as indeed it does to the present day.[61] For a variety of reasons, including its far smaller membership, the College Commission's structure was not centered around state-level activities, but it was as strongly committed as its secondary counterpart to its own autonomy. At first, therefore, it was not clear that the commissions would join the secretary-treasurer in a centralized location.[62]

Nevertheless, both commissions did eventually establish their own offices at the same location as the Association's central office, a change of heart that indicated the strength of the practical and logistical reasons for doing so. For one thing, there was a recognition that the Association's growth had brought a corresponding increase in work and responsibility that was too much to ask of even the most committed volunteers, most of whom held demanding full-time positions as educators and administrators. There was also a sense that the Association's growth required a more orderly and efficient organizational structure. With different committees and commissions operating out of different places, the Association was "scattered" across the South in a variety of institutions prepared to give it space. Records as well as people were "scattered," making their collection and storage difficult. This was a matter of increasing concern as the Association grew in complexity and importance. These arguments were reinforced by the growing sense among those institutions that had given the Association space and assistance that it was time for them to establish their own headquarters. "We began to run into a situation," Albert Geiger recalled, "where institutions that were more or less carrying us along felt it was about time for the Southern Association to walk." Geiger believed that "a lot of people in the Association felt the same way." As Wilson later acknowledged, "the advantages of Atlanta as a center for reaching out over the South," as well as the opportunity it afforded "for greater coordination of all services," finally convinced the two commissions that they should set up house at the central office. In 1951 the College Commission moved into the central office, located by that time on Peachtree Street in Atlanta. The Secondary Commission moved in three years later.[63]

Recognition of the practical reasons for establishing a central office by no means indicated a similar consensus in favor of the philosophical assumptions that underpinned support for greater centralization and coordination within the Association. How much authority the Association should have to speak for all commissions and members remained a live issue. As Geiger later described it, the commissions had come together "physically speaking," but only after a long period of operating "in separate locations as far as any headquarters, if any, were concerned." This physical distance reinforced a sense of separate identity and autonomy that hardly encouraged the kind of "group thinking" Geiger considered necessary to consider how the commissions "might work more as a unit without actually giving up any of the autonomy of responsibility with which they were charged." Geiger agreed with Kirby Walker that the situation was analogous to a building inhabited by "tenants" rather than "a family."[64]

Resistance to greater centralization did not indicate a blanket opposition to cooperation or collective action. Obviously there were many within each commission who favored greater centralization to some degree. And there was general endorsement within the established commissions of their role in providing financial support for the Association and the two new commissions, something they did "very generously," according to William McEniry, himself a proponent of greater centralization. But as McEniry added, they did so "all the time insisting on their autonomy."[65] In some respects, divisions of this kind increased in the period after 1954. Symbolic of the strain and suspicion were the difference that soon developed between Wilson and Geiger over office protocol and responsibilities. Both commissions remained strongly committed to preserving the autonomy and enhancing the influence they built up over the years. Conversely, supporters of greater centralization continued to consider the proponents of commission autonomy too rigidly attached to their own prerogative and priorities.

The following years brought various efforts to lessen conflict and to create a system that would allow for continued autonomy and greater centralization. Support for the idea that the Association should at least present a collective, united front to the educational world grew out of the same awareness of the great changes and challenges facing accreditors that had prompted calls for greater cooperation between different accrediting organizations. The Association's 1959 self-study, called for by Rufus Harris, Association president in 1957-58, addressed this question, along with other issues, including the developing relation to elementary education and the continuing changes in the accrediting aims and practices of the College and Secondary commissions. As was often the case, efforts to find a way forward involved informal discussion as well as formal changes to the constitution and by-laws governing

the Association. A.J. Geiger recalled how a strong element of the
Study Committee had been the bringing together of many different
people "to sit down and discuss and get to know each other better
and have the other group understand their program better."[66] The
self-study also set in motion more programmatic and permanent
efforts to reach a modus vivendi between centralization and autonomy in the form of changes to the constitution and the by-laws.

William McEniry recalled how for those, like him, who
believed the Southern Association should be more "an association
of members" than "a federation of commissions," the "whole
effort in rewriting the constitution and by-laws . . . was to make it
possible for the Southern Association to become an Association
in fact as well as in name." For McEniry, organizational change of
this kind was in keeping with a philosophy of education that
emphasized the "cradle to grave education" of the individual and
the development of a sufficiently diverse and flexible educational
system to meet that demand.[67] One important change designed to
encourage this shift was the creation of the new position of executive director of the Association. The new proposals "provide[d]
constitutional authority" for the new director "and his functions" in
the hope, as James Godard, who chaired the self-study, expressed
it, of giving some needed "central visibility" to the work of the
Association. But the proposals also affirmed the value of "preserving the autonomy of the Commissions in the matter of accrediting," thus also recognizing that the Association was "to a degree a
federation" and needed "to be regarded as such."[68] Those who
favored continued autonomy for the commissions were assured
that the creation of a central office under a director would not
impinge on their responsibilities or independence, especially with
regard to accreditation. As Godard put it, "it was not a line relationship," with the commissions' executive secretaries reporting to
the director of the Association, "except in matters of budget or
broad issues concerning the Association." Changes, and the
responses to them, suggest the continuing need to navigate careful-
ly between the competing demands of autonomy and association.

Many remained unconvinced. Henry King Stanford memorably expressed the continuing skepticism that he and others felt
about centralization. He noted how "the proposed new director of
the Association is told to coordinate the work of the Commissions

charged with accreditive responsibilities." At the same time, "the Commissions are told in an explanatory note that the director will act without in any way denigrating the accreditation functions of the two Commissions and without intruding upon their autonomy in this highly important area." These two aims "pose[d] a dilemma" for Stanford, summarized in the question, "How do you coordinate autonomy?" Stanford's words encapsulated the challenge presented by centralization: How to bring greater coherence to a growing, expanding organization that was, after all, an "association," while at the same time preserving the independence of the commissions that had developed over the years as a consequence of various differences of philosophy, practice and priority.[69]

It seems that members like Stanford found it difficult to get a clear answer to their questions. William McEniry, who chaired the committee that drew up the new constitution, recalled debates in which people would complain, "but you haven't spelled it out." McEniry frankly admitted that the changes contained "various ambiguities," but from his point of view they were constructive ones since they allowed for progress toward a more unified Association. The supporters of change believed that "if we spelled it out, we would never get it passed," and so they focused on setting up a "framework" in which a "second round" of debates "could take place with some possibility of the Association being born." Their approach seemed to work since the document finally passed with "amazing ease." Yet, as McEniry understood, this was largely due to opponents of centralization "recogniz[ing] that the battle was still not joined," and that their "conception of confederation" would not be directly threatened until that "second round."[70]

Further constitutional changes followed a pattern of seeking to formalize a more centralized organization structure for the Association while preserving the autonomy of its constituent parts. Perhaps of greatest significance was the creation of Delegate Assemblies for both the Secondary and College commissions. The head of each member institution became a member of the Assembly. This body, as well as selecting commission members, electing officials and establishing the dues that member institutions should pay, assumed final responsibility for accreditation. These changes strengthened each commission's independence in accrediting matters relating to its own members and mitigated

fears that decisions taken within the commissions might be over-
ridden by the Association acting as a whole. It also had the effect
of encouraging greater participation on the part of member institutions. The membership of the Association's Executive
Committee was also increased in this period to allow for fuller
representation of all the commissions. The revised constitution
also provided for a Joint Council of the commissions comprised of
the chairpersons and executive secretaries of each commission as
well as the executive director, president and president-elect of the
Association. Designed to consider questions of cross-commission
importance, the Council's creation was a further reflection of the
wish to have, and be seen to have, equal representation in the conduct of the Association's business.[71]

Frank G. Dickey, president of the University of Kentucky,
became the first executive director in July of 1963. At that year's
annual meeting, Dickey frankly acknowledged the "differences"
and "grievances" evident within the Association, but expressed the
"profound faith that we can solve these problems." Dickey occupied the office until 1965, when he left to become director of the
National Commission on Accrediting. A brief interregnum saw
Donald Agnew hold the post of acting director until July of 1966,
before Felix Robb, president of George Peabody College for
Teachers, took up the post of executive director.[72] Debate over the
precise responsibilities that should fall to the executive director,
and over the question of whether such a position was even necessary, remained a feature of Association life and work in the coming
years, eventually to be resolved in favor of those who questioned its
necessity. Efforts to smooth relations and increase cooperation
between commissions also continued. The desire for further cooperation was evident, for example, in a new by-law establishing an
Administrative Council of the Association. Composed of the director of the Association, the executive secretaries of the commissions, as well as the director of the Educational Improvement
Program, the Council's aim was to introduce greater coordination
and cooperation between the various commissions' executive staffs
in the cause of advancing the Association as a whole.[73]

Preoccupation with internal struggles did not prevent continued changes within the Association and the commissions designed
to move ever further toward accrediting methods better intended to

serve the cause of educational improvement and, therefore, more likely to preserve the Association's influence and significance in Southern education. One major institutional change came in June of 1963, when the Association was granted a Charter of Incorporation by the Fulton County Superior Court in Georgia. Incorporation came about from the desire, in an increasingly litigious educational environment, to limit the legal liability of the Association and its officers. The Association would still be open to suits as a corporate body, but incorporation did provide officers and individual members with a degree of immunity from lawsuits arising from the Association's activities. Incorporated status had also become necessary to the Association's efforts to compete for funding from foundations, most of which were legally bound not to make grants to unincorporated organizations. The change to the "Southern Association of Colleges and Schools, Inc." meant that the Association's Executive Committee became the Board of Trustees. This change in the Association's status was somewhat ironic given the ongoing battle over the question of how centralized an organization the Association should be. Incorporation brought a level of centralization in law that many would have found unacceptable in practice. As William McEniry pointed out, "The Board of Trustees is the Southern Association. They own its property, they own its bank accounts, they alone are entitled to the name, and there we are, but we sort of backed into it." But as McEniry also pointed out, although the Association had become "an incorporated body with a Board of Trustees which has total authority," it still was composed of "four commissions, not one of which is really prepared to allow that authority." As McEniry suggests, then, this change brought little practical variance to the everyday policies and operation of the Association.[74]

Internal conflicts do not appear to have presented a barrier to significant growth in the Association's membership. During the decade of the 1960s, the Association's total membership doubled.[75] The Secondary Commission almost equaled its greatest decade of previous growth with 716 new members, while the Commission on Colleges added 144 new members by 1969, more than in any previous single decade. Many of the new members of the Commission on Colleges were two-year institutions, and by 1971 they made up 41.6 percent of the Commission's member institutions. Between 1966 and 1971 alone, accredited two-year colleges increased from 143 to 251.[76]

This significant growth was part of the ongoing pattern of change that characterized both commissions in the 1960s and 1970s. This period saw a great deal of further development in the Secondary Commission's personnel, organization and aims. Raymond Wilson retired as executive secretary in 1970. He was replaced by W.R. Goodson of Texas. Goodson had previously been the first person to occupy the position of associate executive secretary, a second full-time position created by the Commission in 1967. Joseph Johnston of North Carolina stepped into Goodson's position and succeeded him again as executive secretary when Goodson retired in 1977. Johnston was a past president of the Association and had also spent three years as Commission chairman. He supported the Commission's continued efforts to develop a more qualitative approach to evaluation and accreditation, along with greater use of educational research in formulating standards.[77] While efforts to develop research-based standards bore little fruit, the Commission did continue to work, through forums such as summer meetings and the new Committee on Standards and Policies, toward more qualitative approaches to accreditation. The Committee on Standards and Policies, which contained a representative from each state committee, proved to be a driving force behind the "massive revision of policies and standards" instituted in 1976.

The Commission on Colleges' gradual movement toward periodic visits, self-evaluation and a more qualitative approach further strengthened the case for corresponding reforms of its standards to bring them up to date with changes in various areas of college life, such as graduation requirements and student-teacher ratios. Approved at the 1962 annual meeting, the new standards reinforced the evolving emphasis on continuous improvement and on methods of evaluation likely to encourage progress along those lines. An introductory section on the "Principles and Philosophy of the College Delegate Assembly in Accrediting" was to carry weight equal to that of the standards themselves. Furthermore, each standard came in two parts, the first of which provided "a generally qualitative statement of principles for evaluating quality," while the second consisted of "illustrations and interpretations" of "norms or benchmarks for various types of institutions." Each institution was now required to have "a well-developed . . . statement of purpose" and to offer educational programs "designed to achieve the stated purpose." This statement of purpose would, in turn, be the basis for evaluating its success or otherwise in meeting the other standards. Inevitably, the transition to new standards brought its share of problems and confusions, prompting further revisions in the light of members' questions and complaints. Member institutions were nevertheless expected to reach full compliance with the new standards by 1966. By 1965, 220 institutions had completed the Institutional Self-Study and Periodic Visitation Program. After an extensive study conducted by Dr. Sidney French of the University of South Florida concluded that it was working very successfully, a decision was made to retain the program permanently.[78]

The College Commission continued its work with historically black institutions, sometimes in the context of wider Association activities. The Clearinghouse Project, supported by a Ford Foundation grant of $60,000 and begun in February of 1968, saw the Association embark on "a three-year program to collect, analyze, and disseminate information about projects, programs and activities designed to assist predominantly black colleges" in areas such as the training of black educators for participation in the newly-integrated accreditation process. Generous grants from the Carnegie Corporation funded a "Special Studies Program" aimed at helping those historically black colleges and universities faced with problems arising from their transition to full participation in the accrediting system of the South. The program was initially directed by Gordon Sweet, a veteran of the Association's growing participation in black education. Sweet was succeeded by black educators Eldridge Scales in 1968 and Joffre Whisenton the following year.[79] In 1971 Dr. Whisenton described how these "challenging" but "rewarding" efforts had resulted in "new confidence, the facing of reality, penetrating self-analysis, clarification of purpose, reorganization of administration, and improvement of instructional programs." With further Carnegie funding, this project carried on into the 1970s.[80]

The Association's expanding involvement in the education of black Southerners, reflected in programs like the Clearinghouse

Project, also suggests something of the organization's recognition that efforts to improve Southern education were necessarily connected to attempts to resolve some of the South's pressing social problems. Another major program established in the 1960s also reflected the Association's desire to address social concerns through educational improvement. With initial financial support from the Danforth and Ford Foundations, the Educational Improvement Program (EIP) began its work in January of 1964. Aimed at assisting Southern students adversely affected by poverty and educational inequality, by the end of the decade the EIP had attracted $29 million in support of various programs such as reading and college preparation projects of benefit to more than 25,000 students at all levels of education from pre-school to college. By 1971, more than $32 million had been invested in a variety of urban and rural educational centers and activities aimed at improving opportunity for the South's disadvantaged youth. The EIP's success was achieved under the directorship of Donald Agnew, whose retirement in June of 1971 brought to an end an extremely valuable and varied career of commitment to the Southern Association and Southern education.[81]

The Association's participation in projects like the EIP, not to mention its involvement in matters such as school desegregation and the North Carolina Speaker Ban conflict, both reflected and reinforced its members' understanding of the connections between questions of educational change and improvement, and the wider social circumstances of the times. Also indicative of this awareness, as well as of its willingness to collaborate with other groups and individuals who shared its broad aims, was the Southern Region Conference on Education sponsored by the Association in 1965, with 400 participants drawn from numerous areas of Southern life, and a high-powered speaker list including Vice President Hubert Humphrey, Georgia Governor Carl Sanders, and his Texan counterpart John B. Connally. The conference's proceedings were published as Education: The Southern Hope, a widely-circulated document that set out an agenda for future action to meet the present challenges facing Southern educators. An Ad Hoc Advisory Committee, established in 1966, focused on how the Association could play a more prominent part in the wider task of helping the South to "solve its problems and fulfill its proper destiny."[82]

Such programs and participation suggest the wider pattern of the Association's involvement in educational endeavors designed to have a positive impact on social development. Furthermore, the title of the conference proceedings "Education: the Southern Hope" suggests the weight of expectation and progress that education was expected to bear in shaping not only the life of the South, but also its "destiny." As the Association approached its seventy-fifth year, the increasingly central role that education was expected to play in Southern life was also reflected in the ever-expanding roles and responsibilities of regional accreditors. As in the past, change and development of the Association's social and educational activities in this period were worked out in a complex, organizational ethos of cooperation and conflict, caution and compromise. If the years prior to the Association's seventy-fifth birthday had seen significant, if piecemeal, change in the organization and activities of the Association in general, and the two commissions in particular, greater changes were nevertheless on the horizon. Of most enduring significance in this regard would be the creation of the Elementary Commission, the subject to which we now turn.

Endnotes

[1] Edwin Mims, "Six Decades of Southern Education," *Proceedings* 60 (1955): 188. In his 1955 address, Mims did recall how he had come "to realize the increasing value of strengthening institutions committed to the training of teachers, and this in turn led me to sympathize with the revision of the constitution that had arisen out of a growing realization of the dominance within the Association of those who had been most active in controlling the administration and objectives of the Association. Indeed, a second period began under the leadership of President Payne of Peabody College, Presidents H.L. Donovan, Doak Campbell, Hubbard and other heads of teachers' colleges (191)."

[2] Lawrence A. Cremin, "The Revolution in American Secondary Education," *Teachers College Record* 56 (1955): 295, Teachers College, Columbia University, New York). Reprinted in Stan Dropkin, Harold Full, and Ernest Schwarcz, eds., *Contemporary American Education: An Anthology of Issues, Problems, Challenges, 2nd ed.* (New York: The McMillan Company, 1970), 133. The continuity between the periods is also suggested by the continued public as well as professional interest in debates stemming from that time. In 1949, for example, the *Saturday Review of Literature* devoted a special issue to the renowned educational philosopher John

Dewey and the "pragmatism" with which he was associated. John E. Ivey, Jr., "Building a Better Region Through Higher Education," *Proceedings* 54 (1949), 208.

3 Henry H. Hill, "Higher Education Unlimited," *Proceedings* 55 (1950), 210-11. Hill presented statistics to show, that by this time, postsecondary students represented 7.6 percent of the total student population at all levels, while the figure for secondary pupils was 20.12 percent. In 1900, in contrast, the respective figures had been 1.39 percent and 4.25 percent. In other words, in 1900 94.36 percent of all students had been in elementary school.

4 Ivey, Jr., "Building a Better Region," 208.

5 Ibid., 209.

6 George Jackson Allen, Jr., "A History of the Commission on Colleges of the Southern Association of Colleges and Schools, 1949-1975" (doctoral dissertation, Georgia State University, Atlanta, 1978), 71-2.

7 Ibid., 74: Allen notes that "there has never been an attempt to differentiate degrees of quality among members in the listing."

8 Ibid., 242ff, for example, discusses growing concern from the 1920s on that accreditation itself was becoming a source of disorder in education.

9 Mark Newman, *Agency of Change: One Hundred Years of the North Central Association of Colleges and Schools* (Kirksville, MO: Thomas Jefferson University Press, 1996), xi. "In a sense," Newman adds, the NCA "pioneered the idea of outcomes evaluation almost fifty years before this term became an educational buzzword."

10 Ibid.

11 *Southern Association Quarterly* (hereafter *SAQ*) 1 (Aug. 1937), 284-85. Cited in *The Southern Study* (Atlanta: Southern Association of Secondary Schools and Colleges) Reprint of "The Cooperative Study for the Improvement of Education: A Staff Report of the Southern Association Study in Secondary Schools and Colleges," *SAQ* 10 (1946), 9. *The Southern Study,* 5, noted how "as a region and states within the region," the South "had cooperatively wrestled with the same problem of improvement; perhaps even more ardently than some because the need was greater."

12 *Proceedings* 40 (1935), 345. Cited in *Southern Study,* 8.

13 Donald C. Agnew, *Seventy-Five Years of Educational Leadership* (Atlanta, GA: Southern Association of Colleges and Schools, 1970), 31. The new Commission received funding from outside bodies such as the General Education Board for many of its projects.

14 It was also instrumental in the Association's growing involvement in elementary education. See Chap. 5.

15 *Proceedings 41* (1936), 138), 3. Cited in *Southern Study, 8.*

16 Ibid., 4.

17 Ibid., foreword.

[18] Cited in ibid., 9.

[19] *SAQ* 1 (Aug. 1937), 284-85. Quoted in *Southern Study, 9.*

[20] *Southern Study, 8.*

[21] Ibid., 12, 10-11, 21.

[22] Frank C. Jenkins, "Future Program of the Commission on Secondary Schools," *Proceedings* 60 (1955), 210-13.

[23] James H. Stiltner, "The Commission on Secondary Schools in Transition," (doctoral dissertation, Georgia State University, Atlanta, 1982), 121-23. At a meeting of the Department of Superintendents of the National Education Association in 1928, Roemer discussed these matters with Dean J.B. Edmondson, Secretary of the North Central Association and Dr. E.D. Grizzel, chairman of the Commission on Secondary Schools of the Middle States Association. The delay was due in part to an agreement to wait until a similar study by the U.S. Office of Education—the National Survey on Secondary Education—had been completed.

[24] *Southern Study,* 4, explicitly recognized the influential role of the *Evaluative Criteria* in its efforts. See also Stiltner, 124 and Earle T. Hawkins "The Evaluative Criteria and Evaluation Practices," *Proceedings* 53 (1948), 213-18. Hawkins was president of the State Teachers College in Towson, Maryland.

[25] Stiltner, 124-26.

[26] *SAQ* (1947), 169. Cited in Stiltner, 125-27.

[27] Stiltner, 137, 142-43. Income from dues had risen from $12,020 to more than $50,000, and the Commission's budget from $8,440 to nearly $40,000 over the same period.

[28] Its cooperation with the Secondary Commission of the North Central Association in formulating accrediting standards had been a consistent feature of the Commission's activities over the years. See Stiltner, 86-7.

[29] Ibid., 224, 114. See also *Proceedings* for 1935.

[30] See Stiltner, 115. The first private CRC consisted of five members from colleges, four private school headmasters and two at-large members appointed by the Commission chairman. By 1955 all members were drawn from either private or parochial schools. See also *Proceedings* for 1935.

[31] In some ways this was already happening. Summer meetings instituted some years earlier, for example, provided the opportunity for the committees' members to get together and discuss current issues of importance to accreditation. Thus, as well as its long-standing duties, the CRC had already gradually developed as a forum for "generating and discussing ideas relative to accreditation and evaluation" and also come to serve "as a liaison between the Commission and state communities." Stiltner, 116-18.

[32] Ibid., 114, 118-20.

33 Ibid., 156-57.

34 Ibid., 157ff

35 Allen, "A History of the Commission on Colleges," 154ff

36 M.C. Huntley, "Commission on Colleges and Universities Past and Future," *Proceedings* 60 (1955), 208. This was a view shared even by representatives of the North Central Association that had been first to respond to these criticisms. Charles E. Friley, president of the Iowa State College, for example, considered the regional associations to be the pioneers, and "still the backbone of the accrediting movement. True, their early quantitative standards left much to be desired, viewed in the light of changes made in the past fifteen years. But their activities, in general, have clearly set the pattern for an acceptable institution of higher education in America and have unquestionably helped the American people generally to understand and appreciate the essentials of a good college or university." Charles E. Friley, "National Trends in Accrediting," *Proceedings* 55 (1950), 196-201.

37 Allen, 75, *Proceedings* 54 (1949): 157.

38 M.C. Huntley, "Commission on Colleges and Universities Past and Future," 208.

39 Ibid.

40 Allen, 72. For a full and detailed account of changes in the Higher Commission's Standards, see Allen, 66ff.

41 Ibid., 85, 88-9; *Proceedings* 62 (1957), 142.

42 The 1939 changes, for example, added a Standard on Instruction that "reflected an uneasiness about the efficiency of predominantly quantitative requirements and provided for methods of evaluating instruction. For the first time, the Standards—Standard Six—required faculty tenure policies." Allen, 71, 76, and Appendix B for the new standard.

43 In 1949, for example, M.C. Huntley in his role as executive secretary had "sounded out Commission leaders" on these matters and found that most members preferred to keep most of the standards' specific quantitative requirements. The resulting Standards for Colleges of Arts and Sciences and Teacher Training Colleges, therefore, "incorporated no radical changes" from those that had been in place previously. Cited in Allen, 76. See Allen, Appendix D, for the complete 1950 Standards.

44 Ibid., 90, 66, and 66ff for a detailed account of the standards and of subsequent piecemeal changes to them.

45 COCU, Council Minutes, Nov. 30, 1955. Cited in ibid., 92.

46 Huntley, "Commission on Colleges and Universities Past and Future," 208-09.

47 Allen, 93.

48 Ibid., 96. Dissatisfaction, or at least confusion, with regard to the existing system

is suggested by the requests in 1955 that an aid to interpreting the standards and understanding the process of accreditation be published. See also ibid., 89.

[49] Ibid, 97; Henry King Stanford, "Report of the Chairman," *Proceedings* 65 (1960), 230. Cited in ibid., 100.

[50] Friley, "National Trends," 197.

[51] Ibid.; Allen, 91, 245ff; Felix C. Robb, "New Plans for Accreditation of Colleges," *Proceedings* 57 (1952), 141-42. This was one of the contributions to a panel discussion on the topic of "recent developments in the formulation of plans in the accreditation of colleges" put on by the CRS. Robb also sympathized with "the predicament of the larger universities," which especially felt "the heavy hand of the multitudinous accrediting bodies that invade their domains" in ways which, "in a sense," he agreed, "threaten their institutional autonomy."

[52] "Resolution Regarding National Commission on Accrediting," *Proceedings* 57 (1952), 74-5.

[53] CIHE, Minutes of the Commission on Institutions of Higher Education, Dec. 4, 1950. Cited in Allen, 82.

[54] See Allen, 78-85.

[55] As Allen, 98, puts it, "Another factor moving the Commission in the direction of new evaluative techniques was the proliferation of many types of post-secondary technical institutes and vocational schools. Commission leaders believed, as did many in other regional accrediting agencies and the NCA, that other agencies might begin accrediting these institutions with little regard for what the regional associations had been devoted to: quality education and the maintenance of a liberal arts core in post-secondary education."

[56] "Resolution Regarding National Commission on Accrediting," 74-5.

[57] See Allen, 241.

[58] Among the principles endorsed was that "accrediting shall be used as a stimulus to growth and development rather than merely inspection and standardization based upon minimum standards." A "corollary" to that principle was that "one of the major aims of the accrediting process shall be institutional self-evaluation, thereby stimulating development through institutional initiative." It was also agreed that "standards of criteria used in accrediting will emphasize qualitative rather than quantitative terms." National Committee of Regional Accrediting Agencies, "Principles Approved by National Committee of Regional Accrediting Agencies," Oct. 25, 1952. Cited in Allen, 92.

[59] Agnew, *Seventy-Five Years,* 44-6; *Proceedings* 65 (1960), 134. The organizational implications of the new constitution, such as the setting up delegate assemblies, the introduction of a director's office, and the preparation for the Elementary Commission's creation, will be addressed in Chapter 6.

[60] Interview with Albert J. Geiger, May 31, 1973, SACS Archive (hereafter Geiger interview), 6. The office was on the campus of what is now Georgia State University.

61 A point Wilson made in 1969 shortly before his retirement when he noted how this commitment still shaped the Commission's "concern not to have too highly a centralized staff." Raymond G. Wilson, "The Commission on Secondary Schools' Some Highlights," (1969), 3-4. Unpublished pamphlet in Southern Association of Colleges and Schools Archive, Decatur, GA (hereafter SACS Archive); Geiger interview, 18.

62 In Raymond Wilson's view, "the record seems clear that neither Commission had any particular intention of consolidating its office with the secretary-treasurer's." Wilson, "The Commission on Secondary Schools' Some Highlights," (1969), 3-4. Unpublished pamphlet, SACS Archive.

63 Geiger interview, 8-10; Wilson, 4.

64 Geiger interview, 25.

65 Interview with J.M. Godard, June 1, 1973, SACS Archive (hereafter Godard interview), 39-40; Interview with William Hugh McEniry, Dec 11, 1973, SACS Archive (hereafter McEniry interview), 27.

66 Geiger interview, 25; The self-study was conducted by a committee of eleven people, chaired by James Godard, representing the Association and the commissions.

67 McEniry interview, 24. McEniry also emphasized that he had come to these views although his own education had been at Birmingham-Southern College and Vanderbilt University.

68 Godard interview, 40.

69 The Report and Stanford's comments on it in *Proceedings* 65 (1960). Cited in Stiltner, 147-148.

70 McEniry interview, 25.

71 Stiltner, 150, 175; Geiger interview, 19; Godard interview, 39-40.

72 *Proceedings* (1963), 150.

73 Stiltner, 165.

74 McEniry, 25-6 Stiltner, 161-62; *Proceedings* 69 (1964) and 68 (1963).

75 A large part of this increase was due to the admission of elementary members. See Chap.6.

76 Agnew, 47; Robert W. Day and Barry L. Mellinger, *Accreditation of Two-Year Colleges in the South* (Atlanta: Commission on Colleges, Southern Association of Colleges and Schools, 1973), 23-4. Of the 251, 192 were public, up from 79, while the number of accredited private colleges had fallen slightly from 64 to 59. The total number of enrolled, full-time equivalent students now in accredited two-year colleges had also greatly increased, from 150,000 in 1966 to 350,000 in 1971. This figure represented 23.2 percent of all full-time equivalent students enrolled in accredited higher institutions in the Southern Association region.

77 Stiltner, 151-53.

78 Allen, 97, 101-04, 110-11; *Proceedings 67* (1962), 184, 220-22. The two existing sets of standards, twenty-one for senior colleges and fifteen for junior, were replaced by one set of fifteen standards intended to apply to all postsecondary institutions. The new standards took effect immediately for new applicants and for existing members who had not yet participated in the new study program. The standards covered areas such as Organization and Administration, Educational Program, Financial Resources, Faculty, Library, Student Personnel, Physical Plant, Special Activities, Graduate Program, and Research. Allen 165ff, provides a full summary of developments within the College Commission up to 1975.

79 "Annual Report of the Director," *Proceedings 29:8* (Aug. 1977), 3; Allen 154.

80 Cited in Allen, 154.

81 Agnew, 50; "A Glance Backward," *Proceedings 23:9* (July 1971), 2; McEniry interview, 31ff; "End of EIP Closes Proud Chapter in Association's 90 Years of Service," *Proceedings 37:3* (Jan.-Feb. 1985), 3-4; Ben Childers, "1984 Achievements Set Stage for 1985 Accomplishments," *Proceedings 37:3* (Jan.-Feb. 1985), 1, for quote on new special program. The EIP was phased out as a consequence of by-law changes in 1984, to be replaced by a special program "responsible for planning, initiating, and implementing educational research and development" for the association.

82 *Education the Southern Hope: Proceedings of the Southern Region Conference on Education* (Atlanta: Southern Association of Colleges and Schools); "A Glance Backward," *Proceedings 23:9* (July 1971), 2, 7. See also Agnew, 47.

Chapter Six

Association Growth: "Cradle to Grave"

In the decades following World War II, the Association's interests and influence expanded in ways both quantitative and qualitative. Growth resulted from the eagerness and ability of growing numbers of secondary schools and postsecondary institutions to join the Association and, as in the case of historically black colleges and schools, the Association's new willingness to admit them. While the admission of black schools and colleges truly reflected a wider social revolution, in terms of their educational practice and philosophy black schools and colleges were in many ways similar to their white counterparts already in the Association. The Association's expansion in the postwar decades also reflected its growing willingness to embrace a wider range of educational institutions within its area of responsibility. In other words it was increasingly open to the admission of large numbers of new *kinds* of institution such as junior colleges and other two-year institutions offering specialized education or vocation training.

This increased diversity in the Association's membership, like its admission of black institutions, had its roots in broader social changes. The ongoing "democratization" of American education in the postwar years, combined with rising economic expectations, led more and more Americans to see education as the necessary foundation for economic prosperity and social status. This expansion found its most significant organizational form in the creation of two new commissions: the Elementary Commission (1965) and the Commission on Occupational Education Institutions (1971). The Elementary Commission in particular represented a distinctive step into a new area of endeavor for the Association, one that remains unique to the present day among regional accrediting associations. The background to the creation of these unique components of the Association, their early activities and subsequent development, and their eventually divergent fates within the Association form an important part of our story in this chapter.

These new departures for the Association blended with ongoing debates and priorities to make the last third of the Association's first century a period of tremendous change for its commissions and its members. Continuing debates and disagreements between advocates of a more centralized association and the defenders of the individual commissions' extensive autonomy of action precipitated further organizational change. Organization changes continued to be bound up with the questions and conflicts long at the heart of Association life: the practice and philosophy of accreditation, accreditation's place within education, and education's role in society. Old questions nevertheless continued to bring new answers, and the further evolution of the Association's thought and action on these issues will also be traced in this chapter. Following a pattern by now familiar, changes in organization, aim and philosophy could not escape the influence of outside events and forces. In this regard, this chapter will also address the Association's growing, often difficult, relation to a federal government whose own power and influence in educational matters has increased dramatically in the second half of the century. Finally, these developments will be placed in the longer context of the organization's history as part of a conclusion that identifies the major issues and themes of the Southern Association's journey from the periphery to the center of Southern education and society.

The Association's most significant expansion, in both social and educational terms, came in the area of elementary schooling, a new involvement eventually embodied in the creation of the Elementary Commission in 1965. The beginning of a new chapter for the Association, the new commission also marked the culmination of the Association's growing participation in elementary education in the years after World War II. This growing interest in elementary schooling had several related sources: social, educational and organizational. There was, for one thing, the fact of sheer numbers. As Henry Hill recognized in 1950, since elementary schools served the great majority of the South's students (23,377,500 or 72 percent), it followed that the vast majority of the South's students attended institutions that the Association did not accredit and, historically, had given little thought to accrediting. What was true of the students was also true of their teachers. Thus, Hill acknowledged that he spoke to a minority of Southern educators when he spoke to a Southern Association that did not accredit the institutions where the majority labored. He expressed to them the hope, however, that "some day we as educators shall demonstrate more effectively that we know the implication of these figures."[1]

Elementary educators themselves needed no urging to take their field seriously or to recognize the problems stemming from its neglect by other sectors of the educational world, including regional accreditors. Some elementary educators worried about the deleterious consequences of what might be called "selective accreditation." Just as non-liberal arts institutions had once complained that the Association's standards and priorities encouraged the diversion of scarce resources away from their areas of concern, so elementary educators feared a similar fate should they remain the only level of education outside the accrediting circle. Albert Geiger remembered how "elementary people in the state Departments [of Education] would see secondary people working in the Association," and began to ask "Why couldn't they have some recognition too? Why shouldn't elementary education be recognized?" Support for accreditation among elementary educators was hardly unanimous. Many harbored the same skepticism as to its value that could be found among some educators in secondary and postsecondary institutions. Nevertheless, those elementary educators who did wish to see it extended, proved to be "instrumental" in encouraging the Association's growing participation in elementary education.[2]

The growing demand that accreditors take a greater interest in the work of elementary educators resonated with powerful trends in educational philosophy and practice generally. Of major significance was the growing commitment, not confined to elementary educators, to the belief that the quality of a child's early education crucially shaped his or her subsequent development as student, citizen and human being. Speaking in 1949 on "The Elementary School of Tomorrow," Henry J. Otto of the University of Texas noted the extent of the "research in child growth and development," as well as its pervasive influence on "every aspect of elementary school practice," especially such key areas as "educational values, curriculum design, and instructional practices." Acceptance of the importance of "early childhood education" had implications for education's social role. Ideally, "academic" and "social" skills would be developed in tandem, and emphasis on "more effective instruction in the three Rs" would exist alongside a strong emphasis on the "physical growth and development, emotional development, and social adjustment and development" of the student. Such an approach, it was believed, would benefit both student and society by providing the former with the "sturdy independence and initiative" necessary to face the problems of the latter as effective citizens. Clearly reflecting the intensifying Cold War atmosphere that provided the wider context for his speech, Otto also claimed that "international goodwill is bred in young children rather than at the college or adult level," and that it began "by being tolerant, understanding, appreciative, and helpful in nursery school and kindergarten." While extravagant in their optimism, Otto's words faithfully reflected the growing belief that in the quality of early education lay the key to personal and political health and progress in the future.[3]

Desire to change educational aims inevitably encouraged debate over how to do so. Educators like Otto assumed that a new approach to early education would "bring new implications for curriculum and instructional practices." In "curriculum design," for example, Otto expressed the widespread view that the emphasis would "shift progressively from subjects taught us in isolation toward a broadly integrated experience curriculum," and focus more on "learning situations" that would encourage students to be more active than the more traditional "assign-study-recite-test formula" allowed for. Teaching practices more attuned to children's individual differences would also be more widely adopted, accompanied by a shift in emphasis from "mass" methods of determining "pupil progress" (such as "the class average") toward "appraisal of individual progress in terms of the unfolding pattern" of each child's individual growth.[4] Thus, the powerful faith that appropriate change at the elementary level would bring tremendous benefit to the individual and society alike also fueled discussions and expectations regarding the means considered most likely to achieve the ideal ends of "child-centered" education. Growing acceptance that the quality of "early childhood" education had a crucial impact on all aspects of a person's future development in many ways reflected the dual emphasis of much educational philosophy since at least the days of John Dewey: on the unique individual on the one hand and the democratizing society on the other. In 1973, William McEniry encapsulated the ideal at the heart of this thinking. He looked with hope to "the last third of the century" as a time of "steady movement toward the revision of the educational fabric" into something "entire and complete," reflecting a pedagogical philosophy in which "a man begins his education with his first breath if not before, and he does not stop, if he does then, until he breathes his last one." Although far from fulfillment as the end of the century approaches, this ideal has proved a steadily growing influence on education in the century's last decades.[5]

The focus on the continuity of the "individual's" education as well as on its profound implications for social progress was bound up with another major theme of educational debate: How to understand and order relations between the different levels and branches of the educational system. The theme of "articulation" was not new of course, but, increasingly, attention focused on the place of elementary schools in relation to the wider educational system. Educators increasingly pointed to the value of recognizing the elementary school as an integral part of a coordinated system covering the period from early childhood to early adulthood, if not beyond. Calls for closer articulation between elementary and secondary levels echoed an assumption often heard at the college level: A college could only be as good as the secondary schools that supplied its students. Similarly, it was insisted that high schools would only meet their full potential when they received students who had benefited from a first-class elementary education. Advocates of elementary education thus emphasized the benefits that would accrue to all levels of the educational system were elementary education to receive the recognition and attention it warranted.

Elementary advocates also emphasized that the connections were between equal parts, not between levels of education that became progressively more important or valuable as the age of the students increased. Hugh McEniry made the case for both stronger connections and greater equality throughout the educational system when he argued not only that "what we do in the first grade has a significant effect on what we do in graduate school," but also that "what we do in continuing education is no less or no more important than what we do in the seventh grade."[6] As with relations between secondary schools and colleges earlier in the Association's history, the task was to acknowledge both the intrinsic importance of each area of education while also recognizing the inextricable connections that existed between them.

With so much of the attention paid to elementary education focusing on "articulation" between institutions and curricular methods and standards within them, it is not surprising that the Association would be drawn into these developing debates. Indeed by the time Otto spoke to the Association in 1949, it had already taken steps toward greater participation in elementary education. The year 1946 was important in raising the Association's profile in elementary circles. That year saw the publication of "Improving Elementary Schools in the Southern Region," a report that grew out of the first sustained, region-wide attention to elementary education. In 1944 a Southern States Work Conference, sponsored by the various state Departments of Education and state Education Associations, initiated a study of the South's elementary schooling, with committees organized in each state to do the research. The resulting report helped greatly to improve elementary education and also proved to be a major step toward the accreditation of that level of education.[7] Within the Association, the 1946 annual meeting heard the elementary schools' version of the "knocking at the door" speech. R. Lee Thomas, director of elementary schools in Tennessee's Department of Education, urged the Secondary Commission to consider accrediting elementary schools. Thomas' speech, according to Donald Agnew, was widely "credited with initiating the elementary program of the Association and establishing the informal ties with the Commission on Secondary Schools" that would continue to strengthen over the coming years. "If not the father, he should certainly be considered the grandfather of the Commission on Elementary Schools," Agnew said of a man who, as well as fulfilling his state-level responsibilities, also played an important role in the Work Conferences, the Commission on Curricular Problems and Research, and the Secondary Commission.[8]

The Association's official involvement began the same year with the decision of the Commission on Research and Service (as the Commission on Curricular Problems and Research had been renamed) to concern itself with elementary education and teaching. In 1948 the CRS began a Cooperative Study in Elementary Education. Conducted with funding from the General Education Board and with the cooperation of the other commissions, the study lasted until 1951. It focused on four main areas of inquiry: evaluation of the elementary school; recruitment, selection and education of teachers, principles and supervisors; the development of an

"Action Program to Discover Promising Practices and Speed Up Improvements in Curriculum and Teaching;" and the collection of data to assist in identifying "critical needs" of school improvement.

Following a familiar pattern, the study sought to involve a variety of educators in the process and to foster cooperative connections among them.[9] The study, according to Charles Spain, its vice-chairman and dean of instruction at Peabody College for Teachers, "was organized from the beginning as a cooperative effort centered at local and state levels." Committees were formed in all eleven states (and, by special request, Oklahoma and Arkansas, too). A Central Coordinating Committee was formed "to stimulate local efforts" designed to educate educators and the public alike about the needs of elementary education in the South. "From its inception," as Harold D. Drummond described it, the Cooperative Study's "distinguishing characteristic" was *"cooperation* at the state level, encouraged and stimulated by the regional organization." Widespread research and debate was pursued by various means, including statewide surveys and studies as well as cooperation with other professional groups and school boards. Various kinds of publications, from press releases to journal articles, were intended to encourage cooperation, including "The Southern Newsletter," which it was hoped would "provide a clearinghouse for promising practices" and "truly mirror the spirit" that had "inspired" and "sparked" the Cooperative Study. The emphasis on building contacts and cooperation was also reflected in the state committees that were encouraged to be as representative as possible. Most, therefore, consisted of educators and administrators from all levels of the system, representatives of relevant state departments and agencies, as well as parents in the shape of state parent-teacher associations.[10]

Workshops, conferences and meetings were also important means to identify, publicize and begin to deal with the problems and challenges facing elementary education. In June and July of 1949, a subcommittee drawn from across the South convened at Florida State University and prepared a two-volume *Elementary Evaluative Criteria*. Similar in purpose to the *Evaluative Criteria for Secondary Schools*, the new guide was intended to help educators assess the current state of their schools and to plan for their improvement. An experimental study conducted in schools in each state was instituted in the following school year (1949-50). In Florida, for example, three schools from three different counties participated. Another valuable feature of the study was the summer workshop held every year at Daytona Beach.[11] Another stated objective of the study, as Charles Spain noted, "was the development of public understanding of the problems and needs of elementary school[s] in the South," the kind of public advocacy role that the Association had not always sought or welcomed. As Spain acknowledged, "long-range improvement" depended on much more than "public relations," but it was also clear that "an awakened and understanding public" held the key to the resources that educators needed to bring about "better opportunities for children in the South."[12]

The study strengthened support within the Association for closer ties to elementary schools. A 1951 Action Program expressed the generally welcome view that the Association should "provide leadership and service" in elementary education. There was also general agreement that this would require "a suitable agency" within the Association with a permanent, full-time staff member "to give general direction" to the Association's elementary education program.[13] There was much less agreement as to how connections should be deepened and over who within the Association should have primary responsibility for overseeing the process. Some proposed a reorganized Commission on Elementary and Secondary Schools. Others favored a federation of state committees coordinated by the CRS, while others still wanted the CRS to assume the task. Some went so far as to call for a new Elementary Commission, but at that time there was still widespread opposition to the Association going so far as to assume responsibility for accrediting elementary schools. Opposition had various sources. An important concern for existing members was that the sheer number of elementary schools would eventually allow their representatives to dominate Association affairs and unduly influence the business of the existing commissions, a fear once expressed by some college members in relation to secondary schools. For their part, some elementary educators worried that accreditation would mean the application of standards, shaped by college and secondary circumstances and priorities, that would be largely inimical to the aims and philosophies of elementary education.

To help settle the question, the Executive Committee of the CRS appointed a working committee to explore the various options and to establish "principles" that would form the basis of the Association's relation to elementary education. The committee produced a tentative proposal that was considered by the representatives of state committees and other "interested organizations" at a three-day meeting held at Emory University in May of 1952. The proposal reiterated the widespread view "that all levels of education . . . are equally important and should be closely related," and unanimously endorsed the belief "that continuing regional action" to improve elementary education "should be fostered" in the interests of all. As H. Arnold Perry, chairperson of the Coordinating Committee and a member of the Working Committee, put it, the proposals would "lead not only to better elementary schools, but will ultimately benefit the entire educational structure" since higher institutions could "never do their best work" without students who had enjoyed "adequate educational opportunity in their elementary school years."[14]

From the Cooperative Study and these subsequent efforts emerged the Cooperative Program in Elementary Education. Created at the 1952 annual meeting, it began work in 1953. Over the coming years, the program, like the study before it, emphasized the importance of cooperation at the local level as a crucial means to achieve school improvement. While majority opinion still held that stronger connections between the Association and elementary education should not extend to the accrediting of elementary schools, the Cooperative Program "provided for the affiliation of elementary schools with the Association" for institutions that participated in its school improvement plan. Affiliation allowed for schools interested in developing standards and practices to work with the Association without first having to meet those standards. Affiliation stopped short of accreditation and so proved acceptable to those who remained opposed to the accreditation of elementary schools.[15]

Opposition to elementary accreditation softened over the coming years as various organizational changes reassured the commissions of their continuing autonomy within the Association and as more elementary educators became convinced of accreditation's value to their field. At the 1958 annual meeting in

Louisville, "the Association authorized the Cooperative Program to accredit elementary schools and systems of elementary schools" according to the standards the Program had developed. Still under the aegis of the CRS, the program accredited its first elementary schools in 1960. Twenty-six school units from Georgia, Kentucky, Louisiana, North Carolina, South Carolina and Texas (comprising ninety-eight schools containing more than 45,000 children) met the standards and were recommended by the state elementary committees. A further thirty units (150 schools and 76,851 students) received accreditation the following year, adding Mississippi and Florida to the states participating in the regional accreditation of elementary education. Pointing "with pride" to other progress made, including the promotion of cooperation and "leadership training" through publications and workshops, increased state-level activity and "improved financial and membership status," the Central Coordinating Committee's 1961 report reflected its members' confidence that the past year had been "among the most successful in the program's history."[16]

The Association's expanded role in elementary education was mirrored by elementary education's growing presence within the Association. Thomas R. Landry, chairman of the Central Coordinating Committee, noted support "on every side" of the Association "for giving the elementary program more status in the organization." In 1962 the Commission on Research and Service was dissolved and a standing Committee on Elementary Education, provided for in the constitutional changes of 1961, established to oversee affairs in that field. These arrangements did "provide an improved basis of operation," but, as Landry also pointed out, failed to "fully meet the needs or the ultimate expectations" of the region's elementary educators. The committee's establishment thus reflected both the Association's closer involvement in elementary education and the continuing reluctance of some within it to establish the distinct commission to oversee it that those disappointed elementary educators were calling for. Nevertheless, the Association's name change in this period (dropping "Secondary" from the title), reflected the significant extent to which it had assumed the same responsibilities in elementary education as it had long had at the secondary and postsecondary level. The name change also pointed to a near future in which elementary school accreditation would occupy an equal role in the life of the now more inclusively named Southern Association of Colleges and Schools.[17]

Demand from elementary schools and systems for membership in the Southern Association of Colleges and Schools soon outstripped the abilities of a standing committee to adequately meet the task. In 1965, by which time the Association already had 1,002 elementary members, the Commission on Elementary Schools was created. Its first executive secretary was Durell Ruffin, who had earlier been the coordinator for elementary schools. By 1970 the number of member schools had doubled, while the combined number of affiliated and accredited members had reached 5,293. In the process of this rapid expansion, the new commission formed its own organizational structure and, through participation in conferences and visiting committees, involved thousands of elementary educators in the ongoing development, revision and application of accrediting standards intended to further the cause of improving elementary education in the South.[18]

Another new commission was created in 1971. The Commission on Occupational Education Institutions, like the Elementary Commission, reflected the impact of changes in the wider educational world on the aims and organization of the Association. The question of how the Association should deal, if at all, with postsecondary institutions that did not meet the founders' idea of a college or university was almost as old as the Association itself. But it assumed added urgency with the blossoming of myriad two-year, special purpose and vocational institutions in the years following World War II. The expansion of occupational education was fueled by public demand, but also by the political and financial backing it received from state and federal politicians eager to respond to their constituents' rising educational expectations. In 1963, for example, the United States Congress passed the Vocational Education Act, and then the Vocational Education Amendments in 1968. State governments in the South had also "assumed a more dominant role in the planning and development of pubic higher education," accelerating its growth as they did so. Georgia, Mississippi and Texas had all set up public two-year institutions in the years between the World Wars, but in most states in the Association's area such systems were the product of "legislation enacted after 1960." These systems comprised three main types of institution: comprehensive community colleges, degree-granting technical institutes and non-degree-granting area vocational schools. Thus, occupational education of one kind or another was offered by a variety of institutions, including four-year colleges offering adult or continuing education, community junior colleges, comprehensive high schools, federally sponsored skill development centers, and proprietary agencies and institutions "offering an almost infinite variety of specialized training."[19]

The first two single-purpose institutions were admitted to membership in 1951. As their names suggest, the Notre Dame Seminary in New Orleans, Louisiana, and the Training School For Christian Workers run by the Southern Presbyterian Church in Richmond, Virginia, devoted their efforts to providing students with specialized training for religious service. Neither admitted freshmen or sophomores and both offered only two or three majors. As the Association considered their applications, J.M. Godard remembered that he and his colleagues were "glad" that, with one institution being Catholic and the other Protestant, the issue was at least removed from "the realm of sectarianism." But it was far from removed from the realm of conflicting educational philosophies. The question of the subjects and majors offered by single-purpose institutions loomed especially large. These institutions' attempt to join the Association challenged what J.M. Godard described as the "unwritten rule" of that time that an institution had to offer at least a basic liberal arts curriculum and "at least eight majors" to be considered for membership. As part of the application process, both the institutions and the general question of courses and majors were thoroughly studied by Association members, especially Gordon Stipe, then vice president of Emory University, and Donald Agnew, president of Coker College. In part because of this thorough preparation, they were admitted with little or no resistance from within the Commission or the Association as a whole. But the admission of these two institutions did effectively end the "unwritten rule" policy. From then on, a new policy allowed for the admission of a single-purpose institution even if it did not offer liberal arts majors, provided its curriculum contained a liberal arts core. At the same time, single-purpose institutions had to meet Association standards in the majors they did offer, as well as in institutional areas such as library and other support facilities.[20]

The prospect of bringing vocational and technical institutions under the Association's accrediting wing did not generate the same atmosphere of calm and compromise. Continued applications for membership throughout the decade from institutions as diverse as music conservatories, medical schools and technical schools kept the issue alive. Arguments for and against considering these applications followed the familiar lines of past Association debates over what kinds of education and institutions should properly be the concern of the Association in general, and the Commission on Colleges in particular. With proliferation and diversification only likely to increase, there were calls for the Association to take a more active role in meeting these institutions' desires for accreditation. Some argued for accreditation on the familiar grounds that if the Association did not do it, some other organizations, perhaps even the federal government, would.

Advocates of occupational education drew on some of the same arguments employed by their counterparts in elementary education. Felix Robb's insistence in 1970 that it was "clearly in the national interest for occupational education to be vastly improved in its quality, availability, and image at every level—from the elementary school through the highest graduate program," was representative of a wider, long-standing view among occupational education's supporters. It was also, according to Robb, in the interests of the millions of Americans whose chances for a rewarding education would be greatly enhanced by such expansion and improvement. For Robb, it was "equally important that occupational education be viewed in a broad context" not as a "thing apart," but as a process that has value for all and particular value for some." Occupational education's integration into the educational system was tied to its improving public image. Robb lauded vocational education's emergence in the 1960s from the "dark ages" of scorn and neglect to which it had often been subjected by critics who associated it with "poverty, delinquency, and limited intelligence." Now, argued Robb, occupational education had strong popular support and was in step with many of the values and aims of modern American life.[21] Many in the College Commission nevertheless remained opposed to institutions with declared missions so far from the liberal arts ideal being admitted to membership.

In 1958, the Executive Council, in cooperation with the other regional associations and the National Commission on Accrediting, set up an investigative committee to explore possible responses to developments in occupational education. The following year, this Committee on the Accreditation of Post-Secondary Specialized and Technical Institutes produced several recommendations, including a set of guidelines for evaluating whether "special purpose institutions" should be considered for accreditation. They should, it was suggested, be nonprofit organizations, require a high school diploma or its equivalent from entering students, and include some liberal arts subjects in its program. Full accreditation and membership would still depend on an institution meeting all other existing standards for colleges. A new standing committee would be responsible for evaluating these institutions, while visiting committees "would include specialists in professional areas and 'generalists' representing non-technical areas." In 1962 the Commission established the category of Special Purpose Institutions for places that qualified for membership on those terms. That same year the Technical Institute of Old Dominion College, in Norfolk, Virginia, became the first degree-granting technical institute admitted to membership in the Commission on Colleges. The Southern Technical Institute of Marietta, Georgia, followed two years later, and from 1964 to 1971 the Commission accredited thirty two-year degree-granting technical institutes. By the 1960s, then, it was accepted that the Commission on Colleges should take responsibility for the accreditation of "degree-granting" technical institutions that retained a liberal arts core, while vocational-technical programs offered at the high school level should be the concern of the Secondary Commission.[22]

The Association's relation to trade and vocational institutions that neither offered any collegiate programs nor granted degrees remained to be settled. Yet the continued growth of these institutions and of vocational programs offered by two-year colleges only added urgency to demands that the Association do something about the accreditation of occupational education. In 1966 a special committee was appointed to explore the question. To assist in its inquiries, the Committee organized a Conference on Occupational Education, held in April of 1967 and funded by the Southern Company and Southern Bell Telephone Company.

Given the sponsors, it was perhaps not surprising that "participants from industry and education urged the Southern Association
to evaluate and accredit vocational institutions." The conference
recommended that the Association establish a commission to
carry out this task.[23] Two months later, the Board of Trustees
appointed an ad hoc committee "comprised of experts in occupational education." Its task was to come up with recommendations
for extending the Association's accrediting responsibilities to postsecondary occupational education institutions.

From these efforts emerged the Committee on Occupational
Education, funded in part by a foundation grant. Its primary
objectives were "to develop, test, and implement a system for evaluation and accreditation of occupational education institutions"
and "to improve the quality, quantity, availability and status of
occupational education in the South."[24] The Committee recognized the difficult and long-term nature of bringing systematic
improvement to occupational education. One way it sought to
encourage this was through the affiliation of institutions not yet
eligible to be accredited by either the College or the Secondary
commissions. Through this process, institutions could, on a voluntary basis, work toward self-improvement and the development
of standards. After one year of operation, the Committee had
ninety-four affiliated institutions.[25] Subsequently the Committee
was authorized to apply the standards eventually accepted to institutions currently affiliated with the Association. Those meeting
them were to be recommended to the Delegate Assembly of the
Southern Association for full accreditation. In 1970 the Committee
accredited its first institutions, sparking the rapid growth of two-
year colleges represented in and by the Association.[26] By 1971, the
Association had 251 members drawn from the ranks of two-year
institutions, including junior colleges (both public and private),
comprehensive multi-campus community colleges, as well as specialized and technical institutions.[27] In November of 1971 the
accreditation of postsecondary, non-collegiate institutions became
the responsibility of the newly-created Commission on Occupational Education Institutions (COEI).

Testing and developing evaluative standards remained a priority of the Commission in its early years. In pursuing this priority,
the Commission took close account not only of the aims and values

of the institutions themselves, but also of the business world they sought to serve. Often, indeed, there was a strong correspondence in the aims and values of both groups, making for very close relations between them. "Both degree and non-degree programs in vocational-technical education," as one study described the relationship existing in most Southern states, were "closely coordinated with local business and industrial needs." In many Southern communities, these "cooperative efforts" had made for a "close 'town and gown' relationship" between business and occupational education. These shared assumptions and close working relationships crucially shaped the content of the education and training that students received, becoming, for example, "a significant factor in the establishment of curricular requirements" designed to be "compatible with professional and paraprofessional requirements."[28]

The desirability of close relations between education and business was also taken for granted by vocational education's supporters within the Association. Representatives of industry had strongly encouraged the Commission on Colleges to assume evaluation and accrediting responsibility for special purpose institutions. For their part, supporters of occupational accreditation within the Association hoped the Committee, and later the Commission, would assume a pivotal role in fostering greater cooperation between education and the business world. Felix Robb, for example, envisioned the creation of "a new kind of business-industry-education relationship" in which, through "advisory councils and boards comprised of leaders in major occupation fields," the Southern Association would receive advice "from 'consumers' of education's projects."[29] Like occupational education, then, the COEI developed an approach that sought to serve, in the words of Ronald B. Storey, the academic manager of the Gulfport, Mississippi, Job Corps Center, "both the needs of the students and those of industry and business."[30] The 1970s also saw the creation of the Vocational-Technical Education Consortium of States (V-TECS), an agency devoted "to establish[ing] definitive catalogs of the skills and competencies required in clusters of occupations." This effort extended beyond the boundaries of the Southern Association to cover 16 states across the nation and continued through the Association's centennial year and beyond.[31] In July 1981, Kenneth W. Tidwell, previously the associate executive director since joining the COEI in 1977, was appointed executive director. Throughout the following decade, the COEI continued to expand both membership and programs.[32] Whatever the growing public approval of and demand for occupational and vocational education, the COEI's members were well aware that many of their fellow educators and accreditors continued to view their work skeptically. Storey reflected this awareness in regretting that "many people still labor under the illusion that occupational education institutions exist only for those individuals who are not capable of succeeding in a 'regular' school environment." This "stereotypical view," was, according to Storey, based on people's memories of high school "shop classes" designed to "occupy" troublesome or underachieving students with bird house building and the like, rather than to prepare them for a real "occupation." The title of Storey's 1985 *Proceedings* article, "They Are Not Building Bird Houses Anymore!" also reflected the widespread desire to replace these outmoded images with a more accurate appraisal of present-day occupational and vocational training. Now it involved the serious training of young people for participation in the work force, but also the re-training of existing workers, offered in a variety of occupational fields, from clerical and business to construction and computing.[33]

Accreditation played the role in this changing and expanding field that it had in other educational areas; encouraging improvement within institutions while also enlarging their prestige in the eyes of potential "consumers" of their services, whether students or businesses. Storey insisted that gaining accredited status "was not an easy process," indeed, because the accrediting process was both "difficult and time consuming" and many institutions were unwilling to embark upon it. Those who successfully did so, however, could reap "rewards" that were "immeasurable." Storey credited the COEI's standards for "many of the improvements" made in occupational education, and also for the improved public status of institutions receiving the Association's stamp of approval. Potential students, anxious to ensure the quality of their "education or reeducation," sought "training at institutions . . . accredited by a nationally recognized organization." Employers, in turn, increasingly looked for the accreditors' seal of approval when hiring new employees or retraining existing workers. As Storey summarized the benefits, "Accreditation adds prestige to the institution and credibility to students who graduate from the institution." Thus, as in other areas of accreditation, institutional improvement and image enhancement proceeded hand in hand.[34]

The addition of two new commissions had a significant impact on the Association's organizational structure, as did the steady expansion of the existing commissions' membership and responsibilities. As in previous periods, the "revolutionary" years of the 1930s for example, significant organizational change was bound up with continuing conflicts of power, principle and philosophy among the individuals and institutions that made up an increasingly diverse and complex association. Whatever the continuing differences and debates among and between commissions on matters both procedural and philosophical, a certain stable balance of interests was nevertheless achieved. The continuing growth and expanding influence of each commission combined with the various organizational and constitutional changes to bring greater coordination of Association activities, while preserving the independence of each commission, especially in accrediting.

As the Association's response to the proliferation of accrediting bodies—a powerful motivation for finding ways to compromise and cooperate both within the Association and across the nation—was the need to respond to wider changes in society and education, changes that often seemed to carry some threat to accreditation. In the 1970s and 1980s, a period of sustained discontent and disruption at all levels of education, the impact of external events on the Association's life if anything intensified. The word "change" was seldom far from the lips of educators or reformers as a widespread sense of crisis pervaded perceptions of the nation's education. Prompted by wider social changes (such as those illuminated by the Speaker Ban controversy in North Carolina) or by conflicts over educational practice and philosophy, this period saw the appearance of all kinds of reports (national, regional, statewide and local) from all kinds of sources (governmental, nonprofit, reform groups and educational "think-tanks"). Indeed, it was fast becoming a full-time job just to keep up with all these reports, a situation the Secondary Commission implicitly recognized when it appointed Hilton Smith as research consultant to read and summarize them all "for busy people with classes to teach and schools to run." Each study in its own way focused on describing the symptoms or prescribing the cures for the sickness at the heart of American education. Each study, whatever its particular emphasis or conclusion, reinforced the belief that, in the words of the U.S. Department of Education's own influential study, when it came to education, America was *A Nation at Risk*.[35]

A persistent complaint from the public, politicians and many educators, too, was that schools and colleges were failing in their responsibilities to develop the skills and intelligence of the students entrusted to them. With schools and colleges seen as failing to meet their primary mission, especially at a time when education had never been considered so central to personal development and social stability, calls for greater "accountability" on the part of educators and their institutions framed much of the demand for radical remedial action. A debate so often focused on how to improve the standards and quality of schools and students clearly demanded a response from accrediting organizations such as the Southern Association, charged with the encouragement and measurement of educational improvement. Thus, troubled educational times provided further motivation for greater cooperation within an Association that saw itself as having a significant role to play in the educational debates and changes of the time.

The Association's members certainly paid close attention to insistent public demands, including those that assigned a share of responsibility for education's problems to people like themselves. As in the past, however, the Association pursued a course that was neither wholly resistant to nor wholly welcoming of calls for educational reform. Some listened with a degree of skepticism regarding the imminence of America's educational meltdown, believing that the criticism was often overblown or ill-informed. The Elementary Commission's John Davis was among those who considered much of the criticism of the present educational system to be overstated and often rooted in ignorance of what actually went on in the nation's schools. But the Association also followed a familiar path in making a priority of examining how accreditation might change in order to improve schools and to maintain the Association's influential role in educational affairs. Lending urgency to these efforts was the recognition that accreditation was often identified as a major source of the nation's educational problems. One strand of this critique was quite familiar, indeed had long been reflected in debates within the accrediting world, and revolved around how to encourage such things as qualitative standards, greater sensitivity to each institution's mission, and continuous improvement toward the fulfillment of that mission. Giving particular force to the continuing critique of accreditation in this period was the wider criticism that educators were failing to focus on the students' development. James D. Koerner, an outspoken critic of regional accreditation, was "struck by the absolute refusal of accreditors to look at what is presumably the most important index of quality in a college or university—the students who come out of the place."[36]

To remedy this, it was widely and increasingly argued, would require less emphasis on "process" and far greater attention to "outcomes," in other words on the skills and abilities developed by the students. New forms of familiar demands and criticisms—calls for "accountability" for "educational outcomes"—helped to shape continuing revisions of the Association's accrediting philosophy and practice. Discussing occupational education, Felix Robb noted in 1970 the "increased public insistence on accountability and the measurement of educational success in terms of a learner's ability to perform."[37] This insistence was felt across the educational spectrum throughout this period. In 1985, Harry Smith, president of Austin College in Sherman, Texas, described how the growing "demand for state and federal funds and rising tuition costs" had left parents and students as well as legislators and educational foundations "anxious to know whether or not they were getting their money's worth out of higher education." Smith acknowledged that the major revision of its Standards for Accreditation set in motion in 1979 by the Commission on Colleges was "spurred on in part by a growing concern about educational quality and the need for greater accountability."[38]

The question of how greater accountability might be achieved was increasingly answered by an emphasis on "outcomes assessment": in other words on measuring an institution's worth not just in terms of its facilities, faculty and finances, but in significant part by the quality of its "finished product"—the individual student. In 1984, the Board of Trustees adopted a resolution on educational outcomes, expressing the Association's broad commitment to developing "accreditation standards and evaluation procedures, which promote the systematic assessment of the outcomes of educational programs," as well as to providing resources and "leadership" to encourage progress toward that end.[39] The mid-1980s Task Force on Planning recommended "establishing goals and objectives for the Association" that "requested" each commission to "establish goals and objectives for itself that supplemented the goals of the Association." These goals included one on "Outcome Measures," which required each commission to develop accreditation procedures that would ensure that member institutions were "implementing a process by which outcomes are measured."[40] By 1985, Executive Director Ben Childers could report that "much has been achieved by all units of the Southern Association in the area of outcome measures," adding however that "extensive follow-up" remained "essential to full achievement." The Elementary Commission had changed its standards to require institutions "to establish measurable objectives, assess student performance, use test data to provide plans for addressing student needs, and report the progress of students to governing boards, staff, and parents." For its part, the Occupational Commission assessed outcomes through monitoring such things as job placements and employer satisfaction. At the same time, the Secondary Commission was working on incorporating ways to measure school performance into its accreditation and evaluation procedures.[41]

The Commission on Colleges' new criteria also encouraged a greater focus on student assessment. Its new criteria revealed a more qualified attachment to "outcomes assessment," placing it within a broader commitment to what was called "institutional effectiveness." After several years of customary research, drafting and consultation (including a series of hearings held across the region), the College Delegate Assembly "approved in principle the proposed new Criteria for Accreditation" in 1983. But it did so with the "stipulation" that the section (Section III) on "Institutional Effectiveness" should be "expanded and clarified in order to de-emphasize outcome assessment as the sole or primary criterion in the accrediting process."[42] Section III was "completely rewritten" and the College Delegate Assembly approved the revised Criteria for Accreditation at the 1984 annual meeting in Atlanta.[43]

Emphasis on "institutional effectiveness" required that "member institutions make explicit the goals they have set for themselves and how they intend to assess their effectiveness in fulfilling those institution-specific goals." It was intended to encourage institutions to examine closely what they claimed to be offering and doing, and then to take a hard and ongoing look at how well they were fulfilling those claims. It encouraged them, in other words, to focus not just on how good an institution's resources might be, but on how well it was using those resources in the pursuit of its stated mission. The new approach also stressed continuous self-assessment on the institution's part, to be carried out every year, not just every decade. The new criteria represented a "radical departure" from the Commission on Colleges' traditional approach to accrediting.

In this period all four commissions continued to expand their activities and interests in ways that reflected a shared desire to respond both to continuing concerns and contemporary circumstances. As they did so, they faced, singly and together, various key issues relating both to the internal relations of the Association and to its connections to the wider worlds of education and society. Major changes in all the commissions' ways of doing things have to be seen in the context of the long-standing debate over quantitative and qualitative methods of measuring educational improvement that had shaped the long-term evolution of regional accreditation. Yet the familiar challenges of reform and relevancy that the Association had faced throughout most of its history were now given new urgency and specific direction by the wider educational ferment of this period. Whatever their motivation, the new emphasis on such areas as educational outcomes, student assessment and institutional effectiveness reflected the commissions' continuing attempts to develop accrediting procedures and processes that took closer account of the individual school or student and encouraged a more continuous and cooperative approach to steady improvement. Thus the mid-1980s (like, for example, the mid-1930s) represents one of the pivotal moments in Association history; in some respects a culmination of past efforts and issues, in other respects the beginning of a new era.

This sense of the mid-1980s as a pivotal moment was reinforced by a changing of the guard among the Association's leadership. At

270 A Centennial History

the end of 1984, Joe Johnston and Gordon Sweet both retired from their posts as executive directors of the Secondary and College commissions, respectively. Durell Ruffin, executive director of the Elementary Commission, retired the following year. All three were made executive director emeriti in recognition of their many years of service. Three new executive directors thus took up their duties around the same time. James Stiltner was appointed executive director of the Secondary Commission as of January 1, 1985. James Rogers left the position of president of Brenau College in Gainesville, Georgia, to become executive director of the Commission on Colleges that summer. Rogers was a past member of the Commission and its Executive Council, and his previous positions had included dean of student affairs at Armstrong State College.[44] After an interim period under the direction of Dr. Henry Ashmore, John Davis, who had served as associate executive director, took over the running of the Elementary Commission, also in the summer of 1985. In the spring of that year, Claude E. Lucas, formerly of Fort Valley State College in Georgia, became the first person to fill the new position of director of finance and administration.[45]

This sense both of consolidation and of new beginnings was further symbolized by the opening of the Association's new headquarters. In 1985, the Board of Trustees "approved a plan to acquire property, secure funding, and construct a building for long-term use of the Association." The Southern Association marked the last decade of its first century by moving into a new purpose-built office building in Decatur, Georgia, in 1988.[46] In some ways the Association's new headquarters also symbolized its permanent and growing role in Southern life. Comfortably settled in a new building, as it entered the century's final decade the Association nevertheless continued to face familiar, often uncomfortable, questions regarding both its internal development and its evolving relationships with other elements of the educational world, including a diverse membership, a burgeoning collection of governmental agencies, other accrediting bodies, and, of course, a wider public focused, as ever, on the state of education.

The changes in accrediting procedures of the 1980s indicate, among other things, the Association's awareness of public attitudes regarding education in general and regional accreditation in particular. As the Association's prominence in Southern education developed, so too its understanding of how it was perceived by the public, and how it *wanted* to be perceived, continued to evolve. With the Association's growing role in the lives of the South's people and its expanding relations with business and government, demand grew for a more concerted and consistent approach to public relations. If the potential for public misconception and criticism evident, for example, during the Speaker Ban controversy, was to be limited, the Association needed to do a better job of explaining itself to the people whose lives its activities affected. The growing desire not just to serve the cause of educational progress, but to be seen to be doing so, is illustrated by the inclusion of a recommendation on the Association's "Image" in the Strategic Action Plan of the 1980s. The recommendation established as a goal for the Association that it come to be "perceived as the primary spokesman for education in the South."[47]

Efforts to fulfill this straightforward, if ambitious, statement of purpose nevertheless suggest the inevitably ambiguous nature of an Association necessarily positioned within the constricting triangle created by the public, by various levels of government, and by its own ever-growing and diversifying membership. For if the Association sought the sweepingly inclusive role of "primary spokesman for education in the South," it already had roles that might not necessarily be in harmony with this broad goal. For one thing, the Association was in one sense an advocate for its members, a group that, however large, was far from synonymous with "education in the South." So while accreditation was widely seen as an instrument for measuring how well member institutions were meeting the demands placed on them by the public, the Association was also perceived as a "spokesman" for those institutions, including on occasions when the Association and its members might consider public demands unreasonable or damaging. Thus arose, and persists, the question: Can the roles of interest group advocate and public servant be consistently reconciled?

One way, of course, in which the Association saw itself as serving the public interest was through its development and application of accrediting processes that not only brought definite improvements to the region's schools and colleges, but provided an increasingly valuable "seal of approval" that consumers—whether students, parents, business or government agencies, or educators themselves—could look to with confidence. A 1981 study conducted by the Commission on Secondary Schools among admissions officers of four-year colleges and universities in the Association's area seemed to bear out the value of the Association's role in this regard. Despite the presence of other factors, such as standardized tests, grade-point averages and college entrance exams, the study found strong support for accreditation as an important measure of incoming students. From this perspective, to serve the Association's members by pushing them to improve was also to serve the public by improving the quality of the educational institutions from which Southerners received their education.[48]

Critics of accreditation were skeptical that the interests of schools and colleges always corresponded so nicely with those of the public that, one way or another, paid for them. One especially hostile critic was James D. Koerner, who launched a sweeping attack against regional accrediting, especially at the college level, in his keynote address to a conference on "Accreditation and the Public Interest" held in Washington, D.C. in November of 1970. Although highly polemical, perhaps designed to provoke strong debate, Koerner's answers to the question, "Who Benefits from Accreditation: Special Interests or the Public?" encompassed many of the general complaints made regarding accreditation.

Koerner began his "attack" on the regional associations by "bluntly" stating his "principle complaint" against them: "They have become nothing but old-fashioned trade associations piously pretending to represent the public interest." Furthermore, the comparison was "inexact" since organizations such as the American Medical Association did not in fact "wield the brute force" of accrediting agencies that—since at least for colleges, membership was no longer really "voluntary"—had come to be "genuinely monopolistic and coercive." Koerner also expressed concern that the regional accrediting bodies had come to "exhibit characteristics of federal regulatory agencies," their "substantial power to regulate higher education" having been "acquired . . . through usurpation and the default of other agencies." Worse still, in Koerner's view, was that, in common with federal regulatory agencies, the regional associations "often use their power less in the interests of the public than in the interests of the industry they are supposed to regulate.

The regional associations often act in effect as licensing bodies that protect the established market in education."[49]

As membership grew to cover thousands of institutions, critics claimed that it was less a case of accreditation being a seal of approval as a *lack* of accreditation being a sign of disapproval. In other words, regional accreditation could helpfully identify the minority of institutions that should probably be avoided, but it provided little, if any, guidance to those looking to choose from among the accredited majority. "Towering above" their other failings, according to Koerner, was the regional associations' "failure to provide the student and his parents with comprehensive and comparative guidance to educational institutions. It's as simple as that and as monumental." Given the diversity of the system and choices they faced, Americans needed this kind of "guidance . . . more than the people of any other country." The diversity Americans faced was, ironically, in large part the product of America's uniquely decentralized approach to education, an approach that had encouraged the creation and rise of the regional associations. Yet, according to Koerner, the very "agencies that are presumed to know the most about the quality and the individual characteristics of all these institutions" were content to "allow the public to wander endlessly in the immense and tractless forest of our schools and colleges" with little more than the advice of friends or "commercial publications" of dubious worth. "The taxpayer," in Koerner's analysis, "is therefore confronted with the absurd situation of having financed the most gigantic educational enterprise in the history of man and having no way whatever of assessing it" or of "matching particular institutions to particular educational needs."[50] So, although the regional associations might have convinced themselves they could represent both the interests of their member institutions and the public interest, in reality, according to the critique voiced by Koerner, a massive conflict of interest existed between the demands of the educational institutions and the needs of the public who sought to evaluate them. In Koerner's view, "If the regional associations took seriously their duties to the body politic, they would long since have developed the means for putting detailed evaluations and comparative commentaries about educational institutions into the hands of the general public. That they have not done so, have no intention of doing so, and cannot do so as long as they are captive trade associations, is, I submit, the most serious indictment that can be brought against them."[51]

Organizations like the Southern Association would doubtless have rejected much of Koerner's attack as closer to caricature than to genuine criticism. And it seems impossible to imagine a situation in which member institutions would have agreed to any kind of ranking system. Whatever the reasons for not ranking institutions within the membership, this unwillingness to differentiate among members was seized upon by critics as further evidence that the Association's primary social and educational function was not serving the public interest, but speaking on behalf of the "special interest group" formed by its members.

The Association and its peers would also, surely, have pointed to the aim of encouraging institutions to improve in terms of their own aims rather in competition with other institutions, and to how the development of new ways of doing so itself illustrated accreditors' openness to criticism and change. Koerner was not impressed by this line of reasoning, lambasting both quantitative and qualitative standards, the former on the familiar grounds that they promoted an unwanted uniformity, the latter on the basis that they were "excessively fuzzy and nebulous." Anyone who had read visiting accrediting teams' reports could not help, Koerner insisted, "being struck by the impressionistic judgments, the arbitrariness, the capriciousness, and the subjectivism that permeate them." In his critique of standards, then, Koerner, perhaps unintentionally, recapitulated both sides of the debate *within* accreditation as to the drawbacks of either quantitative or qualitative standards.[52]

But Koerner made no allowances for those accreditors who had encouraged, or come to accept, a shift toward qualitative evaluation as a means to lead accreditation away from some of the elitism and rigidity inherent in more traditional forms of evaluation that they, as well as Koerner, were concerned about. Rather, Koerner summed up his lengthy attack, "the standards and criteria of the regional associations simply follow usage and form." Contrary to the stated aims and claims of regional accreditors, "In no sense do they 'lead.'" Instead, Koerner found regional accrediting "guilty" of a "complacent" commitment to preserving the status quo, of bureaucratic "arteriosclerosis," as well as of imposing "so-called standards and criteria" with "no basis" in "research or theory," but which reflected merely "the received wisdom of the day," which, in Koerner's definition, was "any practice in which a majority of institutions engage, and often only a minority of prestige institutions, becomes enshrined in the standards and criteria . . . , there to be inflicted on all other institutions." Koerner cited tenure along with "the assumption that certain ways of governing educational institutions are so superior to any other possible ways that they must be made standard" as examples of the "enshrinement of the conventional wisdom by the regional associations."[53]

Koerner was not finished with his cataloging of the ways in which regional accrediting defied, rather than defended, the public interest when it came to education. He expressed his concern that organizations that "resemble cartels in their own region" sought to "extend their monopoly through the creation of national organizations such as the Federation of Regional Accrediting Commissions of Higher Education (FRACHE)." Compounding the dangers of this monopoly power was the "indefensible veil of secrecy" behind which much of it was exercised. In Koerner's view, a tax-exempt educational agency should be as open as possible, not as closed as "the Kremlin" to outsiders seeking information as to its activities and procedures. "This kind of fishbowl operation will no doubt," Koerner felt, "strike any bona fide accreditor as a bizarre and horrifying prospect." From Koerner's viewpoint, however, "tax-exempt monopolies with plenty of power to throw around must be made accountable to somebody besides themselves."[54]

Accreditors would have found much to disagree not only with Koerner's description of their activities, but also to the motives he ascribed to them. Many would surely have felt that he exaggerated their power, and Koerner was less than consistent in his view of whether the membership dominated the Association or the leadership dictated to the institutions. Koerner made few allowances for the kinds of constraints and limitations that accreditors labored under, perhaps especially those arising from the growing role of the federal government in the nation's education. They would surely also have rejected Koerner's implicit argument that accreditation's contribution to the public interest should largely be understood as a source of consumer information. Yet even if accreditors rejected much of the tone and substance of Koerner's critique, he was hardly a lone voice. Others took a more generous view of accreditors' motives and adopted a more sympathetic understanding of the challenges presented by their complex location in the midst of their members, the public and government. Yet surely Koerner and others were right to reject the notion of any easy correspondence between the interests of educators and those to be educated, between the good of the institution and the good of the public within which that institution is located. Given the inevitability of these complex and competing interests, it was just as inevitable that the Southern Association would always occupy an ambiguous role in seeking to serve the interests of the public and the interests of educators.

Feeding the perception among segments of both the public and educators of the Southern Association as a special interest advocate was its increasingly complex relation to federal and, to a lesser extent, state governmental agencies, and its need to take positions on the involvement of those agencies in the running of its member institutions. Throughout its history, the Association and its commissions have had to take close account of the powerful social and political forces shaping education and, therefore, accreditation. While many of the major clashes with government in the past had been at the state level, increasingly the conflicts arose out of federal efforts to shape the nation's education. The GI Bill was the most visible and widespread consequence of this involvement in the immediate postwar period. Loans to students and research grants to institutions and individual academics had a tremendous impact on all levels of postsecondary education. In a variety of respects, the provisions of the GI Bill greatly influenced questions of who would go to college, what kind of college they would go to, and what they would study when they got there. If federal money and involvement brought educators and their institutions closer to the people of America, it also brought them into much closer contact with the expansive and demanding apparatus of central government. Furthermore, the GI Bill proved to be the harbinger of greater federal involvement in education over the coming years, as various pieces of major legislation reflected the growing desire of federal politicians and agencies to shape the educational interest to meet their conception of the national interest. This involvement would have an enduring impact on postsecondary institutions and, therefore, on the Association, especially the Commission on Colleges.

Government involvement in education was often carried out in the name of goals, which most educators, like most Americans, supported. The GI Bill, for example, had "encouraged colleges to continue their wartime stance of service to national goals." As the very name suggests, the National Defense Education Act of 1958 was motivated in great part by continued concern for national security and supremacy in the Cold War. In a war fought in the mind and in space as well as on the battlefields of Korea and Vietnam, education could scarcely have remained as free from federal attention as it had once been. There was much about these goals that educators could support, especially since these wartime aims often meshed with the longstanding commitment to the democratization of education understood as increased social responsiveness on the part of institutions and expanded access to those institutions for the American people. The federal government's intervention in education continued to grow, especially as a consequence of court decisions and legislation of the civil rights era. Subsequent expansion of civil rights legislation to include women, the disabled and other groups continued to expand the roles of the federal government and the judiciary in education, creating many new laws with which educational institutions were required to comply. The role of government agencies in enforcing "non-educational" demands on institutions relating to matters such as workplace health and safety also increased greatly. Again, many of the new requirements imposed by the government or the courts were desirable and were often accepted as such by the institutions involved. Furthermore, from an individual and institutional standpoint, educators and administrators usually proved eager to tap as deeply as possible into the vast reservoir of public money made available by federal funding of everything from student loans to rocket science research, a developing attitude evident from the early postwar years when the opportunity to receive financial support through the GI Bill had "justified acceptance of federal support by private institutions."[55]

Yet administrators and academics were often ambivalent about this new level of federal involvement in their lives. While the idea of the "national interest" or the "public good" might be relatively clear in wartime, it is a far more slippery concept the rest of the time. The hand that encouraged social goals educators endorsed could also encourage aims they opposed. The hand that fed institutional growth was the same hand that could exercise control over the institutions charged with spending public money and abiding by the law of the land. Federal money could fuel an institution's expansion but could also draw it into a complex web of federal funding and compliance. Federal funding could shape institutional development in response to priorities not necessarily formulated by either the institution's administrators and academics, threatening to direct colleges and universities away from their stated missions and to undermine their independence far more effectively than the Southern Association's standards had ever done. Even when they agreed with general aims such as greater equality of access and opportunity, or higher quality scientific research, many educators and administrators worried that government involvement in their institutions presented a threat to academic integrity and administrative independence.

The Commission on Colleges shared its members' concern that government influence on education represented a serious threat to institutions' independence. Thus, the Commission on Colleges found itself increasingly speaking out on behalf of its members and on behalf of itself. The Commission's role as advocate for its members in the face of federal involvement reflected its members' ambivalent attitude toward that involvement. In late 1989, for example, James T. Rogers, the Commission's executive director, warned a Congressional Joint Committee on the Reauthorization of the Higher Education Act of 1965 that "excessive regulation" would hinder the "flexibility, innovation, and access that have been among the beneficial characteristics of our higher education system." On this point, Rogers' views were shared by many leaders of member institutions.[56]

Accreditors' concerns were also shared by many outside education circles that held to the widespread and longstanding view that education should be the responsibility of locality and community, and that the federal government's role in it should be limited at most. At the same time, the Association's more visible role as advocate on behalf of members seeking to limit government influence on their institutions fueled the complaints of those who believed that accreditors had largely become lobbyists for the special interests of the education business. Whether they were viewed positively or negatively, the larger point is that the public image of the College Commission in particular, and regional accrediting in general, inevitably took on much of the complexity and ambiguity that shaped the growing connections between its member institutions and the federal government.

Accreditors were also ambivalent about the government's increasing efforts to influence accreditation. In some respects, federal involvement in education augmented the accreditors' influence. In others, it threatened not only their members' loss of independence, but their own. Yet in many ways, the Association's increased connection to federal activity in education *boosted* its power and influence in Southern education and society. The GI Bill, for example, elevated the accreditors' role as intermediaries between their membership and government.[57] Good standing with the appropriate regional accrediting association was increasingly a prerequisite for the receipt of all kinds of federal funding, from students' loans to professors' research grants. To lose accreditation would be to lose those students and professors as well as the money that went with them, and, in all likelihood to lose the chance to survive in a competitive educational word. In such circumstances, there was very little that remained genuinely "voluntary" about membership in the Association's Higher Commission. This had started to become a factor much earlier of course, as the complaints of some of the denominational colleges and Centre College in the 1920s indicates. But it was fully entrenched as an unassailable fact of life by the time the Speaker Ban Hearings devoted so much time to the issue of translating loss of accreditation into a language—loss of government funding—that everyone could understand.

However, much as the growth of federal involvement enhanced accreditors' influence, they remained concerned that in other respects it threatened to undermine their influence and credibility. As the 1977 director's report expressed it, "government agencies, both federal and state" also presented the "greatest challenges" to voluntary accreditation. In part, that challenge arose from the government's apparent efforts to take on an accrediting function itself. In the 1950s, for example, the Korean War brought forth another GI Bill, which created a new educational role for the federal government. For the first time, the U.S. Office of Education was mandated to produce a nationally recognized list of accrediting associations considered by the Commissioner of Education to be "reliable" judges of educational institutions' quality. While this was not an accrediting role as such, as Jack Allen points out, it did give to a branch of the federal government "the authority to approve the accreditors." This was an unwelcome development for many in the Association and in umbrella accrediting organizations like the NCA and the NCRAA. In part, this was because the government list included accrediting agencies that they had hoped to eliminate. A larger concern was that the list reflected an expanding, if indirect, accrediting role for the federal government, a role that threatened to alter the responsibilities and diminish the power of regional bodies like the Southern Association. Legislation such as the Higher Education Facilities Act of 1963 and the Nurse Training Act of the following year gave the U.S. Office of Education some accrediting powers relative to institutions not already covered by a recognized accrediting body. This expansion of government activity provided a further incentive for the Association to expand its accrediting responsibilities in order to preempt further inroads by government or others.[58]

Yet on the whole, the federal government did not seem inclined to take on an explicit, wide-ranging role in accrediting. No doubt this was due partly to an awareness of the hostility that such involvement would arouse, and not just among accreditors. Historically, American public opinion had been hostile to the idea of the national government becoming involved in matters considered of private or local concern. This suspicion of "big government" was commonplace throughout the nation, but nowhere was it stronger than in the South, where historical circumstances such as slavery, secession and Civil War had transformed a shared national commitment to particular political values into a staunch defense of local independence and states' rights. These attitudes shaped Southern attitudes toward education. Indeed, even the ideal of an educational system administered at county and state level had been a hard sell for the reformers of the nineteenth century. Even as local control subsided in the face of higher standards and greater organization, many people who agreed on precious little else agreed that education was not a job for government, especially not the federal government. And in the South of the civil rights era, many white Southerners saw no reason to change their opinions regarding federal "interference" in the region's schools and colleges. Yet if a *direct* federal role in accreditation was unlikely, an increased government role in education inevitably had a growing impact on the activities of accrediting agencies. If government involvement was shaping the goals of educational institutions, it followed that it must also shape the activities of those with the responsibility of evaluating institutions' success in meeting their goals. This raised the fear that the accrediting process was being co-opted to the service of goals other than those dictated by the Association's own procedures and standards or by the original missions of the institutions themselves. Thus, if government involvement seemed to threaten institutional independence in the way it tied funding to specific kinds of development (a complaint also heard against the Association's standards), it also threatened to diminish the Association's independence by co-opting them as inspectors not of educational improvement in accordance with the Association's standards, but rather of how well institutions were developing in response to the government's goals and incentives. Ironically, a more enduring problem for the Association would be the federal government's desire to use, rather than usurp, its accrediting functions and responsibilities.[59]

And so it proved. A growing body of federal legislation over the years influenced the actions and policies of accreditors. Of great significance, for example, was the passage of the National Defense Education Act of 1958, legislation described by Herbert Kliebard, as "a massive entry by the federal government into curricular matters." This new level of government participation had a tremendous impact on ongoing curriculum conflicts and debates between educators, with the consequence that "the way in which the curriculum of American schools was determined was never quite the same."[60] Legislation that had such an impact on curriculum development inevitably shaped the thought and action of accreditors whose own work had so much to do with what, as well as how, the region's students were taught.

Another key issue was the government's efforts to use regional, and other, accrediting bodies as de facto inspectors of governmental laws and regulations. For all its expansive interests in education, the federal government often lacked the practical means, not to mention the constitutional or political authority, to adopt an official evaluative role in the nation's schools and colleges. In turning to the accreditors to fill this role, federal agencies significantly expanded their efforts, and their ability, to shape accreditors' activities to the service of their own priorities and practices. Thus, it was not simply relying on the Association's judgment as to whether an institution met standards previously worked out between the Association and representatives of its member institutions. Rather, federal agencies increasingly sought to shape accrediting methods and standards to suit their own priorities. James Rogers encapsulated these concerns about federal regulation's direct impact on accrediting during legislative hearings on Capitol Hill in 1989. At that time, the Commission on Colleges was especially worried that the federal government, through its Agency Evaluation Branch, "was either moving beyond its mandate into issues of educational quality, or was proposing that accrediting institutions regulate certain practices that were properly the concern of the federal government or the courts." An Association that had hardly avoided criticism of its own standards was understandably concerned about what it saw as an attempt to enlist regional accreditors as unpaid inspectors and enforcers of the federal government's standards and policies. On this and other occasions, then, the Association, and especially the Commission on Colleges, found much of its time devoted either to meeting or to resisting growing government efforts to shape its aims and practices. In recent years, it has found itself increasingly required to speak for itself as well as its members, on behalf of the accreditors as well as the accredited. The Association's growing, often contentious, relationship with the federal government has continued to be a major element in its activities, especially within the Commission on Colleges.[61]

These kinds of tensions, and the varying appraisals of accreditation arising from them, were hardly the product of increased federal involvement in education alone. For one reason or another, they had always gone with the accrediting territory. Whether dealing with antagonistic governors or suspicious legislators, with anxious students or demanding parents, the Association's members have found themselves operating on the ground between member institutions and the wider society, between varying educational ideals and changing public pressures. In this arena, even shared assumptions and ideals can be the source of difference as debate develops on the particular and practical ways to achieve those goals. Inevitably, one person's legitimate public interest is another person's unwarranted outside interference; one person's commitment to educational independence is another person's ivory tower indifference to the real world. Just as inevitably, the Association's continuing participation in these debates and conflicts will ensure it remains a magnet for both the high expectations and strong criticisms of educators, politicians and members of the public. In a 1980 study, educator Fred Harcleroad concluded that accreditation's "use by all types of enterprise, particularly federal and state governments, has tended to modify its functions and caused changes in its structure and operations." Harcleroad also predicted that "accrediting associations could well be influenced significantly by future altered relationships," a judgment fully borne out by the continuing activities and priorities of the Association as it moved toward its centennial year.[62]

The question of how to respond to the various social forces influencing education and accreditation also continued as a source of debate within the Association, prompting deeper distrust as well as extended cooperation, stronger desire for association as well as greater resolve to preserve, even extend, existing levels of commission autonomy. The extremes of cooperation and conflict are reflected in the developing relations between the two school commissions on the one hand and the two postsecondary commissions on the other. As we shall see, relations between the Elementary and Secondary commissions, in recent times, suggest the potential for blending association and autonomy. The recent history of relations between the two postsecondary commissions suggest the limits of association, where differences of power and principle remain preeminent.

The conflict between the Commission on Colleges and the COEI that eventually ended with the latter commission's departure from the Association had its roots in philosophical differences as old as the Association: differences regarding the appropriate relation between education and the economy. As Fred Harcleroad also recognized, "business" was another major "sector" of American life that significantly affected the development of voluntary accreditation. American business has consistently sought to shape education and accreditation to its own purposes, often encouraged by public opinion and government bodies convinced that a primary function of education should be to improve Americans' ability to find the kind of work or workers required by an always-changing economy. If these perennial issues contributed to the Association's mixed role and perception in education and society, they also had a deep impact on relations within the organization. Enlisting accreditation in the cause of making education more sensitive to the necessities of economic life had its supporters within the Association almost from the beginning. With the creation of the COEI, the Association had a commission wholeheartedly devoted to the cultivation of good relations between business, occupational education institutions and accrediting. To those in the COEI, as we have seen, the closer its relation to business the better. What was good for business was good for occupational education. "The language of occupational education," as Ronald Storey put it, "is the language of today's business and industry."[63]

These efforts have just as surely provoked strong resistance from many educators who have feared the negative impact of commercialism on education and accreditation alike. The "commercialization" of education had, of course, been a long-standing concern throughout the Association's history and was one of the main points of contention between the liberal arts group and the college teachers' group in the 1920s and 1930s. Many within the Association, especially within the Commission on Colleges, remained skeptical that a mutually beneficial relation between the values of the campus and the marketplace could be taken for granted, especially when it came to non-occupational fields of study. Over the years, however, the defenders of the liberal arts tradition had made a series of compromises that recognized changes in the worlds of work and business, increasingly recognizing that postsecondary missions other than the liberal arts ideal had to be accommodated. Yet even as the Association's general accrediting philosophy moved toward greater emphasis on the particular mission of each institution and the Commission on Colleges relaxed its liberal arts requirements for special purpose and two-year colleges, the insistence that degree-granting postsecondary institutions preserve a core of liberal arts or general education courses remained powerful.

Some had hoped that the creation of the COEI would help to resolve long-standing differences of philosophy and priority by separating the accreditation of occupational educational institutions offering certificates and diplomas from that of degree-granting institutions. This did not happen. Despite by-laws forbidding the COEI from seeking to accredit degree-granting occupational education institutions, it was soon making efforts to do so. Much of the disagreement revolved around the question of how "degree" should be defined. The Commission on Colleges remaining adamantly attached to the traditional college-based understanding of degree and argued that it should be their responsibility to accredit any institution offering one. If an institution was offering a qualification that did not meet this definition, then it should not call it a degree, but rather a diploma or a certificate. COEI accreditors, for their part, wanted graduates of their institutions to enjoy the added social and economic advantages they believed came with a qualification characterized as a degree. The dispute, in other words, centered less on the content of the training students would receive than on what the qualification they received for completing that training would be called. It is ironic that educators who had long lamented the unfairness of occupational education being viewed as less valuable or prestigious than a college education nevertheless sought to redress that slight by adopting the semantic trappings of the kinds of education under whose shadow they had long labored. In doing so, they inadvertently endorsed the educational hierarchy they elsewhere lamented.

The two postsecondary commissions' conflicting priorities and philosophies continued to play themselves out in organizational and jurisdictional differences between them. These often heated conflicts were closely bound up with the ongoing contention over autonomy and centralization, with the opposing sides in both cases often containing the same people. Partly resolved by the organization changes that eliminated the executive director position and reduced the size of the Board of Trustees, it was only finally resolved by the eventual departure of the COEI from the Association shortly before the centennial.

If the evolving trajectories of the two postsecondary commissions eventually led them in entirely different directions, those of the Elementary and Secondary commissions have gradually brought the school commissions closer together. Relations between the two commissions, especially in the early years, saw significant problems and conflicts, some of which can be put down to ubiquitous concerns about the unpredictability of change and the perceived need to protect one's own "turf." The most important substantive issue facing the commissions was the issue of systemwide accreditation. Initially, the two commissions had not had much to do with each other since the Secondary people were opposed to any form of systemwide accreditation: that is, accrediting both elementary and secondary together as part of one system. The absence of systemwide accreditation necessarily raised the question of who would accredit the middle schools: institutions consisting of a combination of grades overlapping both areas generally viewed as elementary and secondary. This remained a contentious issue into the 1980s, but due in important part to top-level cooperation, especially between Executive Directors John Davis and James Stiltner, a policy was hammered out whereby each school would decide which commission it wished to accredit them. There was a proviso that schools could not move back and forth between the two in search of more congenial accrediting standards or processes. Opposition to this plan persisted as some members feared that the commissions would seek to "poach" each other's members, but strenuous efforts were made to resolve these differences.

As time passed, however, this most contentious of issues separating the Elementary and Secondary commissions would prove to be the ground on which they would eventually build an extensive framework of cooperation. As accrediting procedures and philosophies in both commissions have evolved toward a similar, more flexible, model emphasizing both student achievement and institutional improvement, cooperation has increased. A very significant program of recent years, especially for the Elementary Commission, in its own right—the Goodlad Project—suggests something of the shared assumptions regarding the aims and purposes of education and accreditation, and also illustrates the deepening inter-commission cooperation in efforts to achieve those aims.

Among the many studies of education published in the 1980s

was a book titled *A Place Called School* (1984), written by John I. Goodlad, a professor in the University of Washington's College of Education. This study would prove to be the most important educational study to emerge from this period as far as the Elementary and Secondary commissions were concerned. John Davis of the Elementary Commission regretted how the inordinate attention paid to what were, in his view, less valuable studies meant that Goodlad's work "did not receive the national attention and recognition that it so rightly deserved." Davis judged Goodlad's book "probably one of the most comprehensive examinations of elementary and secondary education" to be produced "in many decades." Hearing Goodlad speak in 1985 at the American Education Research Association's meeting in Chicago "convinced" Davis that the Southern Association "needed to involve Dr. Goodlad in some sort of project that would serve the cause of school improvement in the South."

Davis' conviction that enlisting Goodlad's "national reputation and . . . expertise" would be good for the Association was strengthened by his belief that "so much" of what Goodlad had to say about school improvement "paralleled the process for school improvement" that he and his colleagues in the Elementary and Secondary commissions had themselves "developed over the years." Goodlad emphasized involving as many people as possible in reform efforts and insisted that the individual school should be the focus of improvement. These priorities meshed well, it seemed to Davis, with the philosophies and practices of the Elementary Commission,[64] and those of the Secondary Commission too, since James Stiltner "readily agreed" to the Secondary Commission's involvement with Goodlad. After an initial meeting in Seattle, Goodlad agreed to work with the Association up to the 1987 summer conference to be held in Charleston, South Carolina. Goodlad agreed to be the keynote speaker at the 1986 annual meeting and to address the Joint Elementary/Secondary Delegate Assembly. This was the beginning of a relationship that would result in the five-year "Goodlad Project," sponsored jointly by the Elementary and Secondary commissions and "designed to provide an alternative to the traditional reaccreditation process" as part of the wider project of school renewal in the South.[65]

The Goodlad Project's initial efforts focused on identifying the recommendations contained in *A Place Called School* and on "establish[ing] procedures and guidelines" to examine whether the existing standards of the Elementary and Secondary commissions supported, contradicted or failed to address Goodlad's research findings. A "Blue Ribbon Task Force" was formed, composed of the executive directors and chairmen of the Standards Committee of both the Elementary and the Secondary commissions and chaired by the Association's president-elect, Ray Bruce. Eventually, fifty-six recommendations and twenty-four criteria for educational improvement were identified. Committees then worked on assessing their compatibility or otherwise with existing commission standards and on building them into the standards of the Elementary and Secondary commissions where appropriate.[66]

In the meantime, the commissions launched a pilot program in the fall of 1987. From the many volunteers, the Association selected seven schools in three states. The pilot schools consisted of elementary, middle and secondary schools from the Fayette County Public Schools in Lexington, Kentucky, and the same combination from the Brazosport Independent School District of Freeport, Texas. The seventh participant, representing private and unit schools, was Norfolk Academy in Virginia. Prior to the project, Davis and Stiltner met with the schools' teachers and administrators to familiarize them with the project and to gather questions for Goodlad to address at the summer meeting in Charleston.[67] The program aimed to determine whether the Goodlad-influenced standards and criteria would provide the participating schools, and by extension the other schools of the region, with "a more effective vehicle for self-renewal."[68]

The pilot schools used the fifty-six recommendations "as values, or goals" to guide their working toward self-renewal in terms of the twenty-four specific criteria.[69] The criteria were grouped into five main areas: School Climate, Planning, Staff Development, Curriculum and Instruction, and Communication.[70] The pilot program included follow-up contacts with both graduates and drop-outs to gather information that might be helpful to future planning. The incorporation of "student achievement results" as well as the insistence that staff development topics should come from the faculty in each school, not from outside, reflected the general beliefs underpinning the renewal project that reform must come from within and must take account of local circumstances.[71] By the summer of 1988, the project was beginning to produce results, according to teachers and administrators in some of the pilot schools. Three new schools, one in Pasco County, Florida, and two in Montgomery, Alabama, joined the pilot program in the coming school year.[72]

Another new aspect of the project was the interest shown in it by the Encyclopedia Britannica Education Corporation (EBEC). The EBEC filmed the Charleston planning sessions involving Dr. Goodlad and two dozen teachers from the pilot schools, and edited versions of these meetings eventually became part of a video series titled "Renewing A Place Called School." The video series dealt with the six broad subjects of Schools and the Freedom to Change; The School as the Unit of Change; Enriching the Curriculum; Improving Instruction; Leadership and Staff Development; Assessment and Long-Range Planning. Accompanied by a sixty-page "leader's handbook," the series was made available for sale to schools considering their own self-renewal projects.[73]

By the end of 1990, John Davis reported that both commissions remained "actively engaged in an alternative route to regional accreditation that includes more than eighty schools throughout its eleven states."[74] The collaborative endeavor with John Goodlad began what John Davis described in 1993 as "a new era" for the Commission on Elementary Schools, one in which accreditation would have "a three-pronged focus" that began with the school as the unit of improvement, insisted that "improvement must be a continuous effort" and operated on the assumption that "student outcomes must be a measure of that improvement."[75] Thus it offers a specific example of how wider social and educational changes combined with changing thinking regarding the purpose and future of accreditation to shape the development of the Association's methods and priorities. In contrast to the irreconcilable differences between the two postsecondary commissions and their leaders, the Goodlad Project also symbolizes the developing levels of voluntary collaboration achievable when anxieties regarding autonomy can be lessened, and accrediting assumptions and priorities increasingly coincide rather than conflict. As the Association's first century in search of educational articulation and improvement drew to a close, questions of how to blend cooperation and independence in the cause of doing so remained as central in 1995 as it had been in 1895.

Thus, as it reached its centennial year, the Association continued to chart its course amidst the shifting tides of organizational, educational and social circumstances that had been part of its history since the beginning. Yet by 1995, the small landing craft that had established a beach-head in the educational world of 1895 had assumed the size and stature of an entity more akin to an aircraft carrier in terms of its size and complexity, but also in terms of its potential reach and power in the related theaters of Southern education and society. When the Southern Association returned to Atlanta for its centennial meeting, it did so as an organization with almost 12,000 members among the region's elementary and secondary schools and its postsecondary colleges and universities, and an operating budget of $4 million with which to pursue its aims and defend its interests in the world of educational research, reform and accreditation. Mere numbers, however, do not do justice to the striking diversity of schools, colleges and individual educators now encompassed by its various commissions, a diversity that would have astonished even those, like Edwin Mims, who lived to see the growth and consolidation of the period spanning World War II. In conclusion, then, as the Association begins its second century, it is of both historical and contemporary value to revisit those themes and issues briefly and to ponder what its founders might have made of its first century of participation in Southern life and education.

Endnotes

[1] Henry H. Hill, "Higher Education Unlimited," *Proceedings* 55 (1950), 210. The figures for 1900-01 were 16.3 million or 94.36 percent.

[2] Interview with Albert J. Geiger, Southern Association of Colleges and Schools Archive, Decatur, GA (hereafter SACS Archive), 14.

[3] Henry J. Otto, "The Elementary School of Tomorrow," *Proceedings* 1949, 191.

[4] Ibid., 1949, 192, 191.

[5] Interview with William Hugh McEniry, Dec. 11, 1973 (hereafter McEniry interview), SACS Archive, 23.

[6] McEniry interview, 23; Otto, "Elementary School of Tomorrow," 192-93.

[7] Donald C. Agnew, *Seventy Five Years of Educational Leadership* (Atlanta, GA:

Southern Association of Colleges and Schools, 1970), 31, 34-35.

[8] Ibid., 34; "Evaluating the Elementary School: A Guide for Cooperative Study," (Atlanta: Southern Association of Colleges and Schools, 1964), 1. Thomas was made an honorary member of the Association in 1964.

[9] See H. Arnold Perry, "Proposals of the Cooperative Study in Elementary Education," *Proceedings* 57 (1952), 151. Perry was professor of education at the University of North Carolina.

[10] Harold D. Drummond, "Next Steps in the Cooperative Study," *Proceedings* 54 (1949), 189-90; Charles R. Spain, "Developing Public Understanding of the Elementary Study," *Proceedings* 54 (1949), 188-89; Agnew, 34

[11] Mabel Jean Morrison and Lucile Williams, "The Florida Elementary-Middle School Committee, Southern Association of Colleges and Schools: A Brief Historical Review, 1944-1991," 11.

[12] Spain, "Developing Public Understanding," 189.

[13] *Proceedings*, 1952. Cited in Morrison and Williams, 24; *Proceedings* 56 (1951), 73, 83-4.

[14] *Proceedings*, 1952. Cited in Morrison and Williams, 24; Perry, "Proposals," 152.

[15] Agnew, 35; *Proceedings* 66 (1961), 170.

[16] Ibid.

[17] *Proceedings* 66 (1961), 174.

[18] Agnew, 35.

[19] Robert W. Day and Barry L. Mellinger, *Accreditation of Two-Year Colleges in the South* (Atlanta: Commission on Colleges, Southern Association of Colleges and Schools, 1973), 16-17; Felix C. Robb, "The Accreditation of Occupational Education," 24 July, 1970, SACS Archive, 4.

[20] Interview with J.M. Godard, June 1, 1973, SACS Archive, 28-31. See also Agnew, 161.

[21] Robb, 1-3.

[22] Day and Mellinger, 18-20; Allen, 162-63.

[23] Allen, 164-65.

[24] *Proceedings*, 23:9 (July 1971), 5.

[25] Robb, 4-5. See also Day and Mellinger 20-21.

[26] "Operational Policies of the Committee on Occupational Education," (Southern Association of Colleges and Schools, 1969), 3-4. See also Allen, 165.

[27] Day and Mellinger, ix. "At the close of fall registration in 1971," according to Day and Mellinger," more than 350,000 full-time equivalent credit students were enrolled in two-year institutions in the Southern region."

[28] Ibid., 26.

[29] Robb, 7.

[30] Ronald B. Storey, "They Are Not Building Bird Houses Anymore!" *Proceedings* 37:3 (Jan.-Feb. 1985), 2. See also, Allen, 165.

[31] "Annual Report of the Director," *Proceedings*, 29:8 (Aug. 1977), 3.

[32] *Proceedings*, 34:6 (July-Aug. 1982), 8.

[33] Storey, 2.

[34] Ibid.

[35] Hilton Smith, "Contemporary Studies of American High Schools," *Proceedings* (Sept.-Oct. 1984), 2ff, and following issues.

[36] James D. Koerner, "Who Benefits from Accreditation: Special Interests or the Public?" Keynote Address at a conference on "Accreditation and the Public Interest" Hotel Dupont Plaza, Washington, D.C., Nov. 6, 1970), 12. Copy in SACS Archive.

[37] Robb, 1-3.

[38] Harry E. Smith, "College Criteria Emphasize Relationship Between Accreditation and Planning," *Proceedings* 37:6 (July-Aug, 1985). Smith was president of Austin College in Sherman, Texas.

[39] Ben Childers, "1984 Achievements Set Stage for 1985 Accomplishments," *Proceedings* 37:3 (Jan.-Feb. 1985), 1.

[40] Ben Childers, "Setting Goals for the Association," *Proceedings* 37:6 (July-Aug., 1985),1.

[41] Ben Childers, "1984 Achievements," 5.

[42] Smith, "College Criteria."

[43] Smith, 2.

[44] See "Rogers to Head College Commission," *Proceedings* 37:5 (May-June 1985), 20.

[45] *Proceedings* 37:6 (July-Aug 1985), 1, for information on Davis and Lucas.

[46] Childers, "Setting Goals," 3.

[47] Ibid., 1.

[48] James H. Stiltner, "Survey Finds Accreditation Still Important," *Proceedings* 33:3 (1981), 3. Seventy-two percent of colleges considered accreditation of an in-state student's high school "very important" or "virtually necessary." The combined figure for out-of-state students was 81 percent, with little difference in response between public and private institutions.

[49] Koerner, "Who Benefits?" 4-5.

[50] Ibid., 5-9.

[51] Ibid., 9.

[52] Ibid., 12.

[53] Ibid., 12, 9-11.

[54] Ibid., 14-15.

[55] Hugh Hawkins, *Banding Together: The Rise of National Associations in American Higher Education, 1887-1950* (Baltimore: The Johns Hopkins University Press, 1992), 165-66.

[56] "Rogers Presents Testimony Before Washington Committee," *Proceedings* 42:1 (Jan.-Feb., 1990), 7.

[57] Hawkins, 165-66.

[58] "Annual Report of the Director," *Proceedings,* 29:8 (Aug. 1977), 3; Allen, 250, 258.

[59] See Allen, 257ff. Association relations to the federal government in the late 1960s and later, as well as the national cooperation it prompted, will be discussed in Chap. 6.

[60] Herbert M. Kliebard, *The Struggle for the American Curriculum, 1893-1958* (New York: Routledge, 1995), xvii.

[61] "Rogers Presents," 7.

[62] Fred F. Harcleroad, *Accreditation: History, Process, and Problems* (Washington, D.C.: American Association for Higher Education, 1980).

[63] Storey, "Not Building Bird Houses Anymore!" 2.

[64] John M. Davis, "The John I. Goodlad Project," *Proceedings* 38:7 (Sept.-Oct.,1986), 2.

[65] Ibid., 2; and quote from "Pilot Schools See Innovation Taking Shape," *Proceedings* 40:4 (July-Aug., 1988), 9.

[66] The Task Force asked each commission member to respond to each of the fifty-six recommendations identified in *A Place Called School* in terms of these three questions: "1) Is this a recommendation you think should exist as a standard for the very best school you can imagine? 2) Is this a recommendation you think is appropriate as a SACS standard for all accredited schools? 3) Is this a recommendation you think will be in conflict with state laws or legislative mandates?" Davis, 2-3; Butler James, "Committee Works to Develop Goodlad Standards," *Proceedings* 39:4 (July-Aug., 1987), 5.

[67] "Goodlad Research Sparks New Approach to Accreditation: Five-Year Study Launched in Three States," *Proceedings* 39:3 (May-June, 1987),9.

[68] Ibid. See also Michael Carr, "Pilot Schools Will Begin With Six Basics," *Proceedings* 39:4 (July-Aug., 1987), 5.

[69] "Goodlad Research Sparks New Approach," 9.

[70] "Pilot Schools See Innovation Taking Shape," 9.

[71] "Goodlad Research Sparks New Approach to Accreditation: Five-Year Study

Launched in Three States," *Proceedings* 39:3 (May-June, 1987), 9.

72 "Pilot Schools See Innovation Taking Shape," 9, 16.

73 "Britannica-Produced Videos Bring Goodlad to Schools," *Proceedings* 40:1 (Jan.-Feb., 1988), 9.

74 John M. Davis, "Five-Year Goals Met; Member Schools Increase to 7,116," *Proceedings* 43:1 (Jan.-Feb. 1991), 15.

75 John M. Davis, "Role of Regional Accreditation Expands," *Proceedings* 45:3 (Spring, 1993), 9.

Chapter Seven

Familiar Themes, 100 Years Later

It is a long way from Atlanta's Georgia Tech chapel to Nashville's Opryland Hotel, site of the first annual meeting of the Southern Association's second century. The historical imagination shrinks before the task of estimating what long-time Nashville resident James H. Kirkland would have made of that massive monument to the city's central role in the mass American culture emerging in the Chancellor's time but now a dominant presence on the national landscape. Yet, however astonishing the father of the Association might have found the location, he would doubtless have recognized many of the themes and concerns addressed there as being quite similar to those that drew the him and a small band of like-minded colleagues to the Georgia Tech campus a century earlier.

The founders would probably have been less surprised by the Association's subsequent development than we might think. In all probability, they would have shared the view of a contemporary participant in the educational ferment of the late nineteenth century that, "whoever thinks that any educational problem is permanently solved deludes himself and misleads others, for problems of education, like problems of philosophy, are always and must be in the process of solution."[1] Thus they would not have been overly startled to see educators at the end of the twentieth century debating many of the questions and concerns that had galvanized them 100 years earlier. At the same time, they would probably have been taken aback by some of the particular answers and responses that familiar questions provoked at different times over the course of a century characterized by incessant change. In the changing educational and social circumstances of the twentieth-century American South, familiar questions and issues often provoked new answers and responses that surely would have tested the imaginative powers of men who, for all their forward-looking hopes, remained very much committed to certain educational ideals and social practices.

In the contrasting fates and relations of the various commissions, Kirkland and his colleagues would have seen the persistence of the enduring philosophical and institutional themes at the heart of the Association's life during their own tenure. The persistent probing of the boundaries of cooperation has been a central theme of the Southern Association's life since its beginnings untary nature of participation in regional accreditation's efforts to improve education. Even at the postsecondary level where accreditation is virtually a sine qua non of survival, individuals and institutions retained a great deal of discretion as to the level of enthusiasm or engagement with which they participated in the accrediting process or worked toward meeting its goals. Hence the inherent caution of many of the Association's aims, but especially of the methods and procedures adopted to meet those aims. Such an approach has often seemed slow and overly bureaucratic even to its supporters, but the forward movement of such a large organization, especially after a more equal relationship developed among its various groupings, could not have been anything other than cautious in its methods.

The very diversity that made the founders' original intention of promoting cooperation and articulation more difficult to achieve nevertheless contributed to the successful fulfillment of another founding aim of the Association's development. William Baskervill's understanding that talk itself could be a form of action in the search for cooperative accomplishment and his hope that the Association would develop as a forum for just such debate into the major questions facing the region's schools and colleges has surely been fulfilled. If the various components of the Association have traditionally been jealous of their prerogatives and duties, the commitment to "association" in the more informal sense of collegiality and sociability has also been an unfailing feature of the organization's history. The larger and more complicated the Association became, the more debate and consultation became the required prelude to concerted action. The increase in "talking" at annual meetings was sometimes bemoaned by older hands, but it also reflected the growing numbers of educators willing to devote their time to accreditation and anxious to participate in research and discussion that might improve the effectiveness of its role in educational improvement.

In this regard, the Association's greater diversity and growing numbers also brought with it new energies and expertise that had been denied a place in times when the definition of an acceptable member was much narrower. This is evident, for example, in the benefits that the membership of black institutions brought not only to those institutions, but to the Association itself. The career of Benjamin E. Mays, one of the century's leading educators, illustrates the great benefits the Association gained from the end of segregation once it was able to draw on the talents and wisdom of black educators. Mays died in March 1984 with his reputation as one of the South's great educators secure. A South Carolina farm boy, he had gone on to Bowdoin College in Maine, then the University of Chicago, where he earned his Ph.D. He later became president of Morehouse College and a major figure in the civil rights movement. Mays became the first African-American member of the Commission on Colleges. William McEniry described him "as one of the great men" he had ever met, an opinion apparently shared by many of his colleagues.

Mays provides a striking example of a phenomenon apparent not only among educators from historically black institutions, but from across the spectrum of Southern education: the vast scope of the voluntarism that has been a central, connecting thread throughout the Association's history. Kirkland and his colleagues certainly spent enough of their own unpaid hours on the Association's work and would probably have expected no less from their successors. Again, however, they would surely have been overwhelmed by the sheer numbers of volunteers who have given their time and efforts over the past 100 years. The Association has successfully attracted the interest and deployed the talents, labor and commitment of thousands of educators and administrators, drawn from all kinds and levels of institution. The consistent ability to do so has been at the heart of its growth and its achievements, from the most controversial of its public actions to the countless acts of local commitment that have often passed unnoticed even by those most affected by them. J.M. Godard believed that of all the regional associations, the Southern Association had the most "vibrant history" when it came to "responding to political pressures" that threatened "academic independence and dignity." Godard ascribed this unique "strength" to the Association's ability to involve "the top leaders of the major institutions" in its work. The active participation of people like the presidents of Tulane or Vanderbilt and the big state universities, public figures with influence and prestige beyond the campus limits, proved a real advantage when confronting the political powers of various states. Godard recalled how this was a feature of the Southern Association that "amazed" members of other associations often mentioned to him.[2]

The active involvement of countless educators at the "chalk face" has also powerfully shaped the Association's educational and accrediting effectiveness. The personal account of Dolly Davis, a teacher at Barnett Shoals Elementary School in Clarke County, Georgia, gives a sense of the Association's dependence on people like her. Davis told of how, like many other teachers, she had received past requests to serve on an Association evaluation team. She had always declined, not wishing to be away from her own class for the time involved and concerned about how much work would be involved. Again asked, and again reluctant, Davis was "urged" by her principal, Sherry Malone, to accept the assignment. Despite the work involved in preparing for the visit and the visit itself, and her initial uncertainty as to what exactly was expected of her, Davis found the experience rewarding. The "excellent group of professionals selected to lead us" made sure that everyone knew what they were expected to accomplish. Among the "many positive outcomes" for Davis was the opportunity "to exchange ideas, practices, and philosophies" with fellow professional educators "from around the state," and to see how things were done in other schools and other classrooms. Those who became involved in evaluating others were, therefore, better placed to participate in and benefit from the evaluation of their own schools.

A further benefit of experiences like Davis' was that it often gave teachers and administrators "a totally different perspective" of the Southern Association. Until Davis' own participation in a visit, "the SACS team had been 'them' coming to give 'us' a hard time." Afterwards, she "realize[d] that the SACS team is a group of 'US,' and the purpose is to help improve education." For Dolly Davis, "firsthand knowledge of how an evaluation team functions in examining programs" had made the process "much less threatening." Changes of heart such as this obviously benefited the Association as a whole, helping to balance the chronic complaints of those who continued to view accreditation visits and processes in terms of "us" and "them."[3] Whatever their own personal understanding of their participation, the thousands of people like Dolly Davis who gave their time every year to the work of the Association had a powerful cumulative impact on the Association as a whole. It shaped not only its activities but its ethos, especially within the large school commissions, an influence suggested, for example, by the prominence that the Secondary Commission's annual *Proceedings* reports gave to noting how many thousands of volunteers had participated in the preceding year's activities.

Davis, the elementary school teacher, and Mays, the leading African-American intellectual, illustrate in their different ways the growth and diversity of the educators increasingly drawn to the work of the Association. They suggest also something of the Association's expanding role in Southern education and growing influence on Southern society as its aims and responsibilities have undergone consistent expansion and revision over the decades. They also embody, in turn, the impact of the educational and social revolutions of the twentieth century on the workings and direction of the Association and its commissions.

The Association's own expansion has also reflected the vast quantitative expansion of education generally over the course of the century. How to respond to an expanding and diversifying educational world is yet another major theme of the Association's history whose persistence the founders might well have expected. Men like Kirkland shared the reforming spirit of their times to the extent that they wanted to see great improvements in the kinds of education they valued. They were also content to see other kinds of educational progress made, provided it did not threaten their own priorities. Yet they were highly skeptical, if not totally opposed, to many of the prevailing reform notions of the time, preeminent among them the growing belief that the nation's education should develop in ways that privileged the practical over the ideal and favored new kinds of education and training over the humanities. They were also deeply committed to resisting what they saw as society's negative impact on education, especially as the economic priorities of production and consumption increasingly threatened to overwhelm all other considerations of what aims and values should animate the pursuit of knowledge. Indeed, a central irony of the Association's growth and development lies in its having been created in the midst of educational and social changes its founders feared would be largely destructive in their impact. This was one reason for their resistance to the admission, and the increasing influence, of educational institutions they believed reflected a "materialistic" understanding of education's purposes. This skepticism, hostility even, is evident in the resistance of the early decades on the part of the liberal arts group to the admission of institutions they did not consider appropriate. Hence, we acknowledge the further irony of an Association that came to life at a time when many of its founders' cherished ideals were threatened by new educational aims and philosophies, yet which owes much of its growth and later prominence to the hard-won and increasing representation of the champions of those very aims and philosophies within the Association.

Whatever their concerns about the impact of social change on education, the educators of Kirkland's generation never doubted that what took place in either realm would have a profound impact on the other. Whatever their commitment to preserving particular educational traditions, they understood that the formulation and preservation of educational ideals and aims could not be separated from the wider circumstances of the society in which educators worked. Nor were Kirkland and his colleagues strangers to compromise with the "spirit of the times," accepting changes small and large as the price to be paid for their continued influence within the Association, and the Association's continued influence on the development of Southern education. The shift to accreditation itself was the most important of these changes in the early decades of the Association's existence, a shift that gave it a radically different social role and image than the one originally envisioned by its creators.

Thus, they would have recognized the continuing efforts of their successors (whatever their conflicting priorities and positions within the Association) to respond to the challenges of retaining educational influence and social relevance. As education has increasingly been asked to be more "relevant" to society (whatever that might mean in any given situation), the Association, in common with similar organizations throughout the nation, has worked to remain relevant to education. In doing so, it has at times become something quite different from the intentions of its founders. This kind of change was evident in the period of the Association's shift *to* accreditation. In recent times, it is to be seen in the changing aims and methods *of* accreditation. The Association's evolution has been shaped by questions of philosophy and power, but also by its members' understanding that being prepared to examine itself and to change when necessary are prerequisites of their organization retaining its relevance in a society characterized by constant change.[4]

For scholars who were also Southerners, the founders' response to the impact of "democratization" on their region's education would surely have been mixed. Coming to educational reform at a time when many believed that its deep poverty was the South's most important distinguishing characteristic, the founders would have been heartened to see the lives and prospects of countless Southerners transformed by improved access to all levels of education. When the Association was founded, a blatant, unequal, segregated educational system not only mirrored, but reinforced and legitimized the prejudices of the wider society. By and large, the founders shared these prejudices. The winning by black Southerners of civil rights in the second half of the century eventually transformed the South's educational climate. It may be that many of the founders, like later generations of educated white Southerners who had long taken black inferiority for granted, would have come to terms with and later come to welcome the end of segregation and the expansion of equality. Maybe some would have resisted it, as they resisted other kinds of change, as dangerous both to the cause of quality education and to social progress as they understood those terms. Whether for or against, it is hard to imagine them being anything less than astonished by the depth of change in the region's race relations. Although contacts between the Association and historically black schools and colleges began during his time, it is unlikely that James Kirkland gave any thought to accrediting African-American colleges or elementary schools, much less envisioned the development of attitudes regarding race and education so different from the conventional white wisdom of his own times. The end of legal segregation did not bring an end to racial discrimination in education, of course, as new forms of de facto segregation emerged. Both the creation of racially exclusive private academies in the aftermath of *Brown* "and the persisting white flight" from the region's public schools contributed to the continuation of racial separation and prejudice. New legal and governmental remedies, such as busing and affirmative action, for past and continuing injustice have in turn prompted further debate, controversy and, often, resistance. Clearly, questions of race remained a prominent element in Southern education and, therefore, a continuing challenge for the Association as it reached its centenary year.

The relationship of race to education was central to the South's distinctive regional character throughout most of the Association's existence. Yet by the Association's centennial year, the relationship of education to race had become an area of thought and action just as likely to illuminate similarities across regions, especially with regard to issues and problems such as affirmative action and the future of the public school system. The South's jettisoning of legal segregation made it more like the North, but in a sense it also made the North more like the South. White Southerners hardly had a monopoly on the desire to live and learn apart from black Americans nor on powerful, even violent, resistance to efforts to encourage them to abandon that wish. As questions of racism and how to counter it moved on to the less clear-cut ground of de facto segregation evident in residential patterns and economic inequality rather than legislation, the national character of the race issue became inescapable. Many white residents of Boston, Massachusetts, proved every bit as strongly opposed to busing as the white citizens of Birmingham, Alabama. Challenges to affirmative action were as likely to arise in California as in Texas. Thus the challenges of bringing about genuine educational integration and of encouraging greater equality of opportunity have increasingly been addressed on a national rather than a Southern stage.

This "nationalization" of the race issue, and in particular its impact on education, points to a wider transformation in American life and education during the course of the century. In 1953, the Association's Henry Hill, the president of Peabody College, expressed the view that "without losing many of its distinctive regional characteristics, the South is rapidly becoming national in its outlook and problems."[5] Although Hill spoke at a time when segregation still dominated the South, he rightly pointed to the tendency of people in the South to view many other issues—the Korean War, Communism abroad, economic development at home, for example—from a national perspective shared with the majority of Americans. Throughout the century of the Association's existence, wars abroad and changes at home have encouraged this development. The patriotic fervor behind the Spanish-American War—fought soon after the Association's founding—helped to replace a sense of sectional grievance with one of national pride. If anything, in recent times, the South has developed a reputation for super-patriotism, more likely to support wars less popular in the rest of the country. More conservative, less ethnically diverse, the South produced less of the opposition to America's wars of the twentieth century than did many Northern communities possessed of larger concentrations of recently arrived Europeans or recently radicalized students. Added to the intermittent impact of war has been the persistent and pervasive influence of commerce and consumption in bringing about an "American" culture, delivered to ever-greater portions of the nation by the century's always-accelerating technological advances.

In the particular realm of education, as we have seen, no force for "nationalization" had greater influence than the federal government. Its expanding influence would surely have intrigued, even as it appalled, the educators of Kirkland's generation. James Kirkland would no doubt have been surprised by the size of the federal government's role in education in the years since World War II. In his presidential address of 1921, he had argued that the "necessity" for standards such as those of the Association "grows out of the impotence of our national education system. What the federal government cannot do, the states and other agencies must do."[6] Thus, Kirkland highlighted a central aspect of the Association's creation and early development: It was born and grew in the space created by both popular and political resistance to the idea of federal or national control of education. Yet, over time, the expanded role of the federal government at all levels of education has led to the Association, especially the Commission on Colleges, becoming enmeshed in relations with the entity whose very non-involvement in education had once created the necessity and the opportunity for the Association's founding. Kirkland might not have appreciated this irony or the circumstances that gave rise to it, but one strongly suspects he would have relished the conflicts of principle and power arising from it.

The nationalizing trends evident in the country's culture and politics have both reflected and shaped the social environment in which the Association's members live and work. Whether analysts see this nationalization as the "Americanization" of the South or, as some have suggested, the "Southernization" of America, the end result has been to lessen the significance of regional differences as a cultural force in matters of education and its improvement. In the context of this increasing nationalization both of American culture and of educational issues, the "Southern-ness" of the Southern Association has gradually declined in importance to a point where the name is now much more indicative of a particular geographic area than it is of a particular set of cultural characteristics or educational priorities. It is difficult to imagine Kirkland, the brother of the wounded Confederate soldier, not evincing some regret at the declining significance of "the South," as he understood that term. But to the extent that he, like other reformers of his time, understood Southern distinctiveness in terms of its widespread poverty, both economic and cultural, he would have been less troubled, perhaps, by the declining significance of the word "Southern" in the Association's name, and more likely to focus on the role the Association had played in ameliorating the negative sources of Southern distinctiveness.

Indeed, whatever the founders' thoughts on the wider transformations that have overtaken Southern society over the course of the twentieth century, they would perhaps have been most taken aback by, and most gratified by, the distance education has traveled toward the center of Southern society and the lives of its citizens. And perhaps it is in this, in the Association's everyday involvement in Southern life, that the founders would have found most to surprise them. Certainly, they held to the belief that the conduct of education was the key to the condition of society. But they had also been keenly aware that theirs was a minority opinion in a culture they believed to be characterized by a profound and destructive neglect of education. A century later, the belief that education is a central influence on all aspects of society has acquired the status of conventional wisdom. If debate continues to rage as to what the interrelation between education and society should be, few deny its centrality to the understanding of both. But if Kirkland and his colleagues would be taken aback by the extent to which, by the late twentieth century, education had become a central fact of the broader society's life, they would surely be heartened by how much of Southern education's journey from periphery to center can be read in the history of the Association they founded in Atlanta, Georgia, 100 years before.

Endnotes

[1] Charles H. Thurber, *Proceedings* of the North Central Association (1898), 38. Quoted in Mark Newman, *Agency of Change: One Hundred Years of the North Central Association of Colleges and Schools* (Kirksville, MO: Thomas Jefferson University Press, 1996), 52. Thurber was a member of the North Central Association, the dean of Morgan Park Academy in Chicago and later a professor at the University of Chicago.

[2] Interview with J.M. Godard, June 1, 1973, Southern Association of Colleges and Schools Archive, Decatur, Georgia, 10-11.

[3] Dolly Davis, "Teacher Wondered if Effort Involved Made Her 'Crazy to Do This,'" *Proceedings* 37:6 (July-Aug., 1985), 3.

[4] Newman, xvi, detects a similar impetus behind the major changes in the North Central Association. Those changes, although taking place at different times than those in the Southern Association, were similar in their major outlines to those of the Association: toward accreditation and then toward new methods of accreditation. The similarities suggest the extent to which the Southern Association was responding to public and educational issues and events that were increasingly national rather than regional in character.

[5] Henry H. Hill, "Education: A Conservative Business Investment," *Proceedings* 58 (1953), 173.

[6] James Kirkland, "Presidential Address," *Proceedings* 26 (1921): 76-77.